REFLECTIVE THINKING IN EDUCATIONAL SETTINGS

This volume examines the role that culture plays in the acquisition of cognitive, linguistic, and social skills. Taking reflective thinking as a central analytical concept, the contributors investigate the role of personal reflection in a series of mental activities, including the creation of social relationships, the creation of a mental narrative to make sense of events, and metacognition. These three types of cognition are usually conceived of as separate research fields.

Reflective Thinking in Educational Settings: A Cultural Framework draws these discrete subfields into dialogue, exploring the connections and interplay among them. This approach yields insight into a range of topics, including language acquisition, cognitive processes, Theory of Mind, cross-cultural interaction, and social development. The volume also outlines the implications of these findings in terms of further research and possible social policy initiatives.

Alessandro Antonietti is a professor of applied cognitive psychology at Catholic University of the Sacred Heart, Milan, Italy.

Emanuela Confalonieri is a professor of developmental and educational psychology at Catholic University of the Sacred Heart, Milan, Italy.

Antonella Marchetti is a professor of developmental and educational psychology at Catholic University of the Sacred Heart, Milan, Italy.

Reflective Thinking in Educational Settings

A CULTURAL FRAMEWORK

Edited by

Alessandro Antonietti
Emanuela Confalonieri
Antonella Marchetti

CAMBRIDGE
UNIVERSITY PRESS

32 Avenue of the Americas, New York, NY 10013-2473, USA

Cambridge University Press is part of the University of Cambridge.

It furthers the University's mission by disseminating knowledge in the pursuit of
education, learning, and research at the highest international levels of excellence.

www.cambridge.org
Information on this title: www.cambridge.org/9781107025738

First published 2014

Printed in the United States of America

A catalog record for this publication is available from the British Library.

Library of Congress Cataloging in Publication Data
Reflective thinking in educational settings : a cultural framework / [edited by]
Alessandro Antonietti, Emanuela Confalonieri, Antonella Marchetti.
    pages   cm
Includes bibliographical references and index.
ISBN 978-1-107-02573-8 (hardback)
1. Critical thinking.   2. Reflective learning.   3. Cognitive learning.   4. Thought
and thinking.   5. Cognition and culture.   I. Antonietti, Alessandro, 1960–
II. Confalonieri, Emanuela.   III. Marchetti, Antonella.
BF441.R395   2014
370.15′24–dc23   2013036429

ISBN 978-1-107-02573-8 Hardback

CONTENTS

CONTRIBUTORS

ALESSANDRO ANTONIETTI, Department of Psychology, Service of Learning and Educational Psychology, Catholic University of the Sacred Heart, Milan, Italy

PIERGIORGIO BATTISTELLI, Department of Psychology, University of Bologna, Bologna, Italy

PIETRO BOSCOLO, Department of Psychology, University of Padova, Padova, Italy

JENS BROCKMEIER, Department of Psychology, University of Manitoba, Winnipeg, Manitoba, Canada

JEROME BRUNER, New York University, School of Law, New York, USA

FELICE CARUGATI, Department of Education, Alma Mater Studiorum University of Bologna, Bologna, Italy

ILARIA CASTELLI, Department of Psychology, Research Unit on Theory of Mind, Catholic University of the Sacred Heart, Milan, Italy

GIULIA CAVALLI, Department of Psychology, e-Campus Studies University, Italy

BARBARA COLOMBO, Department of Psychology, Catholic University of the Sacred Heart, Milan, Italy

EMANUELA CONFALONIERI, Department of Psychology, Centre of Research in Developmental and Educational Dynamics, Catholic University of the Sacred Heart, Milan, Italy

ELEONORA DI TERLIZZI, Department of Psychology, Research Unit on Theory of Mind, Catholic University of the Sacred Heart, Milan, Italy

ANTOINETTE DOYLE, Department of Human Development and Applied Psychology, OISE, University of Toronto, Toronto, Canada

KERSTIN W. FALKMAN, Department of Psychology, Göteborg University, Göteborg, Sweden

GABRIELLA GILLI, Department of Psychology, Catholic University of the Sacred Heart, Milan, Italy

KATHLEEN HIPFNER-BOUCHER, Department of Human Development and Applied Psychology, OISE, University of Toronto, Toronto, Canada

ERLAND HJELMQUIST, Department of Psychology, Göteborg University, Göteborg, Sweden

BRUCE D. HOMER, The Graduate Center, City University of New York, New York, USA

FLAVIA LECCISO, Department of History, Society and Human Studies, University of Salento, Lecce, Italy

BARBARA LUCCHINI, Department of Psychology, Research Unit on Theory of Mind, Catholic University of the Sacred Heart, Milan, Italy

ANTONELLA MARCHETTI, Department of Psychology, Research Unit on Theory of Mind, Catholic University of the Sacred Heart, Milan, Italy

DAVIDE MASSARO, Department of Psychology, Research Unit on Theory of Mind, Catholic University of the Sacred Heart, Milan, Italy

MAREK MERISTO, Department of Psychology, Göteborg University, Göteborg, Sweden

SARAH MIRAGOLI, Department of Psychology, Centre of Research in Developmental and Educational Dynamics, Catholic University of the Sacred Heart, Milan, Italy

DAVID R. OLSON, Ontario Institute of Studies in Education, University of Toronto, Toronto, Canada

JANETTE PELLETIER, Institute of Child Study, Department of Human Development and Applied Psychology, OISE, University of Toronto, Toronto, Canada

SERENA PETROCCHI, School of Psychology, Keele University, Keele, UK

SIMONA RUGGI, Department of Psychology, Catholic University of the Sacred Heart, Milan, Italy

FEDERICA SAVAZZI, Department of Psychology, Catholic University of the Sacred Heart, Milan, Italy

PATRIZIA SELLERI, Department of Education, Alma Mater Studiorum University of Bologna, Bologna, Italy

MICHAEL SIEGAL (DECEASED), Department of Psychology, University of Trieste, Trieste, Italy, and University of Sheffield, Sheffield, UK

LUCA SURIAN, Department of Psychology and Cognitive Sciences, University of Trento, Rovereto, Italy

MARIANTONIA TEDOLDI, Department of Psychology, University of Trieste, Trieste, Italy

ANNALISA VALLE, Department of Psychology, Research Unit on Theory of Mind, Catholic University of the Sacred Heart, Milan, Italy

ACKNOWLEDGMENTS

This book is dedicated to Olga Liverta Sempio, who has recently retired. She was professor of Developmental and Educational Psychology at the Catholic University of the Sacred Heart in Milano. She was the coordinator of the Ph.D. program "Person, Development and Learning" and director of the master course "Counselling and Psycho-educational Intervention in School Settings." She cofounded the research unit on Theory of Mind and was a member of the scientific board of the Research Center on Instructional Technologies (CRIT), later called the Research Center on Developmental and Educational Processes. She was the coeditor of the series Educational Psychology: Development and Educational Processes published by Raffaello Cortina. Her research interests concerned cognitive development (with a special focus on the acquisition of the concept of number), socioemotional development, teaching-learning processes and interpersonal relationships in education, students' difficulties in school, and perspectives and methods to train teachers and educators. Olga Liverta Sempio is a colleague of the editors, and the contributors of this book either worked with her or were in touch with her for academic and scientific reasons. We all thank her for her friendship and for the scientific exchanges we had with her.

We deeply grieve for the loss – which occurred during the editing process – of Michael Siegal, who coauthored one of the chapters and honored us with his intellectual brilliance.

The editors of the book gratefully acknowledge the assistance of Dr. Maria Giulia Olivari and Dr. Valentina Rita Andolfi, who carefully and cleverly helped them in preparing the final version of the manuscript.

Introduction

Do Metarepresentation and Narratives Play a Role in Reflective Thinking?

ALESSANDRO ANTONIETTI, EMANUELA CONFALONIERI,
AND ANTONELLA MARCHETTI

Reflective thinking can mean three different things. A first form of reflective thinking consists in elaborating personal conceptions about the mental activities and abilities and in becoming aware of what occurs in our and other people's minds when we are engaged in intellectual tasks. This form of reflective thinking encompasses the research field usually labeled as "metacognition." A second meaning of "reflective thought" regards Theory of Mind, which concerns more closely the realm of social interactions and relationships. Theory of Mind in fact is conceived as the recognition of one's and others' affective and epistemic mental states as the psychological causes and motives underlying behaviors. Metacognition and Theory of Mind are in part explicit and can be recognized by asking people to express verbally their beliefs about the mind; they are, however, also partially implicit, and they can be detected by observing how people behave – both in natural and in experimental settings – and speak. The third kind of reflective thinking takes the form of narration. In this case individuals reflect on their own and others' mental lives by trying to make sense of what happens within and around them. People's storytelling, on one hand, reveals their naïve psychological ideas and, on the other hand, hints at exploring and understanding their own and other persons' mental states and intentions better.

The forms of reflective thinking mentioned are seen as important competences that are needed to equip an individual to face the demands of reality. Their functional meaning appears in informal settings – such as spontaneous conversations and dialogues – as well as in formal contexts, such as instructional environments. Furthermore, they are shaped by interpersonal relationships and by literacy because an individual is an active partner in social exchanges, belongs to a given culture, and uses specific artifacts in which values, norms, and rules are embedded.

A reflective attitude about our own mental processes is a somewhat "unnatural" attitude. Our mind is set to understand the external reality and not to reflect on itself. The recursive process that causes the mind to focus on itself instead of the external content is the exception and not the rule in psychic activity in general. Only when there are particular difficulties or errors that we find that we have made are we led to ask questions about how we proceed and then induced to reconstruct mentally the paths we have followed or are following. This means that the request to adopt a reflective attitude is not an easy request because this attitude is not the most habitual and familiar to individuals. We must keep in mind possible resistance and failure. The consequence is that we must be prepared for a long period of assimilation and promote the motivation to be engaged in reflective operations.

Second, reflection is an individual activity that is likely to place the subject in an almost solipsistic position. There are certainly moments during the intellectual growth of individuals in which isolation and retreat into themselves are important. In response to intrusive environmental inputs, "closing" the channel of communication with the outside world and reserving space for introspection are steps that now are rarely attempted, but they are essential to preserve the possibility of evaluating, reasoning, and deciding. But we must not forget the natural inclination of the relational subject. Opportunities for sharing the results of our reflections and reconstructing the mental functioning of others can help avoid this individualistic drift. Another antidote to solipsism is the realization that sometimes reflection is developed through social interaction. Awareness about the mental processes involved in an activity sometimes results from discussion, from conversation, or from social comparison. This indicates that much thought is actually incorporated in artifacts and technologies outside the mind. The results of the reflection on one's mental processes, in fact, find expression in artistic works and computer tools. There are paintings and sculptures that depict not only people engaged in reflective activities – thereby signalling the attitudes, even bodily (posture, muscle tension, gestures, facial expressions, etc.) that accompany such activities – but also the consequences of reflective thinking in real life. Today's technology can amplify these expressive possibilities of reflection. What people write in their blogs, chat documents, Web sites, and videos they create to share with friends very often have a reflective component as they include the expression of mental states and processes that accompany experiences of life. Reflection is not so explicit only in the intangible introspections of individuals; it is also detectable in concrete material products, which can provide interesting insights and tools for education and training.

The characteristics of reflection we have mentioned – that is, social sharing and embodiment in cultural artifacts – are well represented by narratives. Narrating is a social act not only addressed to exchanging information, but also to putting in order our experiences and giving them an inner and shared organization. By narrating – and so giving the sequence of their experiences by linking them with temporal connectives and causal relations – people give meaning to their own and others' events. As the Italian writer Alessandro Baricco stated in an interview: "The facts become your life or when you crash, directly, or when someone composes them into a story and sends them to you in the head.... The story, and not information, makes you master of your history." Narrative thinking is closely related to metacognitive reflection. When you tell a story, you are induced to make reference, implicitly or explicitly, to your own mental states (by expressing your own perspective – namely, your intentions, emotions, beliefs, and so on – on the events you are reporting), as well as to other people's mental states (their intentions, emotions, beliefs). When you begin telling a story, you are induced to reflect about why you decided to tell such a story (what is your actual motivation?) and how you are telling that story (am I succeeding in leading my listeners to understand or in impressing, convincing, entertaining them?). Thus, reflective thinking is deeply involved in narrating.

The present book includes a series of chapters addressing different aspects of the role played by reflective thinking in educational contexts such as family, school, and university. The general framework shared by the contributors takes into account the role played by culture in fostering the acquisition of cognitive, linguistic, and social skills. The main aim of the book concerns the attempt to collect in the same volume contributions sharing the common assumptions mentioned, derived from different specific research areas, to allow readers to understand the possible intersections among these areas. Another aim is to show that the core ideas associated with reflective thinking, those resulting from the relationships between meta-representation and narrative, can be applied to different contexts and to different developmental levels.

The main objective is to highlight possible connections among fields that are usually conceived as separate, by assuming a life-span perspective and taking into account different age levels and different developmental issues. Both typical and atypical development, both intraindividual and interindividual processes, both personal and public/institutional factors were considered, and different educational settings, symbolic systems, and learning procedures were analyzed.

The contents of the volume are organized in two parts. Each part is concluded by a commentary in which the authors (respectively, Giorgio Battistelli and Jens Brockmeier together with Bruce Homer) try to consider globally the chapters of the corresponding section, finding possible threads connecting them and discussing the whole picture that emerges.

In the first part the role of representations and metarepresentations is addressed. The first chapter (Social Development and the

Development of Social Representations: Two Sides of the Same Coin?) by Felice Carugati and Patrizia Selleri tries to answer a series of questions often recurring within the approaches to the psychological development: How do children make sense of the social world? How do they represent the various exchanges that characterize the social life where they are embedded? How does their knowledge differ from that of the adults in their communities, and what is the process through which this knowledge is acquired? Development is seen as the outcome of processes of social interaction, dialogue, communication, and conversations, all leading children to reflect on their own mental and interpersonal processes. For this reason, social psychology and developmental psychology are not distinct enterprises. Moscovici's theory of social representations offers a useful theoretical framework to deal with this issue through the conceptualization of three levels in social representation development: the sociogenesis, the ontogenesis, and the microgenesis of social representation (SR). Some examples are offered as regards the level of the ontogenesis of SR (acquisition of social gender identities, representation of intelligence, and school abilities as sociocognitive tools). The process of interpretive reproduction proposed by Corsaro is recognized as a method for the integration of ontogenesis and microgenesis of children's SR within a cultural framework.

The second chapter (Learning from Multimedia Artifacts: The Role of Metacognition), written by Alessandro Antonietti and Barbara Colombo, shifts to the role of metacognition in multimedia learning. Multimedia educational artifacts incorporate cultural assumptions and implicit theories concerning the way people believe such tools should be used. Hence, structuring a theoretical framework focused on the actual role of metacognition in multimedia learning appears to be extremely relevant. The authors tried to understand which models of metacognition are mostly assumed in relation to multimedia artifacts and, more specifically, which roles metacognition has in relation to multimedia, and, finally, which effects, if any, metacognition seems to have concerning different aspects of multimedia. The chapter highlights how studies converged on three main aspects: metacognitive knowledge, metacognitive monitoring, and metacognitive control. Furthermore, it was possible to identify three different perspectives concerning the role ascribed to metacognition: The more simple one sees technology as a tool to promote metacognition; a second perspective sees metacognition and learning as linked, and technology is here intended as a tool to scaffold this twofold relationship; the last perspective sees metacognition and technology as useful to promote effective learning if and when used together. All perspectives but one seem to record both positive and negative results linking metacognition and multimedia. The last perspective, however, appeared to be the most promising since it fostered self-reflection and self-regulation. Yet, it is important not to forget that metacognitive competence is not always necessary or advisable in multimedia learning. A metacognitive attitude has its costs and has to be used only when needed. Pros and cons of metacognition in the field of multimedia learning are discussed by taking into account that media use always occurs within a cultural context, and so cultural meanings associated with the multimedia tools cannot be neglected.

The third chapter (Theory of Mind in Typical and Atypical Developmental Settings: Some Considerations from a Contextual Perspective) by Antonella Marchetti, Ilaria Castelli, Giulia Cavalli, Eleonora Di Terlizzi, Flavia Lecciso, Barbara Lucchini, Davide Massaro, Serena Petrocchi, and Annalisa Valle discusses the more recent theoretical perspectives on Theory of Mind development. From a sociocultural perspective it considers the most innovative contributions available in the scientific literature on Theory of Mind, exploring both typical and atypical contexts of development and education. In particular, the first part of the chapter is dedicated to typical settings and focuses attention on those aspects of development that seem to "contribute to" and/or "accompany" Theory of Mind in terms of precursors as well as interacting abilities. In this sense it discusses the link between Theory of Mind and attachment in familiar and scholastic settings of caregiving and the role of pretense and language in specific relational contexts. The second part of the chapter deals with the atypical development, considering the case of autistic and deaf children, who represent two of the most challenging fields of investigation as regards the topics of deviance versus delay in Theory of Mind development. Finally, the last part of the chapter is about the most recent frontiers of this area of research, which in the employment of highly sophisticated technology (for example, brain imaging) constitute the next step for new insights on Theory of Mind development.

The subsequent contributions included in the first section of the book report the results of experimental studies. The fourth chapter (The Use of Metacognitive Language in Story Retelling: The Intersection between Theory of Mind and Story Comprehension) by Janette Pelletier, Kathleen Hipfner-Boucher, and Antoinette Doyle is focused on the types of adult-child interactions that support the development of early literacy and is aimed at clarifying the relationships between these interactions and reading and writing outcomes in school. Narrative competency, a component of emergent literacy generally measured in terms of storytelling ability, has been the subject of investigation by researchers attempting to elucidate the relationship between the preschooler's skill in interpreting and producing narrative accounts and later reading comprehension. In the past decade, Theory of Mind development and narrative comprehension, as intersecting processes, have become an area of increasing interest to researchers in both fields. In this chapter, the Theory of Mind achievements of typically developing kindergarten children are considered in relation to the transactional processes of meaning making in storybook reading experiences. This chapter shows that four- to six-year-old children bring social understandings to storybook-based interactions in order to construct meaning actively from text and that these understandings are manifested in their appropriate use of metacognitive language. The findings of a cross-sectional study aimed at investigating kindergarten children's production of mental state verbs in a story retell task are presented and discussed in terms of their relation to concurrent measures of narrative comprehension. Implications for educational and instructional practices are discussed as well.

The last chapter of the first part (Language Access and Theory of Mind Reasoning: Evidence from Deaf Children in Bilingual and Oralist Environments) was coauthored by Marek Meristo, Kerstin W. Falkman, Erland Hjelmquist, Mariantonia Tedoldi, Luca Surian, and Michael Siegal. The investigation reported in this chapter examined whether access to sign language as a medium for instruction influences Theory of Mind reasoning in deaf children with similar home language environments. The first experiment involved ninety-seven Italian deaf children aged four to twelve years: Fifty-six were from deaf families and had Italian Sign Language as their native language, and forty-one had acquired Italian Sign Language as late signers after contact with signers outside their hearing families. Children receiving bimodal/bilingual instruction in Italian Sign Language together with Sign Supported and spoken Italian significantly outperformed children in oralist schools where communication was in Italian and often relied on lipreading. The second experiment involved sixty-one deaf children in Estonia and Sweden aged six to sixteen years. On a wide variety of Theory of Mind tasks, bilingually instructed native signers in Estonian Sign Language and spoken Estonian succeeded at a level similar to that of age-matched hearing children. They outperformed bilingually instructed late signers and native signers attending oralist schools. Particularly for native signers, access to sign language in a bilingual environment may facilitate conversational exchanges that promote the expression of Theory of Mind (ToM) by enabling children to monitor others' mental states effectively.

The second part of the book addresses the topic of narrative thinking. It is introduced by a chapter (Narrative, Culture, and Psychology) by Jerome Bruner. In this contribution it is argued that psychology seeks to understand the human condition, but the latter is not easily understood. The human condition is shaped both by the biological constraints inherent in our nature and by the symbolically rich cultures that we humans construct and in terms of which we live our lives communally. Humans are both constrained by our biology and liberated from it by the cultures we create to actualize "possible worlds." Humans are also limited by what we might call the intrinsic constraints of culture. Even when we ignore biological constraints, the human condition, viewed culturally, is an endless dialectic between the already Established and what we imagine to be Possible. This perpetual compromise between the already Established and the imaginatively Possible both generates human troubles and, at the same time, provokes human creativity. The challenge of life is to find a viable compromise between the Established and the Possible. This challenge shapes how psychology goes about or should go about its business in researching the nature of man and his condition. Psychologists should learn that to understand human behavior you should take account of the historical compromise that always exists between the Established and the Possible. We have come to recognize that both Piagetian and Vygotskian approaches are needed in a properly balanced psychology – especially in developmental psychology. And increasingly we are becoming aware of how important it is to take both perspectives into account: our attachment to the Established and our search for the Possible.

These issues are further elaborated in the subsequent chapter (Schooling and Literacy in Mind and Society) by David Olson. In this chapter it is argued that learning to read and write is to discover something about one's spoken language. Literacy contributes to making speech and language into objects of explicit knowledge. Making knowledge explicit is the links among literacy, schooling, and society. How this could be so is the focus of this chapter. Literacy is instrumental in formalizing knowledge and practices in terms of known, explicit rules that can be more or less mechanically applied by anyone trained in the use of those rules and procedures; residual ambiguity is resolved by courts and panels. Bureaucracies are the social systems that result from the application of these principles to complex social goals and problems. They allow the possibility that complex tasks can be dissolved into established rules and procedures carried out by persons trained to play particular roles. These explicit rules and procedures apply not only to the society but to the mental lives of individuals. What the chapter argues is that the institutions of a bureaucratic society are themselves literate institutions. Bureaucracies not only use literacy; they embody the very practices of literacy, practices described in terms of explicit rules and procedures. Thus, literacy plays a role not only in consciousness of language and consciousness of mind, but also in the explicitness of arguments, the uses of evidence, and the forms of discourse appropriate to such specialized institutions as economics, law, science, and literature. A literate society is one that is both societally literate, having in place the infrastructure for the systematic, bureaucratic management of social affairs, and personally literate, composed of a citizenry with the knowledge and willingness to participate fully in these governing institutions. Schools, through their literate activities, provide a bridge between these two.

The third chapter (Teaching Writing to Undergraduate Psychology Students as Socialization to a Genre) by Pietro Boscolo starts by stressing that writing a dissertation or thesis for a graduate degree (M.A.) in psychology is a demanding task for graduate students, who have to use their knowledge and writing skills in a way quite different from high school compositions – in fact, they have to learn a new genre. In this chapter, students' progress and difficulties in their socialization with a new genre are analyzed and discussed on the basis of the author's experience of teaching academic writing to psychology undergraduate students. When learning to write a dissertation, students have to deal with three levels of difficulty. The lowest level regards the structure of the dissertation, which can be a report of an empirical study or a critical review, and must be written according to the rules and norms of the international psychological community. The second level of difficulty regards the communicative nature of the new genre, which requires not only "good" writing, but also the use of rhetorical strategies that underlie the production of scientific papers. Here students have to learn to use strategies and must modify their beliefs about text writing. In particular, the sociocultural approach, emphasizing the meaning of writing as a cultural practice and its role in the academic and scientific community of psychological discourse, represents a source of difficulty. Students tend to view writing as a cognitive process and an individual ability, rather than as a tool for participating in a community. Finally, the third level of difficulty emerges from the constraints of academic writing, on the one hand, and students' need to express their voice and identity when writing, on the other. Obviously these different competencies are closely interrelated.

The fourth chapter (Experiencing Pictorial Artworks: The Role of Intersubjectivity) by Federica Savazzi, Gabriella Gilli, and Simona Ruggi moves to another kind of cultural artifact, namely, visual artistic products. Within the field of aesthetics, recent approaches have stressed the fundamental contribution of intersubjective and relational processes in experiencing art. According to these views, aesthetic experience is not only a complex intraindividual phenomenon characterized by a peculiar weaving of perceptive, emotional, and cognitive processes, but also an intersubjective enterprise. These approaches inherently differ from each other in the conception of intersubjectivity that they adopt. Whereas the cognitive approach stresses the intrinsically communicative nature of art and the importance of an intentional intellectual involvement with the artwork to appreciate it, the embodied approach strongly highlights the precognitive empathetic relation with artwork that, by means of embodied simulation, emotionally engages the observer.

The fifth chapter of the second part (Does Culture Shape the Professional Self? An Exploration of Teachers' Narratives) by Emanuela Confalonieri and Sarah Miragoli reports, as do the last papers of the first section, an empirical study that aims at investigating the role of narrative and reflective thinking in making meaning of teachers' experience and of their vocational and professional Self. Telling the vocational career brings out the daily teaching experience, its vocational dimensions, embedded with social and relational aspects, and inserts it in a cultural framework. More specifically, the study explores the relationship between conceptions of teaching and educational theory and the school level in which the teachers are actually teaching (primary, middle, and high school) using a qualitative research method. Ninety-six Italian teachers were recruited and invited to talk about their practical experience after a specific narrative interview. Results showed that the professional identity of teachers may be related to two aspects: the student and the social context. The vocational competence in fact develops itself through the students' developmental needs and relationships and appears to be strongly connected to the social context in which the teachers live and work.

PART I

REPRESENTATIONS AND
METAREPRESENTATIONS

1

Social Development and the Development of Social Representations: Two Sides of the Same Coin?

FELICE CARUGATI AND PATRIZIA SELLERI

INTRODUCTION

How do children make sense of the social world? How they represent the various transactions and exchanges that characterize the social life where they are embedded? How does their knowledge differ from that of the adults in their communities and, perhaps the most fundamental question, what are the processes through which this knowledge is acquired? What does it mean to speak of children's acquiring social knowledge?

Up until the mid-1960s the analysis of social development across childhood was the province of two kinds of psychological theory, psychoanalysis and behaviorism. The former asked questions about the structure of motives and sought answers in the quality and style of parent-child relations (e.g., Sears, Maccoby, & Levin 1957; Hoffman 1970). The latter asked questions about the origins of social and anti-social habits of behavior and sought answers first in terms of general principles of learning (Aronfreed 1968; Eysenck 1964), supposedly as applicable to children as to other conditionable animals, and then in terms of the behavioral examples or models present in the child's environment (Bandura & Walters 1959). Social development was, in fact, the process whereby children come to resemble the adult members of their society: in character, motives, values, beliefs, or action tendencies; in other terms, social development is seen as a conformist replication of the adult way of life.

By the mid-1970s the diffusion of Piagetian ideas into English-language psychology had transformed the model. The premise of almost all scholars of social development was that individuals think about their experience of social life and that this is the key to everything else. Neither children nor adults are simply, as psychoanalysis claims, creatures at the whim of unconscious or irrational inner compulsions. Nor, as behaviorism claims, are they biological machines reproducing acquired behavioral routines or automated responses to stimuli. On the contrary, human individuals make choices and judgments based on inferences and deductions. Therefore, if you wish to understand why people behave or feel as they do, you must first understand how and why they think as they do. Actions and reactions arise from the intellectual interpretations persons make of circumstances; they arise from the way people think. Of course, the Piagetian perspective does not simply replace an interest in behavior, motivation, or affect with an interest in cognitive process. It also establishes a particular view about the linear and teleological move of development itself. Over decades few areas have not been examined through these researchers' lenses (Doise 1985), and the figure has not significantly changed. In this sense, still applicable are Baldwin's comments (1913, pp. 105–106) concerning "the need of a psychological theory of the social individual. The need became apparent for a genetic and social psychology, which would reveal the state of the individual mind in given social condition; the relation, that is, between individual and collective 'representations', to extend somewhat the phraseology of the French writers referred to in the discussion of primitive thought."

THE FIRST HALF OF THE STORY

Despite their phenotypical differences, these perspectives (psycho-analysis and behaviorism) share two fundamental assumptions about the relations between mind and experience. The first one is that experience presents things that should be understood, in the sense of being "correctly" interpreted. Work in the cognitive-developmental tradition has gradually extended the definition of the experience. In the earliest research, it is no more than other people, undifferentiated and interchangeable. It subsequently became other people differentiated in terms of knowledge, age, gender, nationality, wealth, occupation, and societal role. Ultimately it has come to encompass different kinds of social rules, relationships, social activities such as politics and commerce, and institutions such as government and the law.

The second assumption is that the underlying process of organizing knowledge is self-generated or even the result of the activity of innate modules. Children encounter puzzling experiences, they actively try to make sense of them, and in the course of these activities they manage to assemble for themselves further bits of the reality. Given sufficient time and experience, children will spontaneously and independently arrive at the point most adults have already reached. Processes of human intellectual development are assumed to be universal and invariant among the species. Investigators of adult cognitive processes maintain that they are studying the way the class of organisms called "people" understand, remember, and make social inferences (Flavell & Ross 1981, p. 307). The existence of certain human universals in thought is taken for granted.

This requirement is reflected in the classical constructivist theories of the developmental process: It is the process of adaptation that occurs as long as the individual child actively reconstructs its understanding of the world. Since that world has certain invariant properties, this reconstructive process moves the child by successive steps progressively closer to an adaptive, rational, coherent, and nonarbitrary understanding of reality.

Neither the crisis of Piagetian structural theory nor the more domain-specific approaches to cognition seem to reject the general model of social and cognitive development as a more or less linear and teleological move from action to cognition. But if we scrutinize this move in detail in a longitudinal way, we recognize that children and adolescents (described by developmental psychologists as they reach some kind of concrete cognitive instruments – once they enter school and become subjects for research in learning and teaching) show a different figure of their characteristics. These children and adolescents (who in fact become pupils and students, whereas research rarely acknowledges the influence of this tremendous ecological transition) are described as imbued with misconceptions, mistakes, by some syndrome of nonmotivation; they are novices confronted with experts, they have to change concepts, they are prey to lay epistemologies, and so forth. If these subjects become participants in some experiments in adult social cognition, these young people in the street seem to suffer from a kind of cognitive aphasia: They ignore observations at hand; they prefer concrete to abstract information; they are more inclined to conform their opinions than to verify them critically; they establish illusory correlations; they are mistaken about causes; and so on. In more general terms, we face the problem of whether people apply different mechanisms in dealing with persons versus objects, with abstract tasks versus school or everyday tasks, in situations that do or do not involve social norms. We are confronted with the task of illustrating the divergence between the five senses and common sense, between cognition in general (if it does actually exist) and everyday cognition, when social development is involved in everyday cognition! So far, there is a puzzling result: From the point of view of understanding society, it seems that children follow a teleological route to conform to adult society, but from the point of view of cognitive development, as children grow up, they consistently seem to resist formal reasoning.

Problem Solving or Solved Problems

But this is not the end of the story. Radical individualistic cognitive constructivism, broadly speaking, is a problem-solving model of knowledge. If its roots can be found in Binet's theory of intelligence,

Piaget's own theory is really a perfection of Binet's basic ideas, with the complementary insight that repeated activities of problem solving are themselves the engine that drives cognitive growth. The same kind of analysis that Piaget made of the developing child's relations with the material world has been applied to relations with the social world. The child is assumed to try to solve problems and puzzles, systematically presented by the world, and in doing so he/she gradually transforms the capacities available at any time for their solution.

Three kinds of problems are involved. First there are problems that arise in social relationships from conflicts of interests and values, such as distributive justice concepts (Kohlberg 1984). As for the second, there are problems of social description. Children are confronted with social institutions and practices as much as they are confronted with natural phenomena, like sunsets, lunar eclipses, and so forth. Just as they may try to figure out the principle of buoyancy and balance, they will try to understand commercial transactions or the principles of interest, profit, or social inequalities. Social knowledge is here described in terms of the construction of mental representations of these principles or systems of relationships (Jahoda 1979; Berti & Bombi 1988) and a model of intelligence as individual problem solving is assumed (Dweck & Elliot 1983; Sternberg 1985).

The third issue is that this kind of model underlines that social knowledge is paradoxically knowledge-free. Problem solving instruments are assumed to operate in the absence of any knowledge about the world except what is immediately observable in the problems to which they are applied; problem solvers bring only a set of mental operations to be applied to the facts of each case. This model defines knowledge from the perspective of the "knower as doer." Social knowledge is knowing how to do social things – administer justice, make rules, apportion blame, take the role of the other – how to do things toward and within the social environment.

But it could be assumed that an environment also does things to the individuals who inhabit it; individuals are the target of the action of the environment and not just the agents of action upon it. Then knowledge can also be knowledge about environmental action upon individuals, and this perspective is particularly relevant for children. Children, more than most other groups, are targets of social action. Moreover, problem solving might be seen as a group and not only as a purely individual activity. Solutions of problems are also conserved within a collective memory of groups; not all individuals have to start from scratch, resolving for themselves each puzzle of nature and society. Third, there are few problems, whether of nature or society, that have a single rational answer and so remain decisively and uniquely solved (Billig 1987). Thus we think that the social environment presents children with problems to be solved, but it also presents them solutions and arguments for solutions. As we will discuss later, the development of social knowledge could be seen as the acquisition of one's social group's stock of solutions and arguments for solutions. Different social groups can present different solutions of different arguments, or both.

Interpreting Differences as Developmental

If we take as an example the developmental literature on distributive justice, there is broad agreement that belief in a strictly equal division of resources gives way with age to a belief in distribution according to some standard of relative deservingness, whether based on effort or contribution – the equity principle (Piaget 1932; Damon 1977; Nisan 1984) – or on relative need. Occasional social-class differences have been reported, with working-class children more likely to endorse parity or strict equality (i.e., Enright et al. 1980). In these cases, researchers have assumed that working-class children simply lag behind their middle-class peers in the development of more rational distribution principles, that is, the concept of equity. Similar interpretations have been made about the findings from developmental studies of perceptions and judgments concerning social inequalities. The common finding is that older children are more likely than young children to regard inequalities in wealth as justified, normally by differential contributions to society (i.e., Leahy 1983). In other words, in the case of social justice, children appear naturally inclined to become equity theorists. But equity is also a part of a powerful social myth within each culture studied (Emler & Dickinson 2005). In fact, it is a part of an explanation and justification for inequalities. Among the middle class (more likely to be the beneficiaries of equity), this myth is more extensively developed, and its members are more fully committed to it (Billig 1987).

Failing to Ask the Right Question

Cognitive developmentalists are interested in children's understanding of general principles. For example, they may ask themselves, "At what age does the child understand the general principles underlying social rules?" (i.e., Piaget 1932). They discover that by the age of about eleven years, children recognize that rules are the products of mutual agreements and can be modified on this same basis. However, the relevant question may not be "Can the rules be changed?" but "Who has the power to change them in a particular context?" Another example of the limitations of past research practice has been the tendency to ask children about what *they personally* believe, although their knowledge of the social world includes knowledge about what other people and groups believe, and this in turn shapes their own intellectual and moral commitments. That is, beliefs reflect the way in which we locate ourselves in an ideological space we occupy with others. To return to the case of conventional and principled moral beliefs, people could be asked about which beliefs they thought other people held. Emler, Renwick, and Malone (1983) found very clear representations of the types of moral beliefs held by people of contrasting political orientations. It may be that the basic level at which moral beliefs are structured is not, as Kohlberg suggested, in specific moral theories corresponding to his stages, but in an ideological space that contains these various "theories" as contrasting positions. People then locate their own commitments within what they represent to be the range of options available.

Ignoring Quantitative Differences

The individual constructivist tradition has fostered the view that only qualitative changes in social cognition matter; thus only qualitative cognitive differences between groups count as demonstrations that social influences do operate. But it is not obvious that this is a sensible or even a meaningful restriction. The intention /consequence distinction has been shown to be a matter of the relative weight that older and younger children attach to these two criteria, not an absolute choice of one versus the other (Weiner & Peter 1973). Similar quantitative differences has discourse. Finally, children may have knowledge about the differences between social groups themselves: It could be as relevant to ask children what others believe as to ask about their own beliefs.

Just as advocates of an individual constructivist interpretation of social development began by making their case through a critique of psychoanalysis and behaviorism, so it is useful to submit constructivism to critical scrutiny. In the long run, overcoming cognitive individualism will require a closer relationship between developmental and social psychologies, for the development of social knowledge is as much a matter of the former as of the latter psychology. The individual constructivist's repertoire of cognitive mechanisms – equilibration, cognitive conflict, and so on – can provide only the half of the story. The other half will be provided by some approaches in social psychology.

A POSSIBLE OTHER HALF OF THE STORY

Some thirty years ago Moscovici (1976, p. 254) suggested a distinction between the *logic system* and the *normative system*. During reflexive cognitive work, which is specific to science and philosophy (and which is the paradigm of every individualistic cognitive approach to cognition, be it Piagetian or domain specific) and to all the approaches whose aim is the study of categories of thought, two cognitive systems are at work: One of them makes associations, categorization, deductions; it is the *operatory system*; the other one controls, verifies, selects information, following a variety of rules, logic, or illogic; it could be labeled a *metasystem*, which reworks the products of the first. The rules of a metasystem are normative rules, value-laden rules. A case in point is the logical relation of reciprocity between A and B: It could not be normatively valid when applied, for instance, to the relation Self-Other, as the effect of *primus inter pares* (cf. Codol 1975) vividly illustrates. Social knowledge is arranged in a social hierarchy, where some topics are more value-laden than others; where the combinatory logic between two propositions is not socially equivalent: Some of them are socially legitimate and thus permitted, whereas others are forbidden. There is no logical explanation for the well-known effect of *intragroup favoritism*, which is at work even among children. The more the boundaries between groups are clear, the more the differences between permissions and interdictions are clear, and they have an impact on operative reasoning.

Within this framework it could be supposed that the construction of knowledge in children is a social process, through which what is assembled depends substantially upon the metasystem of rules of the society to which children belong and the position children occupy within it. Through communication and interaction with both adults and other children the child is the target of (and exerts) social influence on the construction of norms and concepts shared within the social groups to which he/she belongs.

A useful theoretical approach for sketching social development from the other side of the coin is offered by Moscovici's (1976) theory of social representations (SR).

When we consider developmental issues in the light of SR it is possible to distinguish three different types of genetic transformations (Duveen & Lloyd 1990). The first is the ensemble of processes through which SR themselves evolve and change: It is the *sociogenesis of SR*. Sociogenesis is the process through which shared representations of different topics are generated. Moscovici's (1976) study of psychoanalysis is an example of the diffusion of scientific knowledge within the Western culture as it is constructed by different social groups (e.g., the Communist vs. the Catholic press in France during the 1950s), but it is not only knowledge originating in scientific discourse that gives rise to social representations; other themes also circulate in society through the medium of SR. In recent years SR of gender have been undergoing transformations, providing another example of a sociogenetic process (Duveen & Lloyd 1986). A third example is provided by De Paoli's study (1990) of social representations of psychology, in which it is clear that representations of clinical psychology held by both psychologists and other professional groups working in the field of mental health have not yet reached a stable organization but are still developing. Sociogenesis takes place in time, so that even when social representations are investigated at a particular moment in time, the resulting description needs to be viewed in a diachronic perspective.

Sociogenesis thus also points to the historical dimension of SR, as Flament claims (1999). A second type of issue arises when the development of individuals in relation to existing SR is taken into account. Human infants are born into a social world that is already organized in term of SR of their communities, cultures, parents, siblings, teachers, and the question to be addressed is how children become both embedded and independent actors in their own worlds. According to Moscovici, the society where children are born is a "thinking environment." Developing the competence to participate as actors in this "thinking environment" implies that children acquire access to the SR of their community (micro- and mesosystems). It is this process that we refer to as the *ontogenesis of SR*, although this ontogenesis is not restricted to childhood, but occurs whenever individual children, adolescents, or adults engage with novel SR in order to participate in the life of different groups or organizations (school system, work). An adequate account of ontogenesis needs to describe how SR become psychologically active in individuals. According to Duveen and Lloyd (1990) ontogenesis is a process through which individuals reconstruct SR, and in doing so they elaborate specific social identities. It is as social identities that SR become psychologically active in individuals. Thus we can say that in expressing or asserting a social identity individuals draw on the resources made available through SR.

The influence exercised by SR on individuals can take different forms. Some SR impose an imperative obligation on individuals to adopt a specific social identity. As in the case, for example, with representations of gender or ethnicity, individuals are constrained to acquire corresponding social identities. The external obligation derives from the ways in which others identify an individual in terms of these social categories. In other cases the influence of SR is exercised through a contractual obligation rather than an imperative one: It is the case when an individual joining a social group may negotiate a specific social identity. SR of psychoanalysis provide an example of such a contractual obligation. As a body of knowledge, psychoanalysis exercises no external obligation on individuals to acquire the categories of analytical thinking as psychologically active categories. But entering some social groups (e.g., that of psychoanalysts themselves, but also other social groups for whom an analytic perspective forms part of their worldview, or job) is dependent upon how individuals (or groups) negotiate the world in terms of psychoanalytic categories.

Construing the ontogenesis of SR provides scholars with a point of view from which to consider contemporary notions of social development. In each case it enables them to ask about what kind of "child" is construed though a particular conceptualization of development.

There is a third genetic aspect of SR that is important to distinguish. This is the genetic moment that arises in all social interactions, the point when individuals meet, talk, discuss, and cope with conflicts; in short, it is the moment or event when people communicate with one another and in which social influences are exerted. This is the *microgenesis of SR.*

SR are evoked and even instantiated in all social interactions as the partners negotiate their social identities and seek to establish some common definition of the matters at hand and of the situation. The evocation of SR in social interactions occurs first of all in the ways in which individuals construct an understanding of the situation and locate themselves and their interlocutors as social subjects. In many circumstances, of course, there will be a mutuality in the understanding constructed by different partners that will obviate the need for an explicit specification or negotiation of social identities, though one can still describe the course of social interactions as the negotiation of social identities in the same sense that one speaks of a ship negotiating its route.

But where the mutuality on understanding cannot be taken for granted, or where an assumed mutuality breaks down, the negotiation of social identities becomes an explicit and identifiable feature of social interaction. In these circumstances the negotiation of social identities may involve the coordination of different points of view and the resolution of conflicts. In every social interaction there is a microgenetic process in which social identities are negotiated and shared frames of reference established, processes for which SR provide the resources.

Language is, of course, a central tool through which social interactions are conducted, and studies in sociolinguistics have emphasized the construction of social identities in discourse (Gumperz 1982), as well as the role of SR (Rommetveit 1984).

Social identities, however, are not fixed attributes that individuals carry into each interaction and remain invariant through the course of interaction. Through the course of social interaction partners may come to adopt positions distinct from those with which they entered the interaction: It is in this sense that microgenesis can be seen as a process of change. In many circumstances the changes that are observed in social interactions are transitory rather than structural as individuals adopt particular social identities in order to pursue specific goals or accomplish specific tasks. Yet social interaction is also the field in which social influence processes are most directly engaged (Moscovici 1976), and in some circumstances the influences at work in social interaction may also lead to structural change in the representations of participants. These changes may be ontogenetic transformations during the development of SR in individual subjects.

Identifying *microgenesis* as the source of ontogenetic transformations serves to remind us that all development is the outcome of processes of social interaction, of dialogue and communication and conversation. From this perspective, social psychology and developmental psychology are not distinct enterprises. They are concerned with the same phenomena.

Let us present some examples that may help to illustrate the relationships among these three types of genetic transformations of SR. Consider first of all a scientist who proposes a new theory, and let us assume that we are dealing with a radical new theory of the physical world or of human experience. Through various forms of social interaction (publications, lectures) scientists try to communicate their theories to colleagues. The communication will have been successful to the extent that other scientists will have understood the concepts being proposed and accepted that these concepts are well founded and not erroneous. The outcome will be ontogenetic transformations in the representations held by these scientists as individuals, as well as a sociogenetic transformation in the representation held by the scientific community as a social group.

By contrast, let us consider developing children as they try to acquire some SR of their community, gender or nationality, for example. For this development to occur children need to receive some communication, whether through interaction with other children or adults or from the public representations presented in the media.

These microgenetic processes will have led to ontogenetic transformations in children's representation of the world, but the SR of their community are unlikely to be influenced by these particular microgenetic processes. In this case there is ontogenesis without sociogenesis, a state of affairs that is a characteristic feature of childhood given the negligible influence that children are able to exert on the representations held by their community.

Construed in these terms, SR may usefully be invoked for explaining the development of children's understanding of the adult community in which they are born. SR regulate children's construction of reality just as in Piaget's analysis of cognitive development the "closed structures" of logical systems regulate the child's (re) construction of logical-mathematical structures. In the developmental reconstruction of the categories of a culture not all categories are equally significant for the child. As already shown, some of them are imposed; others are a result of contractual negotiation.

The particular significance of certain categories is embedded in the social interaction of everyday life. Categories associated with dimensions such as age, gender, ethnicity, and social class exert a great influence on the process of interpersonal interaction, and this endows them with a high degree of salience. The effect of this kind of "social marking" (Mugny, De Paolis & Carugati 1984) of these categories is to offer considerable scaffolding to the young child's effort in the reconstruction. It could be expected that the more salient (or imposed) and socially marked category systems will be the earliest to be reconstructed by young children.

The SR that form particularly significant elements in children's environment are those that provide them with certain positions within the social system: In every culture one cannot be just a human being; one must be male/female; young/old; son/daughter; sister/brother; Italian/French. Membership in specific social categories provide children with both a social location and a value relative to other socially categorized children. Social identities are the basic prerequisites for participation in social life and in the following pages we devote special attention to them.

The Development of Social Gender Identity

The ontogenesis of gender allows children a significant frame of reference, which provides them with the means of interpreting actions and events according to the cultural rule system in which they live; in short, SR of gender provides a shared frame of reference that makes possible the exchange of a semiotic code that allows children to participate in social life by providing an explanatory framework for the interpretation of their own and others' actions, feelings, and thoughts. The systematic marking of children through social relations for gender and the salience that this distinction has in social life ensure that this distinction becomes highly significant for children themselves. One may speak of SR of gender as being instantiated in these systematic markings in everyday life. Social marking, as far as it has been introduced in the theory of sociocognitive conflict (Mugny et al. 1984), is characterized by saying that "it connects relations of a cognitive order with those of a social order" (p. 137). This is indeed what happens very early in children's life: Gender identity is a result of social marking dynamics and one of the earliest conceptual systems children acquire during primary socialization.

Developmentally, the origin of social gender identity is to be sought not only in the adult symbol system (sociogenesis) but also in the emergence of a distinction between self and other in the infant (microgenesis). This distinction in the first years of life, together with adults' marking of gender through routines in everyday life, must be regarded as the precursors of a symbolic gender identity. Within this conceptual framework, it is useful to integrate studies of the early recognition of a representational self and other using mirror techniques (Zazzo 1948; Lewis & Brooks 1975; Stern 1972, inter alia).

Studies of mothers of firstborn six-month-olds (Smith & Lloyd 1978) have demonstrated that gender influences mothers' handling of, and speaking to, six-month-olds. When asked to play for six minutes with an infant presented as "John" or "Jane," these mothers chose the initial toy to match the baby's gender. When babies make gross motor movements, mothers respond with further gross motor behavior if the baby is "John." However, if the same baby is "Jane," mothers attempt to calm "Jane." The mother's accompanying speech emphasizes either "John's" physical skills or "Jane's" cleverness and attractiveness.

In a case of children aged nineteen to forty-two months, Lloyd and Smith (1985), using toys that were rated for gender appropriateness by parents, showed that boys spend more time playing with masculine toys and girls spend more time with feminine toys. Boys' use of masculine toys increases with age, but girls' use of masculine toys shows no systematic variation with age. There are no significant effects of age for either boys' or girls' use of feminine toys. Another interesting result derives from observation of children playing with familiar peers in either same gender or mixed gender pairs. The differences in duration of play with masculine and feminine toys are modulated by the gender of the child's partner; durations of play with their own gender toys are lower in boy-girl pairs. Girls in boy-girl pairs play less with feminine toys and more with masculine toys than girls in girl-girl pairs while boys in boy-girl pairs play less with masculine toys and more with feminine toys. In other words, the regulation of young children's practical activities by SR of gender is susceptible to social influences deriving from the gender of their partner. Two children of the same gender are able collectively to construct a consistent social gender identity as shown in their use of gender-marked toys. The different use of gender-marked toys in boy-girl pairs suggests that these young children find difficulty in maintaining their social gender identity without the support of a same gender peer. As a developmental result, it is possible to maintain that young children (nineteen- to forty-two-month olds) have difficulty in simultaneously coordinating two socially marked dimensions. The social behavior of nineteen to forty-two-month-old children also shows the function of the adult gender system in regulating social interaction. It is well known that adults' stereotypes consistently report that men are judged to be more aggressive, ambitious, assertive, dominant than are women, while women are described as gentle and sympathetic (Archer & Lloyd 1985).

Results presented by Duveen and Lloyd (1986) show that forty-two-month-old children display more assertive behavior than girls and only at this age group girls show more withdrawal than boys. Examination of sequences of social behavior reveal that boys' attempts to be assertive are significantly more successful than those of girls: an interesting illustration that young children's interpersonal behavior is progressively regulated by SR of gender. Assertion by boys comes to be recognized as a legitimate expression of a masculine social gender identity while girls' assertive bids, though more frequent than those of boys, are less successful. The same behavior, assertion, is given a different interpretation according to whether it is the action of boys or girls.

Where SR of gender (sociogenesis) assign different evaluations to male and female activities, differences also emerge in the ontogenesis of young children when they reconstruct these SR.

Economic Life

As for the economic life, studies of development of children's understanding of economic life in middle childhood and adolescence have emphasized, within the Piagetian tradition, the systematic quality of their social knowledge. On the other hand, since the late 1970s it has been reported that children follow adult representations in associating occupations with gender, attributing a greater value to men than women in occupational roles and to women rather than men in domestic roles. Duveen and Shields (1985) found that a majority of three-year-olds could successfully sort a collection of photographs in two groups, those showing people at work versus. at home. In another task three-, four-, and five-year-old children were shown photographs of men at work and asked whether women could perform these roles and were shown photographs of women engaged in domestic activities and asked whether men could perform such roles. Initially children construed contrasting associations of public with male and private with female as constitutive exclusive categories so that gendered distinction between public and private constrained their judgments about the accessibility of work and domestic roles to men and women. Three-year-olds mapped the distinction between work and domestic roles onto that between male and female in a one-to-one correspondence, so that work and domestic roles were perceived as exclusively male and female, respectively. By the age of four, this mapping had become less rigid and domestic roles were seen as being accessible to men. Even at five years women were denied access to work roles. No differences between boys and girls were observed in these results. But this is not the end of the story.

When children were shown photographs of men and women engaged in various work roles and asked whether these figures could also occupy domestic and parental roles, girls recognized a multiplicity of roles for the female figures at younger ages than did the boys. At five years only half the boys recognized that these female figures could take on domestic roles, while 85 percent of the girls made such judgments. For the male figures neither boys nor girls (studied at three, four, and five years) recognized that they could simultaneously occupy both work and domestic roles. Why do girls recognize a multiplicity of roles for women at younger ages than do boys when neither girls nor boys recognize any such multiplicity for men? The male figures presented to children showed them engaged in public "male" occupational settings. In this case, there is an alignment between the gender of the stimulus figure and the gender marking of the setting, an alignment that is also congruent with the social gender identity of both boys and girls. In spite of the lack of alignment between the gender of the female stimulus and the "male" marking of the settings in which they were presented, girls' social gender identity allowed them to accept this discrepancy. Although young girls recognized the gender marking of occupational and domestic settings, they did not construe these markings as establishing exclusive categories. This relative flexibility may derive from the salience that the multiplicity of roles undertaken by women has for girls' gender identity.

Notice that this research was conducted twenty years ago, and no further evidence has been gathered; nevertheless, it still does illustrate how the concept of social gender identity and SR may be used to account for gender differences in the development of children's representations of economic life.

In a complementary way, Emler, Ohana, and Moscovici (1987) add further evidence about the usefulness of the SR approach for the understanding of children's appropriation of the social world. It is in the case of institutionalized relations. The research in social cognition suggests that children do not recognize the formal and the impersonal elements in role relations until they reach adolescence. They are not initially able to recognize that relations between people could be regulated by anything beyond personal inclinations or preferences.

According to Furth (1978, p. 251), societal decisions are thought to emanate from the free will of individuals. This means that the distinction between the formal and the personal is a cognitively complex notion that appears in adolescence. According to Weber's approach (1947) to authority in modern times, impersonal elements in social relations are best understood in terms of authority relations that underpin them, relations that Weber characterizes as "legal-rational" (sociogenesis!). Therefore, how do children come to understand relations of formal authority ontogenesis)? Experience in school might be expected to be particularly formative of children's representations of institutional or impersonal authority. The school is, after all, children's first entry into a bureaucracy. Emler et al. (1987) examined children's representations of their teachers as an organizational role in children in Scotland and France (aged six to twelve). Both categories of children were divided between middle- and working-class backgrounds. Children were asked several questions about teachers' activities: assessing pupils' work, helping pupils with their work, enforcing school rules.

Results suggest a more articulated interpretation of organizational roles in this age group than social cognition tradition allows. By eleven years almost all pupils recognize that there is a hierarchy of authority in the school and that teachers are in their turn subject to the authority of other persons, such as head teachers, and at the same age pupils recognize that teachers do not have the power to alter or ignore any rule. Moreover, most of these pupils also acknowledge that it is wrong for teachers to allow their idiosyncratic preferences to influence decisions about which pupils they will and will not help. Middle-class pupils were more likely to demonstrate these insights than the working-class, and French pupils were more sophisticated about these bureaucratic features than Scottish ones.

Finally, Scottish and French pupils had some different views about the obligations of officeholders. The Scottish pupils (and particularly middle-class and older pupils) believed teachers are bound to enforce regulations whatever their personal feelings about the fairness of these regulations. Almost all French pupils (regardless of class or age) believed teachers should do what was fair, whatever the regulation required. Likewise, while Scottish pupils believed it was appropriate for a teacher to justify her actions by invoking the regulation that required them, the French pupils rejected this idea. Generally, French pupils seemed more sophisticated or expert about French bureaucracy, that is, recognizing its features earlier, but they were also more hostile to it.

What about Income Inequalities?

Turning to children's knowledge of wage relations, the exchange of labor for money, since Piaget this is a topic extensively studied, following his slant on distributive justice. He described three different strategies children apply to problems of distribution. One is to defer to adults as the appropriate authorities on these questions. A second is to demand a strict equality of distribution. The third is to make allowance for such matters as age, special needs, or previous services rendered. These strategies were found by Piaget roughly ordered by age. This figure was also confirmed by Damon (1977). A general shift from a preference for equality to a preference for distribution according to relative deservingness seems to be shared by the social cognition approach.

In fact, as Emler and Dickinson (2005) claim, according to the sociogenesis of representations of labor for money ideology of economics (for instance, Weber's description of the Protestant ethic and the spirit of capitalism), it could be expected to be influenced by membership in distinct social classes, and specifically the middle versus working class, since these are differentiated in terms of income-earning occupations (rather than, for example, source of income: capital vs. labor).

In a series of studies (Emler, Ohana, & Dickinson 1990; with British, French, and U.S. participants), children from different social backgrounds seven to thirteen years old were asked about the earnings of people in different occupations. From the SR perspective, if social class does influence beliefs about income-occupation relations, it will be to the degree that different social classes constitute distinctive social group beliefs and values concerning economic relations. In these studies the basic task was to estimate the weekly (monthly, according to country) incomes of people of different occupations. People were depicted (pictorially) in four different occupations: doctor and schoolteacher (representative of white-collar or middle-class occupations) versus bus driver and road sweeper (blue-collar or working-class occupations). Children were asked to indicate income levels by distributing the appropriate amount of Monopoly money to each character depicted. In addition to income children were asked why any predicted differences in income across the four occupations existed, whether such differences were fair, and whether parity (equity) of income across occupations would be preferable.

Summing up several results, there is a considerable consensus in all three countries as to the rank order of incomes across the four occupations, though this consensus becomes more complete with age and is more extensive among the middle-class children. In no age, national, or social class group were the differences characterized as unfair. The justifications given for inequalities most frequently referred to differences in the respective inputs of the people in these different occupations; in other words, these children were reacting like good equity theorists. There were however, no age trends; younger children were no less likely than older children to refer to differences in inputs as justification for differences in outcomes, and hardly any children invoked differences in need.

What is interesting are the justifications given to the characteristics of occupations. Descriptive explanations (such as "he just drives a bus"; "all he has to do is sweep the road") decline with age, while importance of the job to the society, the difficulty of the work, and skills needed increase with age, but there are a greater use of descriptive explanations by the working-class children and more frequent reference to qualifications or skills by middle-class children. Last and perhaps more interesting are the findings concerning what children believe the income actually to be. In all three countries, the income estimates of middle-class children differ from those of working-class children. In England and the United States the most striking aspect of the difference is the greater degree of income inequality perceived by middle-class children. The anomalous finding in French children is the working-class children's estimate for the road sweeper.

On the face of it, equity theory is supported; a majority of children do refer to differential inputs to justify differential outcomes. Likewise a cognitive developmental interpretation of commitment to the contributions rule is supported; what age-related effects are present appear to be in the direction of increasing support for this rule.

However, there are various reasons to doubt that a cognitive developmental interpretation of equity is entirely appropriate here.

First, it cannot readily account for differences in beliefs about the extent of income inequalities. It might be argued that these differences reflect the fact that more middle-class children have reached the level of proportional equity (Hook & Cook 1979). Thus working-class children are simply producing the appropriate rank ordering of incomes, while middle-class children have moved on to estimation of relativities. If it is the case, differences between middle- and working-class children should be of the same order as those between older and younger children. They are not. In these studies no relation was found between age and the degree of income inequality perceived. Second, children and indeed most adults are seldom in a position to decide about the relative pay for different occupations; they are confronted with an established system of remuneration, and they can do little more than react to the fairness of its outcome. Nor are they in a position to perform the kinds of computation equity theory requires, given that inputs for different jobs are seldom simple, quantifiable, and known. It also seems unlikely that children are comparing the inputs and outcomes in different occupations and concluding that the results accord with the requirements of the contributions rule. For if it is so, it is difficult to see how children with very different beliefs about the relative outcomes could come to such similar conclusions about the fairness of the result. It is also difficult to interpret why children on opposite sides of the Atlantic should have such different views about the kinds of input that justify these inequalities, if they are operating only according to the principles of equity. Finally, in these cases social life does not present children with a problem – how limited resources should be allocated – that children try to solve by the application of abstract reasoning. Income inequality is not a problem in the rational sense; on the contrary, it is a solution, a Western institutionalized long-standing economic practice for which well-developed justifications exist.

A further alternative view of these results may be borrowed from one of the last articles of the social psychologist Tajfel (1984). He argued that people react quite differently in deciding the justice of exchanges among individuals within groups and those between groups. In the former, consideration of equity may be relevant; in the latter they are not. On the contrary, individuals refer to powerful and dominant SR to justify the privileged position of their own group in society or to account for its unprivileged position. In this framework Lerner's "just world beliefs" may be a more useful legitimization for middle-class children than for working-class classmates.

When asked about certain income differences, it is unlikely that children simply may benefit from their own moral judgment capacities, constructed according to universal laws of cognitive organization. It is more likely that children also access their understanding of their culture's framework of legitimization for the status quo: It could be further evidence of the children's reconstruction (the ontogenesis) of the SR concerning income, that is, social inequalities.

There is nothing logical per se about rewarding people with higher income if they take jobs demanding longer periods of training, or about paying them more if their jobs involve helping others or if their jobs require more responsibility. Nor is there anything inherently causal in these occurrences. The very relation here is made by social conventions: They are decisions about social values, and they cannot be predicted from universals in human cognitive organization.

Emler et al.'s (1990) results articulate this argument. In fact, Scottish middle-class children, and to a lesser extent American, are more inclined than their working-class peers to legitimate differences in income inequalities in terms of social classes. So far a plausible conclusion could be offered: Such knowledge, like the wealth to which it refers, is unequally distributed in society, and knowledge (legitimization) about the socioeconomic and class structure of society is distributed among people (in this case, children) according to their own social class position. Children growing up in the middle class have more differentiated representations of inequalities and more extensive legitimizations for these and are more committed to them: Scottish children appear to be particularly marked by inequality of distribution of legitimization.

We are here at the core of theoretical differences between the social cognition approach and the SR approach.

These children do not differ in opinions about the income inequality (the status quo), but in the degree to which dominant SR are elaborated and shared, a result that is consistent with studies of adults (Mann 1970). Thus working-class children, like working-class adults, share less extensively and completely in the systems of SR that serve to legitimate social inequalities; what children do not do to any significant extent is develop oppositional or critical alternative legitimizations/representations.

Moreover, according to Tajfel (1984), income differences generally favor the middle class, and so the middle-class versus working-class differences will be perceived to be greater by middle-class than working-class children, but only when the difference is perceived to be legitimate. In fact, those middle-class Scottish children who regard income differences as unfair also perceive the gap between the earnings of middle-class and working-class occupations to be smaller than children who regard these differences as fair. The effects of perceived group membership may also explain the French results. Road sweepers in France are commonly North Africans, and the white working-class children in Emler's sample may well have regarded North Africans as a subordinate group, whereas the middle-class children would not make this distinction among working-class occupations.

Social Development as Interpretive Reproduction in Peer Cultures

A complementary view of social development in terms of a social construction is offered by a specific sociological slant on childhood, which introduces the notion of *interpretive reproduction*. The term *interpretive* captures the innovative and creative aspects of children's participation in society (Corsaro 1997). The term *reproduction* captures the idea that children are not simply internalizing society and culture, but are actively *contributing to cultural production and change*. The term also implies that children are, by their very participation in society, constrained by the existing social structure and by societal reproduction. That is, children and their childhoods are affected by the societies and cultures of which they are members. Societies and cultures have in turn been affected by processes of historical change. Within this theoretical framework, there are two key elements: the language and cultural routines and the reproductive nature of children's evolving membership in their culture.

As for the language and cultural routines, language is both a symbolic system that encodes local, social, and cultural structure and a tool for establishing (i.e., maintaining and creating) social and psychological realities. These interrelated features of language and language use are deeply embedded and instrumental in the accomplishment of the concrete routines of social life.

Children's participation in cultural routines is a key element of interpretive reproduction. The taken-for-granted character of routines provides children and their partners with the security and shared understanding of belonging to a social group (for instance, the microsystems of family and kindergartner in Bronfenbrenner's (2005) ecology of human development). On the other hand, cultural routines serve as anchors that enable social actors to deal with ambiguities, the unexpected, and the problematic while remaining comfortably within the friendly boundaries of everyday life (Corsaro 1997, p. 19). It is well known that participation in cultural routines begins very early, almost from the minute children are born. At least in Western societies, social interaction proceeds with an *as if assumption.*

That is, infants are treated as socially competent (as if they are capable of social exchanges). Over time, because of this "*as if*" interpretation, children move from limited to full and creative participation in family and kindergartner (cultural) routines. The classic case in point is the parent-infant game of "peekaboo" (Bruner & Sherwood 1976). These scholars note that what the child appears to be learning "is not only the basic rules of the game, but the range of variation that is possible with the rule set" (1976, p. 283). Now to say that adults always strive for shared understanding with children and the adoption of an "*as if*" interpretation in games is crucial in attaining joint activity does not mean that shared understanding is always achieved, but rather that attempts by both partners are always made.

The notion of interpretive reproduction has been presented graphically as a "spider orb web" as a spiral in which children produce and participate in a series of embedded peer cultures (Corsaro 1997, p. 41). Interpretive reproduction is made up of three types of collective action: children's creative appropriation of information and knowledge from the adult world, children's production and participation in a series of peer cultures, and children's contribution to the reproduction and extension of the adult culture. These activities follow a certain progression: Appropriation enables cultural production, which contributes to reproduction and change. The activities are, however, not historically partitioned. That is, children do not proceed through a specific period in which they appropriate all the needed information to produce a peer culture and only then make contributions to reproduction and change in adult culture. Instead these collective actions occur both within the moment and over time. As an example, children do not learn first all the rules of grammar, phonology, and semantics; practice these rules; and only then begin to use them to communicate with others. Instead, children use their developing language skills to communicate at specific moment in time, and they refine and further develop the skills through repeated use in everyday life over time. It is the same for creation of and participation in peer culture. Children appropriate both information and meaning from the adult world to create and participate in a peer culture at specific moments in time. These same collective actions, through their repetition in peer culture over time, contribute to children's better understanding of the aspect of the adult culture they have appropriated. Furthermore, these repetitions over time can even bring about changes in certain aspects of the adult culture.

An amazing example of peer culture's not simply appropriating the adult rule is allowed by the children's secondary adjustments to teachers' rules. According to Goffman (1961, p. 89), secondary adjustments are "any habitual arrangements by which a member of an organization employs unauthorized means, or obtains unauthorized ends, or both, thus getting around the organization's assumptions as to what he should do and get and hence what he should be."

Corsaro's studies have shown that children produce a wide variety of secondary adjustments in response to school rules: For example, children employ several concealment strategies to evade the rule that prohibits taking toys or other personal items from home to school. This rule is necessary: Personal objects are attractive to other children just because they are different from the everyday materials in preschools, and as a result, teachers are constantly settling disputes about these items. Therefore, such objects should not betaken to school; if they are, they have to be stored in children's lockers until the end of the day. According to Corsaro's documentation (1997), both American and Italian children attempt to evade this rule, by taking small personal objects (particularly toy animals, match-box cars, candies, chewing gum) they can conceal in their pockets. While playing, a child often shows his/her "stashed loot" to a playmate and carefully shares the forbidden object without catching a teacher's attention. From the teachers' point of view, they have several strategies to cope with these adjustments: from overlooking these violations (in cases when they interpret them as minor ones), to relaxing the enforcement of school rules, because teachers recognize the creativity of certain features. For instance, teachers may join in children's play. Doing so, teachers themselves appear to be engaged in a secondary adjustment to their own rules and are exposing children to a basic feature of all rules – that is, knowledge of the content of a rule is never sufficient for its application: Rules must be applied and interpreted in a social context.

Insofar as children are social agents, they contribute to the reproduction of childhood and society through their negotiations with adults and through their creative production of a series of peer cultures with other children. This view of childhood as a social construction could replace the traditional notion of socialization as society's appropriating children with the notion of children's interpreting and reproducing (even creatively) the adult world.

Intelligence as a Social Construction

The relatively scant attention to children's ideas of intelligence has focused on tracing age-related differences in the ways in which the difference in the concept corresponds to cognitive stages or periods, as in the Piagetian-like linear approach. As, for example, Lehay, and Hunt (1983) found that the development of concrete operational thought is reflected in an increasing awareness with age of the internal states of people but, at the same time, in an increasing tendency to compare oneself with others in terms of test results, which is by no means an internal state! In the same vein, Nicholls, Patashnick, and Mettetal (1986) show that when children grow older they begin to appreciate abstract over verbal intelligence, thus conforming with formal scientific views.

While acquiring the concept of intelligence, a child appropriates influential meanings and value-bound distinctions inherent in Western culture, such as the differentiation between cognitive-mental and social-practical abilities and between male and female abilities and the related arrangements in education and work. As we have already underlined, growing means coming to participate in the symbolic order of society.

Important changes take place in children's conceptions of ability during the first school years. Children in preschool and to some extent in the first and second year of primary school, too, have a global notion of intelligence that includes social behavior, conduct, and work habits (Yussen & Kane 1983; Bempechat, London, & Dweck 1991, inter alia). Over the years, children's notions of ability seem to become more differentiated by subject matter and more academic, too, containing such academic criteria as normative comparisons, for instance, to the correctness versus incorrectness of the performance.

According to children's drawings, the most common portrait of an intelligent person is an adult male (Räty & Snellman 1997). Comparisons between Finnish grades evidence that this image becomes more pronounced when children grow older. There appears to be a parallel differentiation in that an adult male is prone to become the prototype of an ordinary person. Therefore, we speak merely of *differentiation* instead of the traditional *developmental change* because it is hard to maintain that it would be something more cognitively sophisticated in the *intelligent adult male*, in comparison to *intelligent adult female*.

Apart from Walkerdine (1993), very scant attention has been devoted to this noncognitive result. In fact, the observed interaction between children's gender and grade underlines that it is the girls' views of intelligence that are subject to change, not so much the boys'. This raises the absolutely noncognitive question whether girls' and boys' cultures have different relationships to the social definition (sociogenesis!) of intelligence, including girls' own definition of their intelligence. Since intelligence is a masculine construction, girls' views are formed in relation to the nonfeminine yet dominant masculine culture, whereas boys' views are formed in relation to the own culture. What is worth noting is that both girls and boys favor their own gender as instances of an ordinary person, but not the intelligent person! In fact, for the boys the prototype of an intelligent person is unequivocally an adult male; girls are more open-minded (at least during the first years!) and flexible in that they picture adults and children, male and female. But older girls too associate intelligence with the high-status adult male – expressed by drawing it as a fancy hat and good clothes, and as studying, thinking, reading at a library, with eyeglasses. These cultural attributes are indicative symbols of knowledge: Eyeglasses are an almost archetypal sign of a bookworm, a person absorbed in mental activities (Räty & Snellman, 1997).

How these age-related changes to be interpreted within the individual constructivist framework? Räty and Snellman (1995) and Carugati (1996) have extensively discussed the impact of school and its differential concept of ability in the appraisal of school subjects, reading and mathematics, where the use of social justifications (ability in social relations) almost disappears, giving way to an increased use of performance-based qualitative criteria. On the other hand, there is research evidence that children begin to use the prevailing academic criteria, such as normative comparisons in mathematics and reading, as early as a few months after beginning school (Räty, Snellman, & Kasanen 1999). In the same vein, research on malleability of academic ability in Finnish compulsory school pupils (Räty et al. 2004) shows that boys and girls perceive their potential to improve their performance to be higher in mathematics than in the mother tongue. In the mother tongue, pupils' ratings of their potential for improvement become more pessimistic with advancement in grade level. In mathematics boys rate their potential higher than girls do and trust to exertion as a means of improving their performance more than do girls. The pupils' judgments of ability and its malleability reflect the models of interpretation endorsed by the educational institution and passed on to pupils (Räty, Kasanen, & Snellman 2002). Pupils who are confident in their potential (at the beginning of the school: the optimistic pupils, according to the authors' label) share a number of fundamental principles concerning the *ethos of effort* and assessment methods of the school system; what is worth noting is that this confidence grows stronger with the advancement of grade level! On the contrary, the "pessimistic" pupils are by no means confident in their abilities and give up hope as they advance in grade level. Conversely, the notion of limited scope of abilities is also a predominant interpretation offered by school institutions for those pupils who are unable, for one reason or another, to keep up with classmates. A further interesting result is that the only gender difference does concern the use of effort to explain one's ratings: Boys have a stronger belief than do girls in effort as a way of improving one's performance in mathematics. A complementary result, which sheds light on effort as a way of legitimizing school performances in adults, is offered by Matteucci and Gosling (2004) and Matteucci (2007).

The same issue of effort is shown as influencing the representations of intelligence and cleverness in Italian pupils. The notion of *cleverness* has been studied because it is the most frequent attribute used in everyday discourse toward pupils, at least in Italian compulsory school. Not only does it mean good performance in academic subjects, but it also implies disciplined behavior and "effort," a long-lasting commitment to school demands. Carugati, Selleri, and Bison (1994) studied what pupils of an Italian compulsory school think of intelligence, cleverness, and differences in intelligence and cleverness among classmates. Six hundred forty children (ten to fourteen years old) answered three questions: What does it mean to be intelligent? What does it mean to be clever? Why are some classmates more clever than their peers? The results, obtained by an analysis of multiple correspondences and a cluster analysis, showed that from ten years onward, pupils are aware of school expectations regarding how "clever pupils" should behave: Effort, acquiring learning tools, and everyday life success are cited even by younger pupils, while school success is mentioned more frequently by older pupils. Furthermore, when asked about the origins of differences, younger pupils refer to discipline (a moral approach to cleverness!) while older pupils refer to effort, which is the other side of the same coin! No differences in terms of gender!

In the same vein, the definitions of intelligence vary according to grades, and here also in terms of gender: Boys and older pupils (twelve- to fourteen-year-olds) use more intraindividual definitions than girls and younger pupils; the differences in terms of school abilities are explained in terms of individual effort by older pupils and as a natural gift or as disciplined behavior by younger pupils; finally girls, even the youngest ones, are more prone to define intelligence as *finding one's own way along the life course.*

AS A WAY TO CONTINUE THE DIALOGUE

Individual cognitive developmentalists have proceeded with the assumption that there is an ultimate and teleological structure of social development of knowledge to be acquired, structure that is assumed to be universal, and that (more or less) all individuals progressively recreate this structure for themselves in the course of their own development. In this framework, development simply means passing through different stages or stagelike phases of reconstruction. The view sketched in this chapter claims that the social development of knowledge is a joint enterprise, involving children and their societies, enterprise in which the outcome and not just the pace of development will vary from one social group to another. Moreover, the knowledge organizations (the sociogenesis) that societies offer to children's minds are also different in specific ways by their content. But we are not interested in a psychology of interindividual differences. Examples we have presented here, concerning the acquisition of social gender identities, significance of intelligence, and school abilities as sociocognitive tools, have been discussed within the framework of ontogenesis of social representations, with the aim of sketching a possible integration of process-content interplay. The process of interpretive reproduction (Corsaro 1997) may be seen as a conceptual tool for this integration: The ontogenesis and the microgenesis of children's SR offer appropriate tools for future empirical analyses.

A case in point is the issue of theories of mind. We leave this subject as a way to continuing the dialogue, for several reasons, mainly because we are not experts in the thirty-year body of research (Premack & Woodruff 1978). We only introduce a few notes. Liverta Sempio and Marchetti (1997), according to Bruner and Feldman (1993) and Chandler and Lalonde (1995), postulate a close link between the development of a theory of mind and the child's more general cognitive and social development, which is seen as development-in-context and the importance of belonging to a given culture.

It remains to cope with the issue of sociogenesis as a complementary point of view. A contribution has been offered by research on parents' and teachers' social representations of intelligence and education (Mugny & Carugati 1985; Carugati & Selleri 2004, inter alia) and on pupils' and teachers' social judgment (Amaral 1997, 2002; Amaral, Vala & Carugati 2004; Matteucci & Gosling 2004; Amaral et al. 2006; Matteucci 2007; Amaral, Carugati, & Selleri 2008; Prata Fernandes, Selleri, & Carugati 2008).

What is worth noting is that parents, teachers, and pupils agree that intelligence is a matter of school performance, effort, social comparison, competition, and discipline!

As societal institutions, the family and school system present a variety of social representations to children and pupils, and they do so in ways that both differentiate and assimilate school and family as specific ecological contexts for children. The theoretical approach of social representations could be a fruitful tool for understanding both the processes and the contents of social development of knowledge, as a tool for children to become active members of their own cultures.

REFERENCES

Amaral, V. (1997). A inteligência e o seu desenvolvimento: representações sociais e identidades sociais (Intelligence and its development: social representations and social identities). In M. Monteiro & P. Castro (Eds.) *Cada cabeça sua sentença: ideias dos adultos sobre as crianças* (pp. 33–74). Oeiras: Celta.

Amaral, V. (2002). Teorias implícitas acerca da inteligência: aspectos desenvolvimentistas e de género (Implicit theories about intelligence: developmental and gender issues). *Psicologia, 1,* 237–256.

Amaral, V., Carugati, F., Peixoto, F., & Selleri, P. (2006). Representações sociais como princípios organizadores de conteúdos cognitivos: um estudo sobre as representações sociais da inteligência. Sociedad Portuguesa de Psicologia, VI Simposio Nacional de Investigacao em Psicologia, Atti convegno (pp.100–109), Evora, 30 novembre 2006.

Amaral, V., Carugati, F., & Selleri, P. (2008). Schooling, cognitive development and social representations of intelligence: Their ontogenesis in the realm of school culture (in preparation).

Amaral, V., Vala, J., & Carugati, F. (2004). Perspectivas "desenvolvimentistas" e de género acerca das representações sociais da inteligência (Developmental and gender perspectives about social representations of intelligence). In J. Vala, M. Garrido & P. Alcobia (Eds.) *Percursos da investigação em psicologia social e organizacional* (vol. 1) (2002) (pp. 91–106). Lisboa: Edições Colibri.

Archer, J., & Lloyd, B. (1985). *Sex and gender.* New York: Cambridge University Press.

Aronfreed, J. (1968). *Conscience and conduct.* New York: Academic Press.

Baldwin, J. M. (1913). *History of psychology: From John Locke to the present time* (Vol. 2). London: Watts.

Bandura, A., & Walters, R. M. (1959). *Adolescent aggression.* New York: Ronald Press.

Bempechat, J., London, P., & Dweck, C. S. (1991). Children's conceptions of ability in major domains: An interview and experimental study. *Child Study Journal,* 21, 11–35.

Berti, A. E., & Bombi, A. S. (1988). *The child' s construction of economics.* Cambridge: Cambridge University Press.

Billig, M. (1987). *Arguing and thinking.* Cambridge: Cambridge University Press.

Bronfenbrenner, U. (2005). *Making human beings human.* Thousand Oaks: Sage.

Bruner, J., & Feldman, C. (1993). Theories of mind and the problem of autism. In S. Baron-Choen, H. Tager-Flusberg & D. J. Choen (Eds.) *Understanding other minds.* Oxford: Oxford University Press, 267–291.

Bruner, J., & Sherwood, V. (1976). Peekaboo and the learning of role structure. In J. Bruner, A. Jolly & K. Silva (Eds.) *Play: Its role in developmental and evolution,* New York: Basic Books (277–285).

Carugati, F. (1990a). From social cognition to social representations in the study of intelligence. In G. M. Duveen & B. Lloyd (Eds.) *Social representations and the development of knowledge.* (pp. 126 –143). Cambridge: Cambridge University Press.

Carugati, F. (1990b). Everyday ideas, theoretical models, and social representations: The case of intelligence and its development. In G. R. Semin and K. J. Gergen (Eds.) *Everyday understanding: Social and scientific implications* (pp. 13 –150). London: Sage.

Carugati, F. (1996). Intelligence, school, marks, and pupils: A rejoinder to Räty and Snellman's (1995) 'A social fabric of intelligence.' *Papers on Social Representations*, 5(2), 151–155.

Carugati, F., & Selleri, P. (1995). Diskurse von Eltern und Experten über Entwicklung. In U. Flick (Ed.) *Psychologie des Sozialen* (pp. 218–239). Reinbeck: Rowohlts Enziklopädie.

Carugati, F., & Selleri, P. (1998). Social representations and development: Experts' and parents' discourses about a puzzling issue. In U. Flick (Ed.) *The psychology of the social* (pp. 170–185). Cambridge: Cambridge University Press.

Carugati, F., & Selleri, P. (2004). Intelligence, educational practices and school reform: Organisations change, representations persist. In A. Antonietti (Ed.) *What students and teachers think about learning: Contextual aspects. European Journal of School Psychology* Special Issue (pp. 149–167).

Carugati, F., Selleri, P., & Bison, I. (1994). Compagni intelligenti e compagni bravi a scuola (intelligent and clever classmates at school). *Rassegna di Psicologia*, XI(2),29–52.

Carugati, F., Selleri, P., & Scappini, E. (1994). Are social representations an architecture of cognitions? A tentative model for extending the dialog. *Papers on Social Representations*, 3(2), 134–151.

Chandler, M. J., & Lalonde, C. E. (1995). Folk theories of mind and self: A cross-cultural study of suicide in native and non-native groups. In A. Marchetti & O. Sempio (Eds.), *The development of theories of mind and the construction of cognitive abilities*. Milano: Raffaello Cortina.

Codol, J. P. (1975). On the so-called "superior conformity of the self" behavior: Twenty experimental investigations. *European Journal of Social Psychology*, 5, 457–501.

Corsaro, W. A. (1997). *The sociology of childhood*. Thousand Oaks: Pine Forge Press.

Damon, W. (1977). *The social world of the child*. San Francisco: Jossey Press.

De Paolis, P. (1990). Psychologist: Vocation or profession? In G. Duveen & B. Lloyd (Eds.) *Social representations and the development of knowledge*. Cambridge: Cambridge University Press.

Doise, W. (1985). Psychologie sociale et constructivisme cognitive. *Archives de Psychologie*, 53, 127–140.

Duveen, G. (1993). The development of social representations of gender. *Papers on Social Representations – Textes sur les Représentations Sociales,* Vol. 2(3), 1–17.

Duveen, G., & Lloyd, B. (1986). The significance of social identities. *British Journal of Social Psychology,* 25, 219–230.

Duveen, G., & Lloyd, B. (1990). Introduction. In G. Duveen & B. Lloyd (Eds.) *Social representations and the development of knowledge.* (pp. 1–10). Cambridge: Cambridge University Press.

Duveen, G., & Shields, M. M. (1985). Children's ideas about work, wages and social rank. *Cahiers de Psychologie Cognitive,* 5, 411–412.

Dweck, C., & Elliot, E. (1983). Achievement motivation. In P. Mussen & E. Hetherington (Eds.) *Handbook of child psychology* (pp. 643–692). New York: Wiley.

Emler, N., & Dickinson, J. (2005). Children's understanding of social class and occupational groupings. In M. Barrett & E. Buchanan-Barrow (Eds.) *Children's understanding of society.* Hove: Psychology Press.

Emler, N., Ohana, J., & Dickinson, J. (1990). Children's representations of social relations. In G. Duveen & B. Lloyd (Eds.) *Social representations and the development of knowledge* (pp. 47–69). Cambridge: Cambridge University Press

Emler, N., Ohana, J., & Moscovici, S. (1987). Children's beliefs about institutional roles: A cross-national study of representations of the teacher's role. *British Journal of Educational Psychology,* 57, 26–37.

Emler, N., Renwick, S., & Malone, B. (1983). The relationship between moral reasoning and political orientation. *Journal of Personality and Social Psychology,* 45, 1073–1080.

Enright, R., Enright, W., Manheim, L., & Harris, B. E. (1980). Distributive justice, development and social class. *Developmental Psychology,* 16, 555–563.

Eysenck, H. (1964). *Crime and personality.* London: Routledge and Kegan Paul.

Flament, C. (1999). Freedom of opinion and normative boundaries in social representation: Development and intelligence. *Swiss Journal of Psychology,* 58(3), 201–206.

Flavell, J., & Ross, L. (1981). *Socio-cognitive development: Frontiers and possible futures.* Cambridge: Cambridge University Press.

Furth, H. (1978). Young children's understanding of society. In H. McGurk (Ed.) *Issues in childhood social development.* London: Methuen.

Goffman, E. (1961). *Asylums.* New York: Harper & Row.

Gumperz, J. (1982). *Language and social identity.* Cambridge: Cambridge University Press.

Harris, M. (1991). Sex differences in stereotypes of spectacles. *Journal of Applied Psychology*, 21, 1659–1680.

Hoffman, M. (1970). Conscience, personality, and socialization techniques. *Human Development*, 13, 90–126.

Hook, J., & Cook, T. (1979). Equity theory and the cognitive abilities of children. *Psychological Bulletin*, 86, 429–445.

Jahoda, G. (1979). The construction of economic reality by some Glaswegian school children. *European Journal of Social Psychology*, 9, 115–127.

Kohlberg, L. (1984). Essays on moral development. Vol. 2: *The psychology of moral development*. New York: Harper.

Lehay, R. (1983). (Ed.) *The child's construction of social inequality* (pp. 135–160). New York: Academic Press.

Lehay, R., & Hunt, T. (1983). A cognitive-developmental approach to the development of conceptions of intelligence. In R. Lehay (Ed.) *The child's construction of social inequality* (pp. 135–160). New York: Academic Press.

Lewis, M., & Brooks, J. (1975). Infants' reactions to people. In M. Lewis & L. Rosenblum (Eds.) *The origins of fear*. New York: Wiley.

Liverta Sempio, O., & Marchetti, A. (1997). Cognitive development and theories of mind: Towards a contextual approach. *European Journal of Psychology of Education*, 12(1)3–21.

Lloyd, B., & Smith, C. (1985). The social representation of gender and young children's play. *British Journal of Developmental Psychology*, 3, 65–73.

Mann, M. (1970). The social cohesion of liberal democracy. *American Sociological Review*, 35, 423–429.

Matteucci, M. C. (2007). Teachers facing school failure: The social valorization of effort in the school context. *Social Psychology of Education*, 10, 29–53.

Matteucci, M. C., & Gosling, P. (2004). Italian and French teachers faced with pupils' academic failure: The norm of effort. *European Journal of Psychology of Education*, 19(2)147–166.

Moscovici, S. (1976, 2. ed.). *La psychanalyse, son image, son public*. Paris: PUF.

Moscovici, S. 1984. The Phenomenon of Social Representations. In R. Farr and S. Moscovici (Eds.), *Social Representations*. Cambridge: Cambridge University Press, pp. 3–68.

Mugny, & F. Carugati, (1985). *L'intelligence au pluriel* (Social representations of intelligence) (p. 196). Cousset: DelVal. Cambridge: Cambridge University Press. 1989.

Mugny, G., De Paolis, P., & Carugati, F. (1984). Social regulations in cognitive development. In W. Doise & A. Palmonari (Eds.) *Social interaction in individual development* (pp. 127–146). Cambridge: Cambridge University Press.

Nicholls, J., Patashnick, M., & Mettetal, G. (1986). Conceptions of ability and intelligence. *Child Development, 57,* 636–645.

Nisan, M. (1984). Distributive justice and social norms. *Child Development, 55,* 1020–1029.

Piaget, J. (1932). *Le jugement moral chez l'enfant.* Paris: PUF.

Prata Fernandes, A., Selleri, P., & Carugati, F. (2008). Reference norms: A way for investigating teachers' evaluations of pupils' performances (in preparation).

Premack, D., & Woodruff, G. (1978). Does the chimpanzee have a theory of mind? *Behavioral and Brain Sciences, 1,* 515–526.

Räty, H., Kasanen, K., Kiiskinen, J., Nykky, M., & Atjonen, P. (2004). Children's notions of the malleability in the mother tongue and mathematics. *Scandinavian Journal of Educational Research, 48*(4) 413–426.

Räty, H., Kasanen, K., & Snellman, L. (2002). What makes one able? The formation of pupils' conceptions of academic ability. *International Journal of Early Years Education, 10,* 121–136.

Räty, H., & Snellman, L. (1995). On social fabric of intelligence. *Papers on Social Representations, 4*(2), 156–176.

   (1997). Children's images of an intelligent person. *Journal of Social Behavior and Personality, 12,* 773–784.

Räty, H., Snellman, L., & Kasanen, K. (1999). Children's representations of ability and their changes during the first school year. *Scandinavian Journal of Educational Research, 43,* 249–258.

Rommetveit, R. (1984). The role of language in the creation and transmission of social representations. In R. Farr & S. Moscovici (Eds.) *Social representations.* Cambridge: Cambridge University Press.

Sears, S., Maccoby, E., & Levin, I. (1957) *Patterns of child rearing.* Evanston, IL: Row, Peterson.

Smith, C., & Lloyd, B. (1978). Maternal behavior and perceived sex of infant. *Child Development, 49,* 1263–1265.

Stern, D. (1972). The early development of schemas of self, of other and of various experiences of 'self with other.' In J. D. Licthenberg & S. Kaplan (Eds.) *Reflections of self psychology.* New York: International University Press.

Sternberg, R. (1985). Implicit theories of intelligence, creativity and wisdom. *Journal of Personality and Social Psychology, 3,* 607–627.

Stipek, D., & MacIver, D. (1989). Developmental change in children's assessment of intellectual competence. *Child Development, 60,* 521–538.

Tajfel, H. (1984). Intergroup relations, social myths, and social justice in social psychology. In H. Tajfel (Ed.) *The social dimension* (vol. 2). Cambridge: Cambridge University Press.

Walkerdine, V. (1993). Beyond developmentalism. *Theory & Psychology*, 3, 451–469.

Weber, M. (1947). *The theory of social and economic organizations*. New York: Free Press.

Weiner, B., & Peter, N. (1973). A cognitive developmental analysis of achievement and moral judgments. *Developmental Psychology*, 9, 290–309.

Yussen, S., & Kane, P. (1983). Children's ideas of intellectual ability. In R. Lehay (Ed.) *The child's construction of social inequality* (pp. 109–133). New York: Academic Press.

Zazzo, R. (1948). Images du corps et conscience de soi. *Enfance*, 1, 29–43.

2

Learning from Multimedia Artifacts: The Role of Metacognition

ALESSANDRO ANTONIETTI AND BARBARA COLOMBO

INTRODUCTION

In the modern era the teaching-learning process has always been mediated by artifacts (e.g., Liverta Sempio 1999). This has been particularly true since the beginning of the period (Houston 1988; Burke 2000), but even in ancient times and during the Middle Ages material tools were considered useful aids to learning. For instance, we can consider a dialogue-centered perspective such as Socrates' maieutics. According to this approach, the learner is led to acquire something new, namely, something he/she was not aware of before, by verbal exchange, without using any physical instrument. Anyway, it is possible to notice that sometimes it is relevant to match words with practical exemplification using concrete objects. A good example is the episode reported by Plato in his *Meno*. Socrates made a slave prove that the area of a rhombus inscribed in a square is half the area of the square itself. To do so, Socrates drew the geometrical figures on the sand with a stick and asked the slave to reason about them. Hence, we can see how a technology, even if quite rough, was even used within a teaching tradition based almost exclusively on conversation and was chosen as the preferable methodology on the basis of its dynamic character as opposed to the immobility of text.

Many are the different artifacts that can be used as a support to the learning-teaching process. Historically, the writing text became the main artifact (Ong 1988; Bolter 1991; Groppo & Locatelli 1996).

Yet, it is clear that the simple handwritten or printed word is sometimes barely adequate to lead the learner to comprehend notions and concepts fully. Words must appear together with pictures, drawings, schemes, graphs, and so on, which can represent the abstract information visually. Illustrated textbooks become more and more widespread as time goes on. They can be considered as multimedia tools combining two communicative media: verbal and pictorial (Mandl & Levin 1989; Levin & Mayer 1993; Mayer 1993). Now, new technologies help to strengthen such multimedia artifacts. The verbal part can be presented as a narrated animation, in order to involve the auditory channel, instead of the visual one (which is already involved in decoding illustrations and would be overloaded and disturbed by the additional content). The visual part, on the other side, can be made up of static pictures, but also of dynamic animations (Höffler & Leutner 2007).

Jonassen (1996) proposed that multimodal artifacts are essential when teaching today's video generation. Nowadays, students have the opportunity to take advantage of interactive multimedia tools in order to develop high-order thinking skills. Such skills include the ability to handle and process information from multiple sources within and across different media (Rouet et al. 1996). On the whole, it appears that the design of instructional multimedia that support the development of the skills required in the future is a challenge for current educational research and practice.

Psychological research has identified some criteria to optimize the matching of text and pictures to promote learning, suggesting how these two media can be effectively linked in space and time (Antonietti & Cantoia 2009) and how students can have access to different information formats (Antonietti et al. 2001; Calcaterra, Antonietti & Underwood 2005; Fiorina et al. 2007). It has also highlighted which characteristics each medium should possess both to avoid overloading the cognitive system and to promote the integration between the information conveyed by words and that presented by visuals (Mayer 2001, 2005). Yet, even the best combination of texts and pictures cannot secure the desired learning outcome. As a matter of fact, a multimedia presentation that includes texts and pictures, as with every education tool, may be used in different ways to exploit its potentialities rather than neglect them (Antonietti & Colombo 2008). For example, a learner might omit analyzing the pictures related to the text he/she is reading, even if they possess all the characteristics that should promote learning (no redundant elements, being close to the text they refer to, and so on), forgoing the potential benefits to comprehension and retention that those pictures could have yielded. Or, he/she might first read the whole text and only afterward pay attention to the related pictures – which, on the contrary, have been devised to be considered together with the text to which they refer. Moreover, the learner could look at the pictures at the right time but focus his/her attention on irrelevant elements such as those that cannot be linked to the main topic of the related text (Jamet, Gavotta, & Quaireau 2008).

In short, the efficacy of educational multimedia artifacts does not rely only on the intrinsic characteristics of such tools, but also on the learner's behavior when using them. As Scheiter and Gerjets (2007) have stated, hypermedia tools may be effective only if they are used in a sensible way. Learners' behavior is driven not only by their learning habits (passed on or spontaneously acquired) but also by their metacognitive expertise – defined as a complex of beliefs, awareness, and conscious strategies (Narciss, Proske, & Koerndle 2007). What a learner will do while trying to learn something from a multimedia presentation will actually depend, first, on his/her beliefs about the tool's characteristics and himself/herself as a learner and, second, on what he/she believes to be correct to do in that learning circumstance. For example, if she/he considers pictures to be only an ornamentation that does not add anything important to the written text, he/she will probably disregard them. If the learner sees himself/herself as a visualizer, he/she will pay more attention to pictures, trying to deduce the meaning of the multimedia presentation mainly from them. If the learner believes that the multimedia presentation does not require much effort and time to be comprehended, because of the facilitation provided by the images, he/she will plan the learning activity accordingly (e.g., leaving it as the last job of the day and devoting limited time to it). Second, the awareness of what happens in the mind while people study a multimedia presentation directs their learning behavior. If the learner, while monitoring his/her behavior during the study of the multimedia presentation, feels that he/she does not understand the meaning of a specific word mentioned in the textual part of the presentation, he/she will try to infer the meaning from the related illustration, attempting to deduce which picture element corresponds to the unclear term. Third, the learner has the chance of planning beforehand in his/her mind the strategies he/she will apply when learning from the multimedia presentation and assess their efficacy to modify or replace them – if necessary. For example, the learner may exert control and regulation over the learning from a multimedia presentation by choosing to try systematically to identify all the notions in the picture that are provided him/her by the text.

Hence, metacognition has to be considered to make multimedia presentations efficient supports for learning (Antonietti & Colombo 2008). Metacognitive competence is important because nowadays students are faced with a variety of multimedia educational devices. In some cases, they have the opportunity to choose among them. In these circumstances, in order to select the tool that is more efficient, they must be aware of what a certain kind of instrument involves in terms of cognitive work required, and so on. But when a single tool is available, metacognition is also important, if the tool is to be used in a way that should be consistent with the features of the tool itself, with the learner's personal characteristics, and with the task demands and the goals to be achieved. What does literature tell us concerning the role of metacognition in multimedia learning?

The question of what and how students learn from multimedia tools has been on the agenda since the 1980s (Pea 1985; Perkins 1985). Since multimedia artifacts should be aimed at assisting students in organizing, analyzing, and displaying information, many researchers believe that metacognition should, or could, be helpful in enhancing students' learning. This assumption is particularly important in light of current constructivist theories of learning that emphasize that "learners have to construct their own knowledge – individually and collectively. Each learner has a tool kit of conceptions and skills with which they he/she constructs knowledge to solve problems presented by the environment" (Noddings 1990, p. 3). In this perspective the learner has to find his/her own path of processing the stimuli offered by multimedia environments. Such an attitude could lead the student to develop a strong awareness of the tool, the specific task, and the content he/she is learning; adequate self-awareness concerning strategies to use; and effective self-regulation.

Another peculiarity of multimedia technology is that it has the potential to support learning by creating inherently challenging, meaningful, and motivating instructional situations (Wilson 1996). Moreover, it allows information to be presented in holistic, complex, and networked forms, as it is typically encountered in natural and authentic situations. Different multimedia applications can model and simulate complex problem solving situations and assist learners with different tools to link the information at hand to their conceptual frameworks (Spiro et al. 1991).

It is generally recognized that learning is facilitated if there is a close correspondence between the user's internal representation and the medium's mode of representation. When the match is poor, additional translation is required; that is, externally coded messages often need to be transferred into one's preferred (or "task-required") symbol system (Salomon 1979).

The different channels and structures through which information is presented (such as sound, graphics, animations, charts, and video clips) are thought to support authentic and meaningful learning, allowing many different strategies to be used in the access and handling of information. However, there is the danger that a too-traditional and "fixed" learning context in which multimedia is used might encourage learners to process multimedia-based information in a transmission mode, for example, by memorizing the material. In such a context, multimedia artifacts require the learner's intentional regulation of his/her cognitive activity by monitoring, reflecting, and controlling one's strategic actions; by contrasting the spontaneous tendency to underestimate the cognitive potential of such environments – and assuming accordingly a passive attitude toward them or, where an active involvement is required, a "test and trial" strategy procedure – from an implicit parallelism with video games or naïve computer use (which promote a nonreflective use of the technological tool, giving the user the option of undoing his/her last move).

Successful outcomes in multimedia learning environments are hence dependent not only on the multimedia tool itself but also on the possibility to stimulate the development of the necessary metacognitive skills for learning in order to promote deep information processing and support, thus the acquisition of well-defined knowledge structures (Mayer 1999).

Given this complex picture, a review of the research that has been carried out during recent years with the aim of highlighting the actual direction of the relationships between metacognition and multimedia learning appears to be useful to foster an appropriate use of multimedia tools and to orientate future investigations.

WHICH MODELS OF METACOGNITION ARE ASSUMED IN MULTIMEDIA LEARNING?

An "absolute" definition of metacognition may be seen as arbitrary because the basic concepts of metacognition seem to vary with the purposes of the researchers. In the literature about the relationships between multimedia learning and metacognition, the latter concept appears to be meant both as metacognitive knowledge and metacognitive control.

In some studies we find a plain definition of metacognition's basic components. For example, Fiore, Cuevas, Scielzo, and Salas (2002) referred to metacognition as a multidimensional phenomenon involving both knowledge of one's cognitions and regulation of those cognitions. In more detail, knowledge of cognition refers to one's awareness and understanding of one's own thoughts and cognitive processes; regulation of cognition refers to one's ability to control and manipulate these processes (Schraw 1998).

Hartley and Bendixen (2003) also focused their attention on basic metacognitive components, adding distinctions among different knowledge typologies. They framed metacognition as subdivided into knowledge and regulation of cognition (Jacobs & Paris 1987) and specified that knowledge of cognition refers to a learner's understanding of his/her own thought processes (Schraw 1998). Knowledge of cognition includes declarative (about), procedural (how), and conditional (when) knowledge. The use of a strategy is dependent on the student's awareness of the strategy (declarative), understanding of how the strategy works (procedural), and knowing when to use the strategy (conditional). Regulation of cognition is understood as the set of behaviors that demonstrate control of one's knowledge of cognition and ability to use it. Examples would include students' ability to monitor, evaluate, and set goals for their learning (Schraw 1998). Students who lack skills such as monitoring for understanding and goal setting tend to struggle in many learning environments (Zimmerman & Bandura 1994). Hartley and Bendixen (2003) used a specific instrument to measure students' metacognitive knowledge: the Metacognitive Awareness Inventory (MAI) developed by Schraw and Dennison (1994), in which items are classified into two categories of metacognition (i.e., knowledge of cognition and regulation of cognition). Authors such as Wang, Wang, Wang, and Huang (2004), on the other side, integrated the general metacognitive model adding an explicit theory of the interrelation between metacognition and multimedia environments. Previously scholars generally viewed metacognition as knowledge about executive control systems (Brown, Hedberg, & Harper 1994), monitoring of cognitive processes (Flavell 1976), self-regulation (Osman & Hannafin 1992), and evaluating cognitive states such as appraisal and self-management (Gordon 1996). Wang et al. (2004) shared Hill and Hannafin (1997)'s five metacognitive categories: (a) metacognition, (b) orientation, (c) self-efficacy, (d) system interaction, and (e) subject expertise. Wang et al. (2004) concluded their theoretical overview linking all these suggestions to constructivism, hoping that students' learning in Web-based instruction is meaningful learning, which involves the assimilation of new concepts and propositions into existing cognitive structures (Ausubel, Novak, & Hanesian 1986).

Another perspective sees authors highlighting the role of metacognitive skills. For example, Bannert, Hildebrand, and Mengelkamp (2009) pointed up how in recent research about metacognition the distinction had been made between metacognitive knowledge and metacognitive skills (e.g., Hasselhorn 1992). Whereas *metacognitive knowledge* refers to the individual's declarative knowledge about learning strategies, person, and task characteristics that are relevant in order to master a specific situation, *metacognitive skills* refer to the control, monitoring, and self-regulation activities taking place in learning. Bannert and colleagues roundly stressed the link between metacognition and multimedia, pointing out as recent research reveals that many learners have difficulties in performing metacognitive activities spontaneously, which most probably result in low learning outcomes (Rouet et al. 1996; Hill & Hannafin 1997; Lawless & Brown 1997; Bernstein & Schellhas 1998; Balcytiene 1999; Bannert 2001).

Other authors focused on a specific metacognitive skill, such as metacomprehension. According to Cuevas, Fiore, and Oser (2002), metacognition is a complex construct involving both knowledge of one's own cognitive processes and the ability to control and regulate these processes (Flavell 1979; Osman & Hannafin 1992; Schraw 1998). After this general definition, they called attention to metacomprehension that refers to the "conscious processes of knowing about comprehending and knowing how to comprehend" (Osman & Hannafin 1992, p. 85). Metacomprehension is not limited to one's ability to recognize a failure to comprehend, but also to know when to engage in behaviors to remediate, or repair, this failure in comprehension once it has been recognized (Osman & Hannafin 1992). Metacomprehension is one of the most prominent metacognitive skills, which are important because they have been shown to be critical in a variety of domains, including self-regulated learning (Hofer, Yu, & Pintrich 1998; Winne & Stockley 1998), communication (Flavell 1979), problem solving (Davidson, Deuser, & Sternberg 1994; Mayer 1998), memory (Brown 1978; Bjork 1994), and the development of expertise (Smith, Ford, & Kozlowski 1997; Sternberg 1998). Moreover, metacognitive skills may also interact with other characteristics of the trainee (e.g., verbal ability), influencing the effective use of metacognitive processes (Davidson et al. 1994; Everson & Tobias 1998; Sternberg 1998; Hartman 2001a).

The same perspective was proposed by Cuevas, Fiore, Bowers, and Salas (2004), who referred to metacomprehension (e.g., Maki, Jonas, & Kallod 1994) as a fundamental skill for multimedia learning. Specifically, because of limited external monitoring from an instructor, learning outcomes within learner-controlled computer-based training programs are critically dependent upon how well trainees are able to monitor and regulate their learning process (Osman & Hannafin 1992; Winne & Stockley 1998; Salas et al. 2002). The relevance of this metacognitive ability relies on the fact that, while individuals differ in their ability to monitor their comprehension, studies indicate that metacognitive skills are amenable to training (Volet 1991; McInerney, McInerney, & Marsh 1997; Gourgey 1998; Maqsud 1998; Hartman 2001a, 2001b).

Other authors did not refer explicitly to metacognition, but refer to the same metacognitive processes using different terminology. Kumpulainen, Salovaara, and Mutanen (2001) referred mainly to what Scardamalia and Bereiter (1993) call intentional learning, a process that is segregated from procedural learning and its consequent outcomes. In this line of thinking, significant components regulating the learning processes (and we can intend them as metacognitive control) were found in individuals' conceptions of the nature of knowledge and learning, in the subject-related knowledge base, and in mindful and focused information seeking behavior and reflective activity, including the use of appropriate learning strategies, such as cognitive and metacognitive strategies (Pressley & McCormick 1995; Vosniadou 1996; Young 1997). Such features, identified as being conducive to effective learning interactions in small group learning situations, promote the willingness to speculate, to make hypotheses, and to use valid evidence (Forman & Cazden 1985; Edwards & Mercer 1987; Fisher 1996).

On the other side, Van den Boom, Paas, van Merriënboer, and van Gog (2004) stressed the importance of reflection. They pointed out that theory provides indications that reflection is an important factor concerning the development of self-regulated learning (Boud, Keogh, & Walker 1985; Von Wright 1992; Ertmer & Newby 1996; Lee & Hutchison 1998; Boekaerts 1999; Sobrol 2000). They refer mainly to Borkowski, Carr, Rellinger, and Pressley (1990): According to them, reflection can be conceived as a strategy or skill that operates on other strategies or, in other words, a form of personal mental experiment that is conducted to compare strategies. By reflecting on one's own learning, students become more aware of their learning process and possible alternative study strategies. In the authors' opinion this was important because the perception of choice is a critical aspect of self-regulated learning (Boekaerts 1999), and the awareness of alternatives is a prerequisite for changing less-than-optimal study habits (Boud et al. 1985). On the one hand, reflection promotes the development of the necessary cognitive structures, making them available for learning activities. The quality of students' reflections is supposed to be a factor that influences the development of self-regulated learning. It primarily depends on internal factors such as the available cognitive structures

(Ertmer & Newby 1996) that contain knowledge, experience, and skills regarding learning and studying.

WHAT ASPECTS ARE MOSTLY TAKEN INTO ACCOUNT WITHIN THE RESEARCH FRAMEWORK?

When authors convert the underlined metacognitive aspects into practice, three main focus facets seem to emerge:

- metacognitive knowledge
- metacognitive monitoring
- metacognitive control.

We will now see in more detail how the works examined cope with them.

Metacognitive knowledge plays a crucial role in students' approach to new technologies in education. For instance, beliefs about the quality of information that can be retrieved from the World Wide Web can influence searching strategies on the Internet (Mason & Boldrin 2008). Antonietti and Giorgetti (2004) carried out two studies to investigate undergraduates' representation of the psychological correlates of multimedia computer-supported instructional tools. A questionnaire was devised to induce students to express their opinions about the motivational and emotional aspects of learning through multimedia, the behavior involved in the learning process, the mental abilities and required style of thinking, the cognitive benefits, and the outcomes. The questionnaire was administered to 50 (Study 1) and to 170 (Study 2) boys and girls enrolled in different university courses. Respondents identified a large number of nontrivial instructional opportunities for multimedia learning and demonstrated a system of beliefs about psychological implications of multimedia tools. Findings were replicated in a further investigation when the same questionnaire was administered to a larger number (493) of boys and girls enrolled in university courses. Their conceptions were not consistently affected by gender differences, by computer skills, or by the faculty and the year of the course attended (Giorgetti & Antonietti 2005). It is worth noting that metacognitive knowledge about multimedia learning appears to be rather specific, since students are able to differentiate their beliefs according to different kind of tools (multimedia presentations, virtual reality simulations, written hypertexts, and so on) (Antonietti et al. 2000; Antonietti, Colombo & Lozotsev 2008; Antonietti et al. 2011). These are common conceptions of multimedia learning that are analogous to those exhibited by teachers (Antonietti & Giorgetti 2006).

A recent series of investigations were carried out by employing various methods. Colombo and Antonietti (2006) deepened the analysis of people's naïve ideas about multimedia learning by making reference explicitly to the cognitive principles devised by Mayer (2001). Students were presented with Mayer's research protocols and asked to guess the research outcomes. More precisely, they were asked to read the texts used by Mayer in his experiments, together with the questions he used to assess learning outcomes. Then they examined the paper reproduction of five pairs of multimedia presentations; the presentations used were the same (as format and contents were concerned) as those used by Mayer in his studies. Each pair of presentations was focused on one of the multimedia principles devised by Mayer and was structured to offer both a version coherent with the target principle and a version opposed to it. The principles examined were exemplified in the following demonstrative presentations:

- *Spatial contiguity principle*: separated book-based presentation with words far from pictures (incoherent) vs. integrated book-based presentation with words close to pictures (coherent);
- *Temporal contiguity principle*: presentation with words first and then pictures (incoherent) vs. simultaneous presentation of words and pictures (coherent);
- *Coherence principle*: book-based multimedia presentation with text and schematic pictures integrated (coherent) vs. book-based

multimedia presentation with text and detailed pictures integrated (incoherent);

- *Modality principle:* animation with words presented as narration (coherent) vs. animation with words presented as on-screen text (incoherent);
- *Redundancy principle*: animation with words presented as narration (coherent) vs. animation with words presented as narration and as on-screen text (incoherent).

Participants' ratings were compared with those actually achieved by Mayer. First of all, students, when asked to judge the presentations' efficacy, always tended to rate higher the presentations coherent with Mayer's principle, rather than the incoherent examples. The sharp majority of undergraduates agreed with Mayer's first three principles (spatial contiguity, temporal contiguity, and coherence), recognizing their efficacy when compared with different cognitive organization of the same multimedia materials. With reference to the other two principles (modality and redundancy), the percentages of agreement were lower, but even so the percentages of disagreement remained low. The overall picture suggests that Mayer's multimedia principles are not so counterintuitive as the author himself believed. A second study was carried out by employing an interview technique based on specific pictures taken from actual textbooks so to highlight illustrators', teachers', students', and other people's opinions about the role that images play in facilitating learning. Participants' responses were always coherent, indicating the systematic nature of the underlying implicit conceptions. Findings seem to disprove Mayer's (1993) pessimistic claim that the commonsense theory of multimedia learning fails to match experimentally supported principles. On the contrary, it appeared that interviewees were spontaneously very close to the researchers' multimedia theory, which states that students learn better from words and pictures than from words alone if pictures are chosen according to the cognitive processes they can elicit and respect specific cognitive principles.

As far as *monitoring* is concerned, it seems to be a key aspect of several studies. According to Wang, Wang, Wang, and Huang (2004), metacognitive strategies are defined as the monitoring of cognitive learning processes. Specifically, they believe metacognition to be the high-level behavior of monitoring cognitive processes and results and they define it by four dimensions (purpose-setting, self-monitoring, self-modifying, and self-evaluation), where self-monitoring appears to be the key aspect. Kramarski and Ritkof (2002) also define metacognition as investigating and monitoring the learning process. In their method the metacognitive questions focus on (a) comprehending the problem/task, (b) making connections between previous knowledge and the problem/task at hand, (c) applying strategies, and – especially – (d) reflecting on the solution processes. The research plan carried out by Kumpulainen, Salovaara, and Mutanen (2001) also stressed the monitoring aspects of metacognition. The participants had sixty minutes to investigate, observe, discuss, and reflect on their understanding and representation of the concept of "energy" in the form of text, pictures, graphs, and so on, on a joint poster. A joint poster task was considered to create interdependency among the students, leading to intensive collaboration and social meaning making. Furthermore, the design of a poster in a multimedia-based small group learning context was regarded as an enabling activity for the students to reflect and reconstruct their understanding of the concept of "energy."

Other authors, on their side, stressed more the *control* aspects. For example, Cuevas, Fiore, Bowers, and Salas (2004) reported how for their second SKATED study (reported in Cuevas et al. 2002; see later discussion), they turned their attention to investigating how individual differences (verbal comprehension ability) may interact with training format (presence or absence of diagrams) to alter not only participants' cognitive (knowledge acquisition and mental model development) but also metacognitive (metacomprehension accuracy) processes. What is critical for novices' learning complex tasks is training that supports the development of knowledge structures that allow them to manage effectively (and therefore control) the requisite higher-order processes as they acquire task expertise. The same is true for Howard-Jones and Martin (2002). They did not mention it specifically but instead reported that reflective questions may encourage backward processing in a multimedia learning environment and involve readers in organizing and repeating previous prose content or, through forward processing, optimize behaviors on passages following the questions (Rickards 1979). It would appear that higher-order questions support the learning of concepts more effectively than lower-order questions (Andre 1979; Hamilton 1985) and demand greater attention from the learner (Halpain et al. 1985). Both Felker and Dapra (1975) and Watts and Anderson (1971) found that students' problem-solving abilities were improved if the text to be learned was punctuated by questions requiring the application to novel examples. Possibly, this improvement is achieved by inducing the learner to consider the given concepts within new settings (Tennyson & Parks 1980) – and thus to control the strategies used in the learning process. It has also been shown that embedded questions involving novel examples help students to identify more clearly their level of understanding (Glenberg et al. 1987), thus encouraging a more selective and efficient review of the text (Walczyk & Hall 1989). There is also evidence that questions that require the students to generate their own information can support the retention of that information (Greene 1988; Garner 1989). In some studies various aspects of metacognition combined. For instance, Bannert (2002) merged *monitoring* and *control* aspects. In her research the focus was (as we saw in the previous paragraph) on the metacognitive skills (control, monitoring, and self-regulation activities taking place in learning and problem solving) of students. Other perspectives, instead, tended to merge the aspects of *metacognitive knowledge* and *metacognitive control*. Fiore, Cuevas, Scielzo, and Salas (2002) focused – as we already saw – on metacomprehension, a principal component of metacognition involving both the ability to recognize a failure to comprehend (knowledge of cognition) and knowledge of when to engage in behaviors to repair this failure (regulation of cognition: Osman & Hannafin 1992). They justified their choice by reporting how metacognitive skills, such as metacomprehension, had been shown to play an important role in self-regulated learning (Gourgey 1998), problem solving (Mayer 1998), and the development of expertise (Sternberg 1998).

Hartley and Bendixen (2003) selected as a starting point for their empirical work two attributes that may impact the use of comprehension aids: *metacognitive knowledge* and *epistemological beliefs* (Hartley & Bendixen 2001). In particular, students' metacognitive knowledge significantly mediates success in most learning environments (Schraw 1998). Defining these aspects more specifically to frame their empirical design better, their study looked at two proposed facets of metacognition: regulation/control of cognition and knowledge of cognition. Also, according to Van den Boom et al. (2004), reflection can be conceived of as the bridge between *metacognitive knowledge* and *metacognitive control* (self-regulation), facilitating the transfer of metacognitive knowledge to new situations (Ertmer & Newby 1996).

WHAT ROLE HAS METACOGNITION IN RELATION TO MULTIMEDIA?

When metacognition is put into a relationship with multimedia, different kinds of reciprocal relationships can be outlined – combining different roles that can be ascribed to the artifact (A), metacognition (M), and learning (L). In this section we will explore how these three aspects have been combined by the authors examined.

Metacognition Promoted by Multimedia

A first perspective sees technology as a way to promote or enhance metacognition (see Figure 2.1).

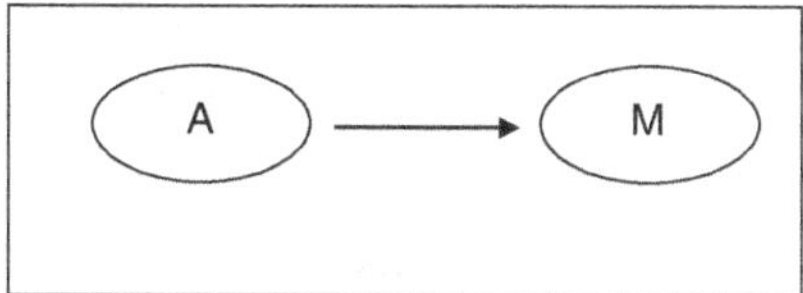

FIGURE 2.1 Artifact (A) as a tool to promote metacognition (M).

Cuevas, Fiore, Bowers, and Salas (2004) seem to share this perspective. In their paper, they described the results of programmatic research efforts aimed at investigating the use of interactive computer-based training technology to support knowledge acquisition and integration for complex task training environments. How did they measure the effects of the technology used on metacognitive processes? The program they used, SKATED (Supporting Knowledge Acquisition through Enhanced Displays), was aimed, in terms of metacognitive processes, at assessing the effect of diagrams associated with texts on participants' metacomprehension accuracy (i.e., their ability to monitor their comprehension accurately while learning new materials). For this measure, they calculated the correlation between their subjective assessment of performance and actual performance (Maki et al. 1994). To assess participants' metacognitive processes better, they further refined their metacomprehension measure (using "dynamic distributed decision making" – DDD) (Kleinman & Serfaty 1989), focusing on metacomprehension bias, that is, the remarkable difference between a participant's prediction and/or postdiction of performance with the actual performance (Maki 1998). Larger bias scores indicated poorer ability to gauge one's understanding of the material, with negative or positive values indicating either underconfidence or overconfidence, respectively. They also included, to increase stress on the link between technology and metacognition, a measure of general metacomprehension predisposition (the Metacomprehension Scale (MCS) developed by Moore, Zabrucky, & Commander 1997) to assess how individual differences in innate metacognitive skills may alter outcomes in computer-based training environments.

In terms of metacognitive processes, Cuevas et al. (2002) reported that diagrammatic presentation led to significant correlations between metacomprehension predictions (subjective assessments of future performance) and actual performance on the knowledge assessment measures (composite score of the declarative and integrative knowledge questions). They also found that generalized metacomprehension predisposition, as indicated by responses on the MCS, significantly influenced metacomprehension accuracy. Specifically, participants reporting higher metacomprehension behaviors were more accurate in gauging their comprehension of the concepts presented in the training. Substantial research has shown that the characteristics (i.e., aptitudes) that learners take to the training environment not only determine their ability to profit from instruction (Fleishman & Mumford 1989), but may also interact with alternative instructional treatments, producing differential results in learning (Jonassen & Grawboski 1993; Proctor & Dutta 1995; Snow 1997). Accordingly, training designers need to determine how instructional technologies can best be used to foster successful learning outcomes, in terms of both cognitive and metacognitive processes, as well as develop plans for adapting instruction to the needs of the learner. In support of this notion, the results of their second SKATED study (Cuevas et al. 2002) provided further evidence for how training interventions can be successfully employed to augment learners' metacognitive processes, leading to higher metacomprehension accuracy and transfer task performance. Diagrammatic presentation was shown to enhance participants' metacognitive processes effectively by increasing the accuracy of their comprehension monitoring. Moreover, in the DDD study (Fiore et al. 2002), metacomprehension accuracy was found to be positively influenced by greater similarity to an expert model and mastery of integrative knowledge as well as general metacomprehension predisposition.

A similar view appears to be shared by Kumpulainen, Salovaara, and Mutanen (2001). In fact, in their research, the main foci in the evaluation of posters (prepared by a small group of students around the science topic they were exploring in a multimedia format) were the logical structuring of knowledge, the demonstration of the students' own ideas and knowledge versus direct copying of text, and clear and coherent illustration of information. Their analyses tended to link technology and metacognition since they covered examination of the students' navigation and information handling processes in multimedia, construction of understanding of the scientific concept of energy to be learned as manifested in the students' posters, social interactions, questionnaires, and stimulated recall interviews.

The cross-analyses of the whole data sample revealed that students' activity was mostly directed to the management and organization of working processes and to the procedural handling of multimedia-based science material. The nature of the students' social interaction appeared to be composed of sequences indicating rather procedural, surface-level activity. The general observation was, however, that students' navigation and search strategies in processing multimedia-based science materials were not very effective. In summary, the students' cognitive activity could be characterized as product-oriented with little evidence of exploratory activity relevant for knowledge construction. Interaction episodes typical of meaningful learning such as thinking aloud, commenting on observations, questioning, social construction of information, evaluation, and connecting new information to preexisting knowledge were rare. The nature of students' cognitive activity was also reflected in the quality of the posters, showing in many cases direct copying of text from the encyclopedia and incoherent conceptual representations. In fact, it appeared that the learning task was conceptualized by the students as a learning activity that required procedural working and presenting of material rather than investigating and criticizing it. Interestingly, the social working mode appeared to increase this type of activity even among those students who adopted a more active, inquiry-based role while working individually on the task. In general, students seemed not to consider the fact that, when information is presented in a networklike structure, the reader has to be even more active and strategic in order to create coherent representations of the topic under investigation (Foltz 1996). The learner must constantly be able to evaluate the meaningfulness of the information presented, consider where to move next, and conceptualize holistic entities from discrete pieces of information (Hammond 1993).

Learners' conceptions of knowledge and learning, as well as their expectations based on earlier experiences about the task and its goals, played an important role in defining the nature of the constructive activity in a learning situation. These features also regulate the nature of learning resulting from a particular activity (Baker & Brown 1984). On the basis of these findings, it appeared that the students' conceptions of the task goals and of effective learning activity patterns contrasted with the intended goals and activities of the instructional setting. The results of this study also demonstrated that students are likely to need support for their strategic activity in multimedia-based learning. While the use of multimedia tools enables learner's control, information processing within multimedia environments may be particularly difficult for learners limited in both domain knowledge and cognitive skills.

Wang et al. (2004) integrated the metacognitive questions proposed by Hsiao (1997) and the writing design mentioned by Gordon (1996). Metacognition strategies should be improved by using the technological system based on interaction with an Internet database which had been devised by the authors and which was called FFS. The goal of such design in Web-based instruction was to help learners develop reflective thinking, express their own ideas about learning contents, modify old thoughts or information to form new ideas, and compare new and old concepts to promote active self-construction. In other words, they hoped that learning in Web-based instruction with FFS system was "meaningful learning," involving the assimilation of new concepts and propositions into existing cognitive structures (Ausubel, Novak, & Hanesian 1986). They intended thus to examine whether the FFS teaching module could enhance the four dimensions of metacognition behavior. The entire FFS teaching module was designed with several important goals: (a) building personal portfolios, (b) developing a sense of personal responsibility toward learning, (c) prompting more prudence in learning, (d) helping learners grasp the ideas in the text, (e) inducing discussion among classmates and cooperative learning in groups, and (f) offering learners enough room for learning feedback.

Positive results were achieved by the authors. As previously seen, their questionnaire was designed to examine whether the FFS teaching module could induce the four dimensions of metacognition behavior. The participants were generally inclined to agree that, in the process of Web-based instruction, the FFS teaching module facilitated metacognition. The questionnaire designed for examining the degree of participants' satisfaction with the FFS teaching module revealed that it was effective in facilitating meaningful learning. The questionnaire designed for examining the influence of the FFS teaching module on learners' learning styles and learning efficiency revealed that learners became more active than they were in the traditional teaching classroom.

The FFS teaching module motivates learners to use metacognition strategies. It can also train and influence the learners' metacognitive behavior, including purpose setting, self-monitoring, self-modifying, and self-evaluation. Students can develop the ability to employ metacognitive strategies if they are trained for an extensive period. They can reflect on their own learning and, thus, effectively avoid the possible confusion caused by stimuli provided through multimodal sources of information.

Multimedia as a Tool to Promote the Link between Metacognition and Learning

Another perspective sees metacognition and learning as linked (higher levels of metacognition yield better learning results) – technology is

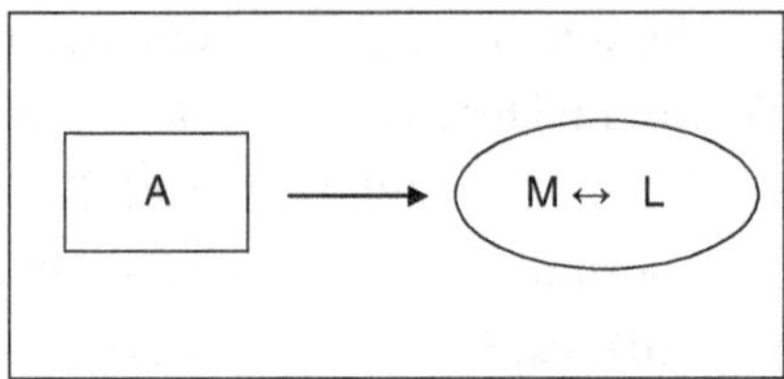

FIGURE 2.2 Artifact (A) as a tool to scaffold metacognition (M) and learning (L).

here considered a tool to scaffold and promote this twofold relationship (see Figure 2.2).

The primary purpose of the paper of Cuevas, Fiore, and Oser (2002) was to investigate how instructional strategies may be incorporated into complex task training to scaffold learners' cognitive and metacognitive processes, particularly in cases of low ability learners. In the first section of their work they discussed how diagrams associated with text can be used to facilitate knowledge acquisition and to highlight how a multifaceted approach to assessment is critical to detect learning gains. The next section provided an overview of the importance of metacognitive skills to successful learning outcomes (M-L). They finally described a study conducted to evaluate the differential benefit of a multimedia tool integrating text and diagrams in supporting knowledge acquisition and metacognitive processes in different populations of learners [A → (M-L)]. A testbed for teaching introductory concepts associated with the principles of flight was developed for this experiment. The technological part relied on two versions of an interactive tutorial (diagrams present or absent) to explore the differential benefit of diagrams in facilitating knowledge acquisition, mental model development, instructional efficiency, and metacomprehension accuracy.

Positive results were reported by the authors. Diagrams effectively supported participants' metacognition. More importantly, this effect was found to be strongest in participants with low verbal comprehension ability. Furthermore, the results demonstrated that these differences in verbal comprehension ability and metacomprehension accuracy translated to task performance. In low verbal comprehension ability learners, the facilitative effects of diagrams served not only to enhance metacognition (improving metacomprehension accuracy), but also to improve acquisition of integrative knowledge. The results of this study suggest that additional experimentation should more systematically attempt to support metacognition for learners of differing ability levels. Moreover, this study focused only on one component of metacomprehension, namely, learners' ability to detect failures in their comprehension. It is also necessary to investigate how instructional strategies can prompt learners to control and regulate their comprehension. In short, the findings reported previously highlight the importance of designing training to support not only the learners' knowledge acquisition, but also their metacognitive processes (Mayer 1999). As advances in instructional design and computing technologies increase the reliance on computer-mediated distance learning approaches (Brown & Ford 2002), training designers need to understand more fully the cognitive and metacognitive processes involved in learning within such environments and how individual differences impact these processes (Annett 1989; Jonassen & Grabowski 1993).

The same perspective can be found in Fiore, Cuevas, Scielzo, and Salas's (2002) study. These authors investigated the feasibility and utility of cognitive diagnostic assessment of problem solving when training for distributed team tasks. They utilized multimedia computer-based knowledge elicitation methods (A) to assess both relational problem solving, requiring the semantic integration of concepts, and dynamic problem solving, requiring the ability to integrate and apply these concepts. Additionally, they addressed how metacognitive processes interact with learning outcomes (M-L) when training for complex synthetic task environments. To evaluate these knowledge requirements adequately, they decided to assess learning via two distinct forms of computer-based problem-solving tasks. Both methods view learning as knowledge construction, whose success involves the active integration of concepts (Mayer 1996; Baker & Mayer 1999), and, as such, the assessment of learning must adequately gauge this integration. Their first measure involved a computer-based knowledge elicitation method to assess a form of relational problem solving requiring the semantic integration of concepts. For the second measure they assessed learning via a dynamic, animated problem-solving task where successful resolution required the ability to integrate and apply concepts from the tutorial. Such measurement was aimed to determine the degree to which metacomprehension predisposition and metacomprehension accuracy were related to knowledge acquisition and application in complex synthetic task environments. They first assessed whether self-reports of one's predisposition toward metacomprehension behaviors may diagnose metacomprehension accuracy. Then they determined the accuracy of participants' judgments of comprehension of the presented material to gauge the relation between problem solving performance and metacognitive judgments.

They predicted that, when to a degree metacomprehension behaviors generalize the learning for a complex synthetic task environment, responses on the metacomprehension scale would be related to metacomprehension accuracy with their experimental testbed. They found that general metacomprehension predisposition was related to metacomprehension accuracy in training for synthetic task environments. Furthermore, by determining metacomprehension bias, they documented how inaccuracy in this process is directly related to poorer performance overall.

Their findings about metacomprehension support the argument that training designers should assist trainees in their attempts to monitor their subjective learning experience better, namely, their metacognitive processes (Bjork 1994). For example, their bias scores illustrate the relation between poor metacomprehension and low task performance. This suggests that those with higher bias may be less efficient learners in online environments. In particular, such learners may spend too much, or not enough, time with the materials depending on the degree to which they over- or underestimate their comprehension. They also documented the utility of using dynamic problem solving methodologies to assess knowledge acquisition and application when training for complex distributed team tasks. These findings are compatible with the arguments of Bennet et al. (1999), who illustrated the benefits of multimedia testing. They additionally found that metacomprehension processes involving both – one's predisposition to such processes as well as one's accurate use when engaged in training for synthetic task environments – are indicative of successful knowledge acquisition.

From an analogous perspective, Howard-Jones and Martin (2002) reported on the effects of asking learners to answer questions when learning in a multimedia environment, even when no immediate feedback was given to learners about the appropriateness of their responses.

In the first study participants answered multiple-choice questions that encouraged analysis of examples within a multimedia learning environment. This first study included a questioning activity that would encourage a higher-order activity such as analysis. To investigate the effects of such questioning, two environments were prepared. The "no response" learning environment (N) consisted of a simple linear presentation of rules and examples with an analysis and solution of each example provided directly underneath it. The A-MCQ learning environment required students to respond to a multiple-choice question questionnaire that demanded that they analyze, in turn, each of the ten examples before they were allowed to see each solution. The solution was provided on a separate screen shown when the analysis question of the example was submitted. It was hoped that this analysis would serve as a discriminative stimulus that would cue processing behaviors. In the second study, participants were asked to summarize the information illustrated by the examples; learners were asked to generate their own rules, thus exploiting the generation effect. The method followed for the second study was identical to that for the first, except for the following changes. A new Rule-Generating (R-GEN) learning environment was devised that did not include the prescribed rules, but displayed the examples (as in the N environment) with a single question asking the student for five rules that would account for the ten examples shown. In both studies metacognitive activity (namely, reflection) was supposed to improve learning (M-L) and the effects to be higher by working within the multimedia environment (A). Unfortunately the results were not as positive as those of the previous investigations. In the first study a significant decrease in learning occurred when students were using the A-MCQ environment, compared with the N environment that required no response. In the second study, instead a significant increase in learning emerged when students were using the R-GEN environment, compared with the N environment. The detrimental effect of the A-MCQ condition was unexpected. It was hypothesized by authors that the format of the questions might have increased the cognitive load by presenting unrelated issues that might otherwise not have been considered, or, by reducing the number of options, they decreased the challenge, engagement, and learning. However, it seems more likely that the reduction in learning observed in subjects using the A-MCQ environment was due to questions focusing only on the first part of the problem solving process (the analysis). The A-MCQ environment, indeed, required learners only to analyze the problem and thereby identify clearly the preceding conditions. It was hoped, originally, that this would prompt learners to consider more carefully how these conditions were related to the successive solution revealed on the next screen. However, by focusing attention on an analysis not yet fully related in the learner's mind to the subsequent solution, a depressive effect that reduced the attention paid to the subsequent text encoding the solution might have occurred. Similar negative effects had been observed in some studies involving prequestions (Anderson & Biddle 1975). Despite some inaccuracy in the rule generation, however, concept learning in the R-GEN environment was significantly improved, presumably because of the generation effect discussed previously. The second study demonstrated that gathering the type of responses that may suitable for monitoring learning can also enhance it directly. However, no formal evaluation of the effectiveness of the approach in terms of monitoring was made here, since the study focused only on the immediate learning effects of two types of questioning about concept learning within one particular context. The negative correlation between pretest and learning scores indicated that, in both studies, those who benefited most were those who knew less to begin with.

Another key factor in this perspective – as highlighted in more recent studies (e.g., Meyer et al. 2010) – is that a multimedia tool (such as an e-portfolio, which can be seen as both a multimedia container for student work and a tool to support key learning processes) has a positive impacts on students' literacy and metacognitive skills when it is used regularly and integrated into classroom instruction.

Metacognition and Multimedia Together Can Promote Effective Learning

Another perspective sees metacognition and multimedia artifacts to be useful to promote effective learning if they occur together (see Figure 2.3).

A pilot experiment by Colombo and Antonietti (2010) showed that people spontaneously base their behavior, while they are learning from a multimedia presentation, on their metacognitive knowledge and awareness, even though this is not optimal. By taking multimedia presentations used by Mayer (2001) in his experiments as a reference prototype, the authors devised two presentations comparable to Mayer's in terms of text length, structure, and complexity. For each topic an audio format and a video format were devised. A total of four presentations were obtained (two topics times two formats). Each participant was shown two presentations, one in audio format and one in video format. During the presentation of each topic, the participant,

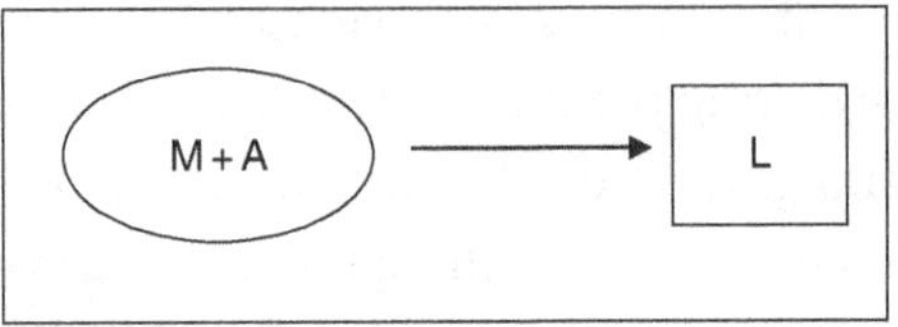

FIGURE 2.3 Metacognition (M) and artifact (A) are useful to promote effective learning (L) if they occur together.

while listening to the text or reading it, could ask for the corresponding picture by pressing a key every time he/she thought he/she needed it. The requests for pictures and the timing of such requests were recorded. This allowed assessment of whether and how participants exerted metacognitive control on the strategies used to benefit from the presence of pictures. Afterward an interview was done in order to lead participants to explicitate the reasons that induced them to ask for pictures. Finally, they were tested on comprehension of the presentations' contents. The results show that, faced with a multimedia presentation and being free to explore it as they like, individuals tend not to respect Mayer's principles. Participants, however, changed strategies according to the features of the multimedia presentation. Even though their metacognitive awareness failed to reflect the different features of multimedia presentations, participants' judgments about such features tended to be internally coherent, suggesting that people are aware of the actual potentialities of multimedia.

From this study it appears that freely browsing multimedia presentations requires that relevant metacognitive knowledge be activated, as well as adequate metacognitive awareness and control. Even if other studies point out how students appear to be able to use metacognitive skills effectively in order to monitor their learning process (Mengelkamp & Bannert 2009), if these are lacking, external support has to be provided. In these cases, metacognitive prompts have been proven to be extremely useful in online environments (Stahl & Bromme 2009); in fact, some investigations directly tested the effects of such kind of support on learning.

The aims of Kramarski and Ritkof (2002) were to investigate the effects of metacognition and e-mail interaction among teachers and students on a specific kind of multimedia learning (i.e., interpreting and constructing graphs) and to describe the e-mail interaction on different levels. They took as a starting point the work of Mevarech and Kramarski (1997), who developed the IMPROVE method, which encourages interaction in order to help people become metacognitive learners in mathematics. IMPROVE involves the following teaching/learning stages: Introducing the new topics to the whole class; Metacognitive questioning in small groups/individualized activities; Practicing; Reviewing; Obtaining mastery on higher and lower cognitive skills; Verifying and Enrichment. By this method students learn to formulate and answer metacognitive questions that guide the interaction. In the present research, metacognitive instruction was based on the IMPROVE technique. A series of four self-addressed metacognitive questions were used: comprehension, connection, strategic, and reflection questions. The comprehension questions were designed to prompt students to reflect on the problem/task before facing it. The connection questions were designed to prompt students to focus on similarities and differences. The strategic questions were designed to prompt students to consider which strategies are appropriate to face the given problem/task and for what reasons. The reflection questions were designed to prompt students to reflect on their understanding and feelings during the solution process. The metacognitive questions were used in students' small group/individualized activities and in writing in their booklets. In addition, the teacher modeled the use of the metacognitive questioning when she introduced new concepts. The link between metacognition and artifact, which should lead to better learning, was stressed in the experimental condition that combined EMAIL and META condition. Positive results were obtained: students who were exposed to spreadsheet software embedded within e-mail interaction and metacognitive instruction (EMAIL + META) outperformed students who were not exposed to metacognitive instruction

(EMAIL). In particular, the effects were observed on students' ability to explain mathematical reasoning and on reducing misconceptions regarding graphs. These findings are in line with other results that showed that metacognitive instruction enhances mathematical problem solving as well as the ability to explain mathematical reasoning (Kramarski 2000). Concerning the written interaction, it seemed that the EMAIL + META condition succeeded in building a mathematical community where students expressed their mathematical ideas fluently and flexibly using various levels of interactions. By formulating written explanations, students learned valuable lessons about the need for accuracy, precision, and completeness in their answers. The findings also showed that more students (44 percent) who were exposed to EMAIL + META interaction used a metacognitive level of interaction than did EMAIL students (8 percent).

According to Bannert (2002), although metacognitive knowledge and skills are not only needed when learning through technology, technology makes the students' reflective behavior about their own way of learning more salient. She thus highlighted the strong link between metacognition and technology to enhance good learning. For example, in a multimedia learning environment, a successful learner has to decide continuously where to go next and to evaluate constantly how the information retrieved is related to his/her actual learning goal (Schnotz 1998). Considering that many students have difficulties in strategic and metacognitive learning (Simons & De Jong 1992), the aim of Bannert's study was to provide appropriate support for metacognitive reflection when learning with multimedia artifacts. It was assumed that successful learning with hypermedia or Web-based environments is not a matter of trial and error but rather a set and specific sequence of metacognitive activities that has to be performed (Schnotz 1994; Astleitner 1997). Ideally, a successful learner performs different metacognitive activities when using a multimedia tool. He/she first analyzes the situation before he/she starts with the execution of information processing. He/she will orient him/herself by skimming through task, instruction, and resources; specify the learning goals or even break them down into subgoals; and plan the ongoing procedures. On the basis of these analyses, the student must search for the relevant information and judge whether the information found is really relevant to the learning goals. He/she then has to extract information and elaborate it. At the end he/she has to evaluate the learning product, again with respect to the learning goals. These activities are constantly monitored and controlled. Learning processes appear to be not so easy for the average students, who may also be not so expert in facing multimedia environments. The aim of Bannert's study was, hence, to provide metacognitive support for learning with multimedia tools. Reported results showed that participants who received metacognitive support performed more metacognitive activities during learning. They also showed better transfer performance, especially if they complied with the offered support in the intended way. The author claimed that offering metacognitive prompts was not sufficient; care had to be taken that these instructional prompts were performed in the intended manner in order to increase learning outcomes. Prior knowledge was the most important factor to help compliance. According to Hartley and Bendixen (2003), in multimedia environments users are faced with a constant barrage of decisions to be made – a perspective similar to Bannert's. These concerns have led to a number of studies attempting to incorporate metacognitive strategy instruction into multimedia instructional materials to improve learning outcomes (Puntambekar & duBoulay 1997; Hartley 2001). However, research to support the notion that metacognitive knowledge positively impacts achievement in a multimedia environment is not yet available, although it is likely to be more important in contexts where learners have more control over the sequence of instruction and the use of comprehension aids. Bendixen and Hartley (2003) focused, more specifically, on the direct impact of metacognitive knowledge and epistemological beliefs on the use of comprehension aids (to improve learning outcomes) in a multimedia tutorial. Metacognitive knowledge, as exemplified by students who are more actively engaged in materials, should impact the use of comprehension aids and lead to deeper and more effective learning. Thus a positive correlation between the use of comprehension aids and metacognitive knowledge has been hypothesized. The study provided mixed results in terms of the relationships among epistemological beliefs, metacognitive awareness, and tutorial use. Yet, the apparent lack of significant correlations between the participants' knowledge and the regulation of cognition was best interpreted by the authors in the light of the task. While one can easily recognize the importance of regulatory skills such as goal setting on course grades or even the likelihood of earning a diploma, the same skills may not be as immediately rewarding when using a short multimedia tutorial.

A similar perspective seems to be shared by Van den Boom et al. (2004). In agreement with Butler (1998), they hypothesized that the reflection prompts used to provoke students' reflections are well suited to embed the different aspects of self-regulated learning into instruction, especially for electronic environments in which reflection prompts can serve as cues to elicit students' self-regulated learning strategy construction (Winne & Stockley 1998; Schunk & Ertmer 2000; Seale & Cann 2000). Their study was designed to investigate the impact of reflection prompts and feedback on the development of students' self-regulated learning. They hypothesized that learners working on study task variants with embedded reflection prompts would gain more development on self-regulated learning than learners studying the task without these prompts. Also they hypothesized that the effects of reflection prompts would vary as a function of the tutor feedback in such a way that the impact of the reflection prompts increases if in addition tutor feedback is provided on the resulting reflection expressions. Results yielded an overall positive picture. The main findings indicated that the intervention with reflection prompts and tutor feedback differentially affected the development of self-regulated learning. The two groups that received feedback from a tutor showed an increase on all three subscales related to metacognitive regulation strategies. The group without the tutor feedback showed a decrease on self-regulation and external regulation and an increase on the lack of regulation. The learning performances were not differentially affected by the study condition. Evaluation of the reflection prompts and tutoring showed that there were no differences in appreciation of the reflection prompts by the students. Students seemed to be aware of the fact that their reflection provoked by the irrelevant prompts and the associated feedback were not relevant to the learning process. When a prompt was perceived as relevant for the task, the students judged the resulting reflection and the associated tutor feedback as helpful. In summary, this study offers indications that reflection prompts, especially if combined with tutor feedback, have positive effects on the development of students' self-regulated learning.

CONCLUSIONS

In this chapter our starting point was recognizing how nowadays multimedia educational artifacts – in the form of both illustrated textbooks and computer-supported hypermedia – are widespread. Such instruments, as all artifacts do, incorporate cultural assumptions and implicit theories concerning the way people believe such artifacts should be used. The frameworks where they are employed, in turn, reinforce those assumptions by the way of suggesting particular modes of using them. Multimedia tools, however, especially in their more technologically advanced forms, present themselves as "open tools," both because users can find modes – not contemplated originally by designers, producers, or trainers – of using them and because users are expected to employ those tools according to their own motivations, goals, and cognitive characteristics. Instructions on how to use a multimedia tool are not totally embedded in the instrument itself, but should be perfected by each user. To do so, a learner should control his/her behavior while using the artifact and develop adequate beliefs about and a sufficient level of awareness of the mental processes involved so to be enabled to self-regulate the application of relevant learning strategies. Hence, metacognitive competence plays an important role in determining the efficacy of the multimedia artifacts. While research concerning the best way of devising appropriate text-picture combinations has a long history, the investigation of the impact of metacognition on multimedia learning is more recent and not so widely applied. With reference to studies where the relationship between multimedia learning and metacognition has been taken into account, we discussed how – though starting from quite different theoretical perspectives (justified by dissimilar definitions of metacognition and of metacognitive processes, or at least from the different emphasis given by authors to the broad and general theme of metacognition) – several works converged to focus empirical research on three main aspects of metacognition: metacognitive knowledge, metacognitive monitoring, and metacognitive control. Research studies examined three different perspectives: The simpler one sees multimedia artifacts as tools to promote or to enhance metacognition. A second perspective sees metacognition and learning as linked Artifacts are here defined as tools to support and promote this twofold relationship. The last perspective sees metacognition and multimedia artifacts as useful to promote effective learning if and when they are used together.

Analysis of the results that we encountered showed a somewhat mixed picture. All perspectives but one seem to record both positive and negative results linking metacognition and multimedia. The last perspective, instead, appear to be the most promising – returning overall positive feedbacks.

Though further research in this specific field is indubitably needed, the data we have at hand suggest that metacognition and multimedia should be considered as strictly linked to promote effective learning. Metacognition should therefore be embedded in multimedia devices, and they should be designed by paying attention to metacognitive awareness. Focusing predominantly on a single aspect, even if linked with the other one, can be chancy and lead to negative learning outcomes.

The picture that emerges suggests that the metacognitive competence required by multimedia learning needs to be trained and enhanced, since the spontaneous beliefs, the degree of awareness, and the repertoires of regulation strategies possessed by the learner are not always adequate. A way to fulfill this need consists in providing multimedia tools with prompts (Stadtler & Bromme 2008), maps (Scott & Schwartz 2007), helps, tutorials, or other supporting systems. In this way, however, we may face the same problem. The learner, in fact, should self-regulate the use of these aids, for instance by choosing whether and when to use them. Metacognitve competence, which is actually lacking, would be useful to employ those additional devices efficiently. We are hence facing a vicious circle (the additional devices are designed to supply the lack of metacognitive competence, but this competence is prerequisite to use of such devices) or an infinite return (such devices should require further devices to assist learners while using them, and so on). More promising appears to be the choice of trying to make the learner be more independent in using multimedia tools, by developing internal metacognitive competence instead of relying on external aids.

Yet, it is important not to forget that metacognitive competence is not always necessary or advisable in multimedia learning. A metacognitve attitude has its costs and hence has to be applied only when needed. If the strategies for use of a multimedia artifact, once proved to be effective, are stabilized and automatized, it is no longer necessary, unless changes occur, to control them metacognitively. This is what actually happens (Green & Azevedo 2007; Moos & Azevedo 2008a): The more practice in learning with hypermedia increases, the more self-regulation decreases. Also the knowledge about the topic to be learned reduces the demand for metacognitive strategies (Moos & Azevedo 2008b). Research points out how metacognitive competence is especially useful when the task is new and complicated.

It is possible that in the future a new culture will develop inside and around the artifacts – a culture that will be adequate to direct relevant use of such tools implicitly (Liverta Sempio 1995). Now we are still stuck in a phase where best practices for each category of learners and for each kind of goal have not yet been determined. In this phase it is interesting to realize how, when facing multimedia artifacts that possess potentialities to promote new ways of learning, students try to find the best way to self-regulate their interaction with such artifacts.

REFERENCES

Anderson, R. C., & Biddle, W. B. (1975). On asking people about what they are reading. In G. Brown (Ed.) *The psychology of learning and motivation* (Vol. 9) (pp. 85–132). New York: Academic Press.

Andre, T. (1979). Does answering higher level questions while reading facilitate productive learning? *Review of Educational Research, 49*, 280–319.

Annett, J. (1989). Training of skilled performance. In A. M. Colley & J. R. Beech (Eds.) *Acquisition and performance of cognitive skills* (pp. 61–84). New York: John Wiley & Sons.

Antonietti, A., & Cantoia, M. (2009). Media and learning: What can cognitive psychology suggest to multimedia education? *Research on Education and Media, 1*(1), 47–62.

Antonietti, A., & Colombo, B. (2008). Computer-supported learning tools: A bi-circular bi-directional framework. *New Ideas in Psychology, 26*, 120–142.

Antonietti, A., Colombo, B., Iannello, P., & Inal, Y. (2011). Students' metacognitive knowledge about distance education in virtual communities and multimedia environments: A cross-cultural study. In C. F. MacTeer (Ed.), *Distance education* (pp. 199–211). Hauppauge, NY: Nova Science.

Antonietti, A., Colombo, B., & Lozotsev Y. (2008). Undergraduates' metacognitive knowledge about the psychological effects of different kinds of computer-supported instructional tools. *Computers in Human Behavior, 24*, 2172–2198.

Antonietti, A., & Giorgetti, M. (2004). Students' conceptions about learning from multimedia. In H. Niegemann, R. Brünken & D. Leutner (Eds.) *Instructional design for multimedia learning* (pp. 249–265). Münster-New York: Waxmann.

Antonietti, A., & Giorgetti, M. (2006). Teachers' beliefs about psychological aspects of learning through multimedia. *Computers in Human Behavior, 22*, 267–282.

Antonietti, A., Imperio, E., Rasi, C., & Sacco, M. (2001). Virtual reality and hypermedia in learning to use a turning lathe. *Journal of Computer Assisted Learning*, 17, 142–155.

Antonietti, A., Rasi, C., Imperio, E., & Sacco, M. (2000). The representation of virtual reality in education. *Education and Information Technologies*, 5, 317–327.

Astleitner, H. (1997). *Lernen in Informationsnetzen: Theoretische Aspekte und empirische Analysen des Umgangs mit neuen Informationstechnolgien aus erziehungswissenschaftlicher Perspektive*. Frankfurt: Europäischer Verlag der Wissenschften.

Ausubel, D. P., Novak, J. D., & Hanesian, H. (1986). *Educational psychology: A cognitive view* (2nd ed.). New York: Holt, Rinehart & Winston. Reprinted, New York: Werbel & Peck.

Baker, L., & Brown, A. L. (1984). Cognitive monitoring in reading. In J. Flood (Ed.) *Understanding reading comprehension: Cognition, language, and the structure of prose* (pp. 21–44). Newark, DE: International Reading Association.

Baker, L., & Mayer, R. E. (1999). Computer-based assessment of problem solving. *Computers in Human Behavior*, 15(3), 269–282.

Balcytiene, A. (1999). Exploring individual processes of knowledge construction with hypertext. *Instructional Science*, 27, 303–328.

Bannert, M. (2001). *Eine explorative Studie zur spontanen Lernwegplanung und gestaltung in vernetzten Lernumgebungen*. Vortrag auf der 60. Tagung der Arbeitsgruppe für Empirische Pädagogische Forschung (AEPF), 19–21 March 2001, Bamberg.

(2002) Managing cognitive load – recent trends in cognitive load theory. *Learning and Instruction*, 12, 139–146.

Bannert, M., Hildebrand, M., & Mengelkamp, C. (2009). Effects of a metacognitive support device in learning environments. *Computers in Human Behavior*, 25(4), 829–835.

Bendixen, L. D., & Hartley, K. (2003). Successful learning with hypermedia: The role of epistemological beliefs and metacognitive awareness. *Journal of Educational Computing Research*, 28, 15–30.

Bennett, R. E., Goodman, M., Hessinger, J., Kahn, H., Ligget, J., Marshall, G., & Zack, J. (1999). Using multimedia in large-scale computer-based testing programs. *Computers in Human Behavior*, 15, 229–283.

Bjork, R. A. (1994). Memory and metamemory considerations in the training of human beings. In J. Metcalfe & A. P. Shimamura (Eds.) *Metacognition: Knowing about knowing* (pp. 185–205). Cambridge, MA: MIT Press.

Boekaerts, M. (1999). Self-regulated learning: Where are we today? *International Journal of Educational Research*, 31, 445–457.

Bolter, J. D. (1991). *Writing space: The computer, hypertext and the history of writing*. Hillsdale, NJ: Lawrence Erlbaum Associates.

Borkowski, J. G., Carr, M., Rellinger, E., & Pressley, M. (1990). Self-regulated cognition: Interdependence of metacognition, attributions, and self-esteem. In B. Jones & L. Idol (Eds.) *Dimensions of thinking and cognitive instruction* (pp. 53–92). Hillsdale, NJ: Lawrence Erlbaum Associates.

Boud, D., Keogh, R., & Walker, D. (1985). What is reflection in learning? In D. Boud, R. Keogh & D. Walker (Eds.) *Reflection: Turning experience into learning* (pp. 85–90). New York: Nichols.

Brenstein, E., & Schellhas, B. (1998). *Lernstrategien in hypermedialen Lernumgebungen*. Vortag auf dem 39. Kolloquium zur Lern- und Lehrforschung. Universität Potsdam.

Brown, A. L. (1978). Knowing when, where, and how to remember: A problem of metacognition. In R. Glaser (Ed.) *Advances in instructional psychology* (Vol. 1) (pp. 77–165). Hillsdale, NJ: Lawrence Erlbaum Associates.

Brown, C. A., Hedberg, J. G., & Harper, B. M. (1994). Metacognition as a basis for learning support software. *Performance Improvement Quarterly, 7*, 3–26.

Brown, K. G., & Ford, J. K. (2002). Using computer technology in training: Building an infrastructure for active learning. In K. Kraiger (Ed.) *Creating, implementing, and managing effective training and development* (pp. 192–233). San Francisco: Jossey-Bass.

Burke, P. (2000). *A social history of knowledge: From Gutenberg to Diderot*. Oxford-Cambridge: Polity Press-Blackwell.

Butler, D. B. (1998). A strategic content learning approach to promoting self-regulated learning by students with learning disabilities. In D. H. Schunk & B. J. Zimmerman (Eds.) *Self-regulated learning: From teaching to self-reflective practice* (pp. 160–183). New York: Guilford Press.

Calcaterra, A., Antonietti, A., & Underwood, J. (2005). Cognitive style, hypermedia navigation and learning. *Computers and Education, 44*, 441–457.

Colombo, B., & Antonietti, A. (2006). Are the cognitive principles underlying multimedia learning counterintuitive? A study of undergraduates' folk conceptions. In G. Clarebout & J. Elen (Eds.) *Avoiding simplicity, confronting complexity. Advances in studying and designing powerful (computer-based) learning environments* (pp. 67–76). Rotterdam: Sense.

Colombo, B., & Antonietti A. (2010). Self-regulated strategies and cognitive styles in multimedia learning. In G. Dettori & D. Persico (Eds.) *Fostering self-regulated learning through ICT* (pp. 54–70). Hershey, PA: IGI Global.

Colombo, B., & Antonietti, A. (2013). Naïve conceptions about multimedia learning: A study on primary school textbooks. *Frontiers in Psychology. 4* (450), doi:10.3389/fpsyg.2013.00450.

Colombo, B., Lissoni, M., & Antonietti, A. (2009). Do illustrated instructional books promote multimedia learning? In O. Demir and C. Celik (Eds.) *Multimedia in educational and special education* (pp. 39–57). Hauppauge, NY: Nova Science.

Cuevas H. M., Fiore S. M., Bowers C. A., & Salas E. (2004). Fostering constructive cognitive and metacognitive activity in computer-based complex task training environments. *Computers in Human Behavior*, 20, 225–241.

Cuevas, H. M., Fiore, S. M., & Oser, R. L. (2002). Scaffolding cognitive and metacognitive processes in low verbal ability learners: Use of diagrams in computer-based training environments. *Instructional Science*, 30, 433–464.

Davidson, J. E., Deuser, R., & Sternberg, R. J. (1994). The role of metacognition in problem solving. In J. Metcalfe & A. P. Shimamura (Eds.) *Metacognition: Knowing about knowing* (207–226). Cambridge, MA: MIT Press.

Edwards, D., & Mercer, N. (1987). *Common knowledge*. London: Methuen.

Ertmer, P. A., & Newby, T. J. (1996). The expert learner: Strategic, self-regulated and reflective. *Instructional Science*, 24, 1–24.

Everson, H. T., & Tobias, S. (1998). The ability to estimate knowledge and performance in college: A metacognitive analysis. *Instructional Science*, 26, 65–79.

Felker, D. B., & Dapra, R. A. (1975). Effects of question type and question placement on problem solving ability from prose material. *Journal of Educational Psychology*, 67, 380–384.

Fiore, S. M., Cuevas, H. M., Scielzo, S., & Salas, E. (2002). Training individuals for distributed teams: Problem solving assessment for distributed mission research. *Computers in Human Behavior*, 18, 729–744.

Fiorina, L., Antonietti, A., Colombo, B., & Bartolomeo, A. (2007). Thinking style, browsing primes and hypermedia navigation. *Computer and Education*, 49, 916–941.

Fisher, E. (1996). Identifying effective educational talk. *Language and Education*, 10, 237–253.

Flavell, J. H. (1976). Metacognitive aspects of problem solving. In L. Resnick (Ed.) *The nature of intelligence* (pp. 231–235). Hillsdale, NJ: Lawrence Erlbaum Associates.

Flavell, J. H. (1979). Metacognition and cognitive monitoring: A new area of cognitive developmental inquiry. *American Psychologist*, 34, 906–911.

Fleishman, E. A., & Mumford, M. D. (1989). Individual attributes and training performance. In I. L. Goldstein (Ed.) *Training and development in organizations* (pp. 183–255). San Francisco, CA: Jossey-Bass.

Foltz, P. W. (1996). Comprehension, coherence, and strategies in hypertext and linear text. In J. F. Rouet, J. J. Levonen, A. Dillon & R. J. Spiro (Eds.) *Hypertext and cognition* (pp. 109–136). Mahwah, NJ: Lawrence Erlbaum Associates.

Forman, E., & Cazden, C. (1985). Exploring Vygotskian perspectives in education: The cognitive value of peer interaction. In J. V. Wertsch (Ed.) *Culture, communication and cognition: Vygotskian perspectives* (pp. 323–347). Cambridge, MA: Cambridge University Press.

Garner, R., Gillingham, M. G., & White, C. S. (1989). Effects of "seductive details" on macroprocessing and microprocessing in adults and children. *Cognition and Instruction, 6,* 41–57.

Giorgetti, M., & Antonietti, A. (2005). Come gli studenti si rappresentano il ruolo della multimedialità nella formazione tools in education (How students conceive the role of multimedia). *Rassegna di Psicologia, 22*(1), 141–159.

Glenberg, A. M., Sanocki, T., Epstein, W., & Morris, C. (1987). Calibration of comprehension. *Journal of Experimental Psychology: General, 116,* 119–136.

Gordon, J. (1996). Tracks for learning: Metacognition and learning technologies. *Australian Journal of Educational Technology, 12,* 46–55. [Online]. Available: http:// cleo.murdoch.edu.au/gen/aset/ajet/ajet12/wi96p46. html

Gourgey, A. E. (1998). Metacognition in basic skills instruction. *Instructional Science, 26,* 81–96.

Greene, J. A., & Azevedo, R. (2007). Adolescents' use of self-regulatory processes and their relation to qualitative mental model shifts while using hypermedia. *Journal of Educational Computing Research, 36*(2), 125–148.

Greene, R. L. (1988). Generation effects in frequency judgements. *Journal of Experimental Psychology: Learning, Memory and Cognition, 14,* 298–304.

Groppo, M., & Locatelli, M. C. (1996). *Mente e cultura: Tecnologie della comunicazione e processi educativi.* Milano: Raffaello Cortina Editore.

Halpain, D. R., Glover, J. A., & Harvey, A. L. (1985). Differential effects of higher and lower order questions: Attention hypotheses. *Journal of Educational Psychology, 77,* 703–715.

Hamilton, R. J. (1985). A framework for the evaluation of the effectiveness of adjunct questions and objectives. *Review of Educational Research, 55,* 47–85.

Hammond, N. (1993). Learning with hypertext: Problems, principles and prospects. In C. McKnight, A. Dillon & J. Richardson (Eds.) *Hypertext: A psychological perspective* (pp. 51–69). New York: Ellis Horwood.

Hartley, K. (2001). Learning strategies and hypermedia instruction. *Journal of Educational, Multimedia and Hypermedia, 10,* 285–305.

Hartley, K., & Bendixen, L. D. (2001). Educational research in the Internet age: Examining the role of individual characteristics. *Educational Researcher, 30,* 22–26.

(2003). The use of comprehension aids in a hypermedia environment: Investigating the impact of metacognitive awareness and epistemological beliefs. *Journal. of Educational Multimedia and Hypermedia, 12,* 275–289.

Hartman, H. J. (2001a). Developing students' metacognitive knowledge and skills. In H. J. Hartman (Ed.) *Metacognition in learning and instruction: Theory, research, and practice* (pp. 33–68). Amsterdam: Kluwer Academic.

Hartman, H. J. (2001b). Metacognition in science teaching and learning. In H. J. Hartman (Ed.) *Metacognition in learning and instruction: Theory, research, and practice* (pp. 173–201). Amsterdam: Kluwer Academic.

Hasseelhorn, M. (1992). Metakognition und Lernen. In G. Nold (Ed.) *Lernbedingungen und Lernstrategien. Welche Rolle spielen kognitive Verstehensstrukturen?* (pp. 35–63). Tübingen: Hogrefe.

Hill, J. R., & Hannafin, M. J. (1997). Cognitive strategies and learning from the World Wide Web. *Educational Technologies Research and Development, 45,* 37–64.

Hofer, B. K., Yu, S. L., & Pintrich, P. R. (1998). Teaching college students to be self-regulated learners. In D. H. Schunk & B. J. Zimmerman (Eds.) *Self-regulated learning: From teaching to self-reflective practice* (pp. 57–85). New York: Guilford.

Höffler, T. N., & Leutner, D. (2007). Instructional animation versus static pictures: A meta-analysis. *Learning and Instruction, 17,* 722–738.

Houston, R. A. (1988). *Literacy in early modern Europe: Culture and education 1500–1800.* London-New York: Longman.

Howard-Jones, P. A., & Martin, R. J. (2002). The effect of questioning on concept learning within a hypertext system. *Journal of Computer Assisted Learning, 18,* 10–20.

Hsiao, Y. (1997). *The effects of cognitive styles and learning strategies in a hypermedia environment: A review of literature.* [Online]. Available: http://www.edb.utexas.edu /mmresearch/Students97/Hsiao

Jacobs, J. E., & Paris, S. G. (1987). Children's metacognition about reading: Issues in definition, measurement, and instruction. *Educational Psychologist, 22,* 255–278.

Jamet, E., Gavota, M., & Quaireau, C. (2008). Attention guiding in multimedia learning. *Learning and Instruction, 18,* 135–145.

Jonassen, D. H. (1996). *Computers in the classroom: Mindtools for critical thinking.* Columbus, OH: Merrill/Prentice-Hall.

Jonassen, D. H., & Grabowski, B. L. (1993). *Handbook of individual differences, learning, and instruction.* Hillsdale, NJ: Lawrence Erlbaum Associates.

Kleinman, D. L., & Serfaty, D. (1989). Team performance assessment in distributed decisionmaking. In R. Gibson, J. P. Kincaid & B. Goldiez (Eds.) *Proceedings of the Interactive Networked Simulation for Training Conference* (pp. 22–27). Orlando, FL: Naval Training Systems Center.

Kramarski, B. (2000). The effects of different instructional methods on the ability to communicate mathematical reasoning. In T. Nakahara, & M. Koyama (Eds.) *Proceedings of the 24th conference of the International Group for the Psychology of Mathematics Education* (pp. 167–171). Hiroshima: Hiroshima University.

Kramarski, B., & Ritkof R. (2002). The effects of metacognition and email interactions on learning graphing. *Journal of Computer Assisted Learning,* 18, 33–43.

Kumpulainen, K., Salovaara, H., & Mutanen, M. (2001). The nature of students' sociocognitive activity in handling and processing multimedia-based science material in a small group learning task. *Instructional Science,* 29, 481–515.

Lawless, K. A., & Brown, S. W. (1997). Multimedia learning environments: Issues of learner control and navigation. *Instructional Science,* 25, 117–131.

Lee, A. Y., & Hutchison, L. (1998). Improving learning from examples through reflection. *Journal of Experimental Psychology: Applied,* 4, 187–210.

Levin, J. R., & Mayer, R. E. (1993). Understanding illustrations in text. In B. K. Britton, A. Woodward & M. Binkley (Eds.) *Learning from textbooks: Theory and practice* (pp. 95–119). Hillsdale, NJ: Lawrence Erlbaum Associates.

Liverta Sempio, O. (1995). Contesto e processi cognitivi. Dalla cognizione intraindividuale alla cognizione situata. In O. Liverta Sempio & A. Marchetti (Eds.) *Il pensiero dell'altro: Contesto, conoscenza e teorie della mente* (pp. 3–40). Milano: Raffaello Cortina Editore.

Liverta Sempio, O. (1999). *I processi di insegnamento-apprendimento come interdipendenza di menti.* Lecture held at the Convegno di Psicologia Culturale, Firenze, 4–5 May 1999.

Maki, R. H. (1998). Metacomprehension of text: Influence of absolute confidence level on bias and accuracy. In D. Medin (Ed.) *The psychology of learning and motivation* (pp. 223–248). New York: Academic Press.

Maki, R. H., Jonas, D., & Kallod, M. (1994). The relationship between comprehension and metacomprehension ability. *Psychonomic Bulletin & Review*, 1, 126–129.

Mandl, H., & Levin, J. R. (1989). *Knowledge acquisition from text and pictures*. Amsterdam: North-Holland.

Maqsud, M. (1998). Effects of metacognitive instruction on mathematics achievement and attitude towards mathematics of low mathematics achievers. *Educational Research*, 40, 237–243.

Mason, L., & Boldrin, A. (2008). Epistemic metacognition in the context of information searching on the web. In M. S. Khine (Ed.) *Knowing, knowledge and beliefs: Epistemological studies across diverse cultures*. (pp. 377–404). New York: Springer.

Mayer, R. E. (1993). Illustrations that instruct. In R. Glaser (Ed.) *Advances in instructional psychology* (vol. 4, pp. 253–284). Hillsdale, NJ: Lawrence Erlbaum Associates.

Mayer, R. E. (1996). Learning strategies for making sense out of expository text: The SOI model for guiding three cognitive processes in knowledge construction. *Educational Psychology Review*, 8, 357–371.

(1998). Cognitive, metacognitive, and motivational aspects of problem solving. *Instructional Science*, 26, 46–63.

Mayer, R. E. (1999). Instructional technology. In F. T. Durso, R. S. Nickerson, R. W. Schvaneveldt, S. T. Dumais, D. S. Lindsay & M. T. H. Chi (Eds.) *Handbook of applied cognition* (pp. 551–569). Chichester, UK: John Wiley & Sons.

Mayer, R. E. (2001). *Multimedia learning*. Cambridge: Cambridge University Press.

(2005). *The Cambridge handbook of multimedia learning*. Cambridge: Cambridge University Press.

McInerney, V., McInerney, D. M., & Walsh, H. W. (1997). Effects of metacognitive strategy training within a cooperative group learning context on computer achievement and anxiety: An aptitude-treatment interaction study. *Journal of Educational Psychology*, 89, 686–695.

Mengelkamp, C., & Bannert, M. (2009). Judgements about knowledge: Searching for factors that influence their validity. *Electronic Journal of Research in Educational Psychology*, 7(1), 163–190.

Mevarech, Z. R., & Kramarski, B. (1997) IMPROVE: A multidimensional method for teaching mathematics in heterogeneous classrooms. *American Educational Research Journal*, 34, 365–394.

Meyer, E., Abrami, P. C., Wade, C., Aslan, O., & Deault, L. (2010). Improving literacy and metacognition with electronic portfolios: Teaching and learning with epearl. *Computers & Education*, 55,1, 84–91. doi:10.1016/j. compedu.2009.12.005

Moore, D., Zabrucky, K., & Commander, N. E. (1997). Metacomprehension and performance in younger and older adults. *Educational Gerontology*, 23, 467–475.

Moos, D. C., & Azevedo, R. (2008a). Monitoring, planning, and self-efficacy during learning with hypermedia: The impact of conceptual scaffolds. *Computers in Human Behaviour*, 24(4), 1686–1706.

(2008b). Self-regulated learning with hypermedia: The role of prior domain knowledge. *Contemporary Educational Psychology*, 33(2), 270–298.

Narciss, S., Proske, A., & Koerndle, H. (2007). Promoting self-regulated learning in Web-based learning environments. *Computers in Human Behaviour*, 23(3), 1126–1144.

Noddings, N. (1990) Constructivism in mathematics education. *Journal for Research in Mathematics Education*, Monograph 4, 7–210.

Ong, W. J. (1988). *Orality and literacy: The technologizing of the word*. New York: Methuen.

Osman, M. E., & Hannafin, M. J. (1992). Metacognition research and theory: Analysis and implications for instructional design. *Educational Technology Research and Development*, 40, 83–99.

Pea, R. D. (1985) Beyond amplification: Using the computer to reorganize mental functioning. *Educational Psychologist*, 20, 1967–1182.

Perkins, D. N. (1985) The fingertip effect: How information processing technology shapes thinking. *Educational Researcher*, 14, 11–17.

Pressley, M., & McCormick, C. B. (1995). *Advanced educational psychology for educators, researchers and policy-makers*. New York: Harper Collins College.

Proctor, R. W., & Dutta, A. (1995). *Skill acquisition and human performance*. Thousand Oaks: Sage.

Puntambekar, S., & duBoulay, B. (1997). Design and development of MIST: A system to help students develop metacognition. *Journal of Educational Computing Research*, 16, 1–35.

Rickards, J. P. (1979). Adjunct questions in text: A critical review of methods and processes. *Review of Educational Research*, 49, 181–196.

Rouet, J. F., Levenen, J. J., Dillon, A., & Spiro, R. J. (Eds.) (1996). *Hypertext and cognition*. Mahwah, NJ: Lawrence Erlbaum Associates.

Salas, E., Kosarzycki, M. P., Burke, C. S., Fiore, S. M., & Stone, D. L. (2002). Emerging themes in distance learning research and practice: Some food for thought. *International Journal of Management Review*, 4, 135–153.

Salomon, G. (1979). Media and symbol systems as related to cognition and learning. *Journal of Educational Psychology*, 71, 131–148.

Scardamalia, M., & Bereiter, C. (1993). Technologies for knowledge-building discourse. *Communications of the ACM, 36*, 37–41.

Scheiter, K., & Gerjets, P. (2007). Learner control in hypermedia environments. *Educational Psychology Review.* Special Issue: *Interactive Learning Environments: Contemporary Issues and Trends, 19*(3), 285–307.

Schnotz, W. (1994). *Aufbau von Wissensstrukturen.* Weinheim: Beltz.

Schnotz, W. (1998). Strategy-specific information access in knowledge acquisition from hypertext. In L. B. Resnick, R. Säljö, C. Pontecorvo & B. Burge (Eds.) *Discourse, tools, and reasoning: Essays on situated cognition.* Berlin: Springer.

Schraw, G. (1998). Promoting general metacognitive awareness. *Instructional Science, 26*, 113–125.

Schraw, G., & Dennison, R. S. (1994). Assessing metacognitive awareness. *Contemporary Educational Psychology, 19*, 143–154.

Schunk, D. H., & Ertmer, P. A. (2000). Self-regulation and academic learning – self efficacy enhancing interventions. In M. Boekaerts, P. R. Pintrich & M. Zeidner (Eds.) *Handbook of self-regulation* (pp. 631–649). San Diego, CA: Academic Press.

Scott, B. M., & Schwartz, N. H. (2007). Navigational spatial displays: The role of metacognition as cognitive load. *Learning and Instruction, 17*(1), 89–105.

Seale, J. K., & Cann, A. J. (2000). Reflection on-line and off line: The role of learning technologies in encouraging students to reflect. *Computers and Education, 34*, 309–320.

Simons, P. R. J., & De Jong, F. P. (1992). Self-regulation and computer-assisted instruction. *Applied Psychology: An International Review, 41*, 333–346.

Smith, E. M., Ford, J. K., & Kozlowski, S. W. J. (1997). Building adaptive expertise: Implications for training design strategies. In M. A. Quinones & A. Ehrenstein (Eds.) *Training for a rapidly changing workplace: Applications of psychological research* (pp. 89–118). Washington, DC: American Psychological Association.

Snow, R. E. (1997). Individual differences. In R. D. Tennyson, F. Schott, N. M. Seel & S. Dijkstra (Eds.) *Instructional design: International perspectives.* (Vol. 1): *Theory, research, and models* (pp. 215–241). Mahwah, NJ: Lawrence Erlbaum Associates.

Sobrol, D. T. (2000). An appraisal of medical students' reflection-in-learning. *Medical Education, 34*, 182–187.

Spiro, R. J., Feltovich, P. J., Jacobson, M. J., & Coulson, R. L. (1991). Cognitive flexibility, constructivism, and hypertext: Random access instruction for advanced knowledge acquisition in ill-structured domains. *Educational Technology, 31*, 24–33.

Stadtler, M., & Bromme, R. (2008). Effects of the metacognitive computer-tool metaware on the Web search of laypersons. *Computers in Human Behaviour*, 24(3), 716–737.

Stahl, E., & Bromme, R. (2009). Not everybody needs help to seek help: Surprising effects of metacognitive instructions to foster help-seeking in an online-learning environment. *Computers & Education*, 53(4), 1020–1028.

Sternberg, R. J. (1998). Metacognition, abilities, and developing expertise: What makes an expert student? *Instructional Science*, 26, 127–140.

Tennyson, R. D., & Parks, O. (1980) Teaching concepts: A review of instructional design research literature. *Review of Educational Research*, 50, 55–70.

Van den Boom, G., Paas, F., van Merriënboer, J. J. G., & van Gog, T. (2004). Reflection prompts and tutor feedback in a Web-based learning environment: Effects on students' self-regulated learning competence. *Computers in Human Behaviour*, 20, 551–567.

Volet, S. E. (1991). Modelling and coaching of relevant metacognitive strategies for enhancing university students' learning. *Learning and Instruction*, 1, 319–336.

Von Wright, J. (1992). Reflections on reflection. *Learning and Instruction*, 2, 59–68.

Vosniadou, S. (1996). Towards a revised cognitive psychology for new advances in learning and instruction. *Learning and Instruction*, 6, 95–109.

Walczyk, J., & Hall, V. (1989). Effects of examples and embedded questions on the accuracy of comprehension self-assessments. *Journal of Educational Psychology*, 81(3), 435–437.

Wang T. H., Wang W. L., Wang K. H., & Huang H. C. (2004). A case study of Web-based Instruction (WBI): The effectiveness of using Frontpage Feedback System (FFS) as metacognition strategy for freshmen biology teaching. *International Journal on E-Learning*. April–June, 18–27.

Watts, G., & Anderson, R. C. (1971). Effects of three types of inserted questions in learning from prose. *Journal of Educational Psychology*, 62, 387–394.

Wilson, B. G. (Ed.) (1996). *Constructivist learning environments: Case studies in instructional design*. Englewood Cliffs, NJ: Educational Technology.

Winne, P. H., & Stockley, D. B. (1998). Computing technologies as sites for developing learning. In D. H. Schunk & B. J. Zimmerman (Eds.) *Self-regulated learning: Self-reflective practice* (pp. 106–136). New York: Guilford.

Young, A. C. (1997). Higher-order learning and thinking: What is it and how is it taught? *Educational Technology, 37,* 38–41.

Zimmerman, B. J., & Bandura, A. (1994). Impact of self-regulatory influences on writing course attainment. *American Educational Research Journal, 31,* 845–862.

3

Theory of Mind in Typical and Atypical Developmental Settings: Some Considerations from a Contextual Perspective

ANTONELLA MARCHETTI, ILARIA CASTELLI, GIULIA CAVALLI, ELEONORA DI TERLIZZI, FLAVIA LECCISO, BARBARA LUCCHINI, DAVIDE MASSARO, SERENA PETROCCHI, AND ANNALISA VALLE

This chapter is a combined effort, and it is distinct in two ways. On the one hand, it proposes the most recent theoretical perspectives on Theory of Mind[1] development within a contextual view. On the other hand, the following pages discuss the work of those people who, over the last fifteen years, have collaborated with Olga Liverta Sempio, to whom this book is dedicated. Without her valuable, thoughtful work and her continuous intellectual input, the Theory of Mind Research Unit (directed by Olga Liverta Sempio and Antonella Marchetti) would not have been set up within the Department of Psychology at the Catholic University of the Sacred Heart in Milan. Each section of the chapter is by those researchers who contributed significantly to investigation of the topic, for the most part with Olga Liverta Sempio and Antonella Marchetti.

[1] ToM, ToM understanding, ToM comprehension, mentalization (ability), and mind reading are here used as synonymous.

THERE IS NO PLACE LIKE ... "FAMILY." IS THIS TRUE?

Flavia Lecciso

The parent-child relationship is the first socially affective experience, and it may be considered a template of what children can expect from others and how they can meet other people's expectations. In terms of this perspective, the primary relationship may be studied not only as the environment in which a child can or cannot learn about mental states, but also as the context that determines the degree to which the social environment can be analyzed and processed.

Over the last ten years a lot of studies have underlined the role of attachment in Theory of Mind (ToM). In particular, the authors agree that secure attachment is linked to good performances on ToM tasks (generally false belief tasks). In other words, the quality of attachment facilitates the development of mentalization, leading an individual to pass the false belief tasks successfully. This theoretical assumption has been confirmed by numerous empirical studies; however, the authors disagree as regards the explanation of this link and have formulated suggestive hypotheses that appear rich in implications from both a theoretical and an educational point of view.

In this section – despite stating that the studies are still in progress – we will present a brief review of two of these perspectives, which may be considered as the main and representative approaches in the literature. We will also present a recent issue of the *Theory of Mind Research Unit*, which attempts to suggest that interpersonal trust is a "bridge (concept)" between ToM and attachment.

Elizabeth Meins (Meins et al. 2002, 2003), from a Vygotskian perspective, explains the link between ToM and attachment through a model that Fonagy defines as "indirect." In this model security of attachment acts on the mentalization ability of a child through the mediation of different kinds of social processes, such as pretend play, language, and interactions with peers (Meins 1997). It is important to point out that Meins emphasizes, in this indirect link, the role of maternal sensitivity as defined in terms of mind-mindedness, that is, the propensity to think of a child as a person or a mental agent. This capacity is exerted in the proximal development zone, fosters a secure attachment, and facilitates a child's greater understanding of his/her mind and the minds of other people. Meins has shown through numerous studies that this propensity is not the same for every mother: There are varying degrees of it, so it is necessary to assess these individual differences. Meins and colleagues, in the initial studies (i.e., Meins & Fernyhough 1999), assessed the mind-mindedness "offline": They did not measure the interaction between mother and child; however, they asked mothers to describe their children verbally. Their responses were then codified as being general, physical, behavioral, or mental. In a subsequent piece of work, Meins and colleagues (Meins et al. 2002) measured the mind-mindedness "online," by codifying the mothers' appropriate mind-related comments during twenty minutes of free play with their children. The mind-related comments of the mothers were shown to be longitudinally predictive of attachment security and child's mentalizing ability at forty-five to forty-eight months.

Peter Fonagy (Fonagy & Target 1997), within the psychoanalytic framework, considers the link between both ToM and attachment through an "indirect model," which is similar to that described earlier, and through a "direct model." In the latter, the security of attachment indirectly facilitates a child's mentalization ability. We will briefly present the latter for its innovativeness and possible pedagogical implications. From this perspective, the role of maternal sensitivity is also very important; Fonagy has defined maternal sensitivity in terms of Reflective Function: the capacity of the caregiver of the secure child not only to view him/her as a mentalizing human being, but also to reflect on this image by means of mental containment processes. According to Fonagy, attachment is the result of successful mental containment, which occurs when the mental state of a child is correctly reflected by the mother, who is capable of "containing" those states of affection that are intolerable for the child and of dealing with them and handing them back to the child as physical care in a suitable form. Insecure attachment is considered to be a defensive mechanism in which intimacy (in the avoidant child and distanced adult) and independence (in the ambivalent child and anxious adult) are forgone. The security of attachment becomes the mental security: The secure child, through exploring his/her caregiver's mind, finds him/herself as a mental agent, so he/she develops his/her mentalizing ability. Fonagy and colleagues devised an "offline measure": a scale to assess the Reflective Function on the Adult Attachment Interview (AAI) transcripts, particularly in the answers to those questions that require reflection and analysis of complex unobservable mental states. These answers allow us to evaluate an individual's ability to think about the parental mental experience and to describe the link between this experience and self-experience. In other words, the Reflective Function assesses an adult's ability to reflect on childhood relationships with parents in mental terms.[2] The Reflective Function scale showed enormous variations in the reflective capacities of individuals. Fonagy and colleagues underline that the most adaptive level of a caregiver's propensity is the moderate one, or, in other words, the "good enough" level, while both excessive mentalizing (which can lead to paranoid reasoning) and deficient mentalizing (which can lead to concrete reasoning) are just maladaptive ways of parental mentalizing (Fonagy, Gergely, & Target 2007). The model by Fonagy and colleagues is not restricted to a theoretical level. Recently it also underlined the underpinned pedagogical stance (Fonagy et al. 2007). Indeed, Fonagy and colleagues (2007) assume that a caregiver with a "good enough" Reflective Function behaves toward the child and

---

[2] Recent studies (Slade et al., 2005) introduced a new index of Reflective Function, assessing the reflective processes on the Parent Development Interview. This permits the analysis of the caregiver's mental propensity within the context of the relationship with the child. The scope of this section does not allow further consideration of these studies.

speaks to him/her in an appropriate and adaptive way. This allows a child gradually to "think" about him/herself and others in mental state terms. From this perspective, the caregiver is a pedagogue, playing the role of a "teacher." Such considerations seem to make it necessary to interpret the development of ToM not simply as an individual aspect, but also as a relational ability or an intersubjective process that involves both relational partners. Two different circles that involve mother and child develop in this framework: a virtuous circle, in which the "good enough" mother's Reflective Function allows the child's good mentalization, and a vicious circle, in which a maladaptive mother's Reflective Function is linked to the child's poor mentalization ability. On this basis, every form of intervention could focus on the "vicious or virtuous circle" in the dyad, bearing in mind the interaction between the mentalizing ability of the child and that of his/her caregiver.[3]

In the final part of this section we intend to present a recent attempt by the Theory of Mind Research Unit to link attachment and ToM through the concept of trust. In the literature, trust is analyzed in cognitive or affective terms. However, Bernath and Feshbach (1995) underlined the need to jointly study the cognitive, emotional, affective and behavioral manifestations of trust. We (Lecciso, Petrocchi, Liverta Sempio & Marchetti 2011) are currently using a new semi-projective task, which analyzes the links among trust, attachment, and ToM in typical development. The task evaluates several dimensions, which are usually analyzed separately: the trust versus no trust dimension regarding the story of interactions, other individuals' perspective taking, and the ability to interpret characters' actions on the basis of

---

[3] The considerations on the existence of a vicious versus virtuous circle allow us to underline the role of the adult, which is, therefore, of fundamental importance in situations of typical development and, more significantly, in atypical development. We will see these circles in paragraph entitled Language and Theory of Mind: Deafness as a Benchmark where we analyze the case of deaf children and their hearing mothers.

previous interactions. The innovative aspect of such a piece of work is that the task allows us to assess the different dimensions mentioned together. The results indicate that the trustful profile is an important element capable of accounting for mentalistic ability. Trust, which derives from a relationally secure context, leads the child to evaluate the behavior of other people in terms of beliefs, emotions, or mental states.

THEORY OF MIND AND SCHOOLING

Giulia Cavalli

When children go to school they already have a well-developed understanding not only of the world, but also of their own mental state and the mental states of others (cognition, emotions, and motivational states). Research on Theory of Mind within an educational context has focused on studying both how children use the mental state of comprehension during school activities and how school can affect ToM development (Lecciso, Liverta Sempio, & Marchetti 2005).

In particular, the interest of researchers in recent years has been directed toward the links between ToM and schooling. There are actually a lot of situations in the school lives of children in which the ability to reflect on the content of one's own mind and the minds of others is involved. This occurs, for example, when children are required to learn from textbooks, from what the teacher says, (Olson & Astington 1995), or during interaction with peers and teachers, which involves cognitive and affective aspects (e.g., during debate, in cooperative and competitive activities) (Tomasello 2001; Astington & Pelletier 2005).

For example, peer acceptance, which requires the ability to interact adaptively with others, seems to be interlinked with mentalization ability: Activities such as peer collaboration or discussion can be easy for children who have a good ToM, so they experience more acceptance and school success than children who have a poor mental state of comprehension. Furthermore, ToM can help children to make sense of their school experience: School is mainly a context in which children build knowledge, form or revise their beliefs about the world, compare their beliefs with those of others, and understand the differences between people with the knowledge of how to do things (e.g., to complete homework).

As regards the two basic processes in education, that is, learning and teaching, it is evident that they are closely connected to the ability to share mental states: Learning implies the ability to reason about the mental states of teachers (intentions, goals, and so forth) and teaching is based on assigning the specific mental states of ignorance or false belief to a pupil's mind (Liverta Sempio 2004). Children must, on the one hand, be aware that there is a difference between the knowledge of a teacher and that of a learner, and they must be aware that a teacher performs a series of intentional actions aimed at increasing children's knowledge. On the other hand, a teacher must recognize the ignorance of other people and her own knowledge (or lack of ignorance) (Ziv & Frye 2004). For instance, it was discovered that from three to seven years of age, children improve their ability to teach others, thus passing from modeling and demonstrating strategies – typical of children who lack a well-developed ToM – to the verbal instruction teaching strategy. This is used a lot more by children who are able to understand mental states (Strauss, Ziv & Stein 2002).

ToM influences not only children's understanding of teaching and their use of teaching strategies, but also their learning strategies. According to Tomasello, Kruger, and Ratner (1993; Tomasello 2001), there are three different types of learning, which can be considered as folk models of the mind: by imitation, by instruction, and by collaboration. They require a developing mentalization ability (and language ability, too, as underlined by Astington & Pelletier 2005). Indeed, imitation only requires the ability to understand a teacher's intention and to imitate her/his intentional actions; learning by instruction is based on recognizing the difference between the beliefs of a teacher and those of children (it involves first-order false belief comprehension); learning collaboratively requires the ability to understand different points of view and to use them to create one's own ideas.

A new topic in this domain of study, which contributes to a deeper analysis of the psychological functioning of a student, has recently been introduced: the link between the motivation to learn and ToM (Liverta Sempio & Cavalli 2007). As the ability to impute mental states with the aim of understanding behavior implies recognizing the motives for people's observable actions, ToM can deal with motivation that directs the learning behavior of an individual. Results showed that school-age children who are extrinsically motivated or externally regulated (i.e., children who find reason to study in some external – not psychological – aspects, such as to obtain a reward or to avoid a punishment) show poor ToM ability (Liverta Sempio & Cavalli 2007; Cavalli & Liverta Sempio 2007).

In conclusion, it seems that ToM though it does not guarantee a child an easier life at school, can facilitate the ability of a child to act in the school context (Astington & Pelletier 2005).

Up to this point we have discussed how children use ToM at school; the other question is how school can help development of ToM. This matter is not easy to study: It is a complex process (Lecciso, Liverta Sempio, & Marchetti 2004). It may be suggested that the affective relationship between a teacher and a pupil (e.g., attachment relationship; Pianta 2001) and the way in which a teacher looks after the mental states of children (e.g. asking them what they think, know, believe, feel and using mental language during interaction with them) help children in the learning process and influence their mentalization ability (Liverta Sempio 2004; Astington & Pelletier 2005).

PRETENSE AND CHILDREN'S LITERATURE

Davide Massaro

The progressive shift in the studies from the fundamental steps of ToM development to an evaluation focused on interpersonal differences has driven researchers to investigate the presence of possible precursors. The "classic" precursors (pointing, shared attention, pretense, etc.) may be defined as behaviors that a child acts out before the critical age for the acquisition of ToM, that is, four years. These behaviors would hide the seeds of ToM, those things that could also be called "assumptions of competence" that anticipate and prepare the appearance of the real mentalistic ability. Although the concept of precursor intuitively finds space both in the theoretical reflection and in the empirical investigation, a more analytic evaluation of the meaning of precursor as well as the investigation of the nature of each precursor raise at least two questions: (1) If a precursor and ToM share a specific basic cognitive competence, why should ToM not appear in concomitance with the precursor? (2) If the period of development that precedes the appearance of ToM appears to play an important role in terms of predictive effect on the acquisition of this competence, what are the educational implications regarding the relationships in which the child is involved?

The first question leads to theoretical reflection and stimulates a critical evaluation of the concept of ToM and precursors. ToM is the ability to predict and interpret behavior on the basis of mental states; it implies the presence of a metarepresentational cognitive ability that makes the person able to manage different representations of the same reality simultaneously. This is a good approximation of the definition of ToM, which is widely shared by a large number of authors; its core element is the metarepresentational mechanism that guarantees a disjunctive and joint management of different representations of the reality experienced and allows the person to hypothesize behaviors based on false beliefs, even if true beliefs are available.

The concept of precursor and its meaning in ToM development need to be discussed in light of these considerations about mentalistic ability.

What do the constructs of ToM and precursor really share? Which aspect of the metarepresentational mechanism involved in the ToM usage does the precursor anticipate?

The main difficulty is identifying the criteria and competences that define the real value of the precursor and explaining the developmental link (and, thus, the distance) between a precursor and Theory of Mind.

Specific precursors more closely touch particular problematical aspects of the aforementioned argument, following a developmental trend. Indeed, the more praecox competences (shared attention, pointing, etc.), on the one hand, pose a small risk of construct overlapping, whereas they increase the problem of specifying these behaviors as real precursors, rather than as behaviors that have a simple predictive value concerning the appearance of ToM.

In other words, the question concerns the nature of the link between ToM and the precursors – rather than any other behavior – if the presence of a specific shared cognitive mechanism is excluded.

On the other hand, "late" precursors, closer in time to the appearance of ToM, point out the problem of the partial or total overlapping of the constructs. This is in the case of pretend play, one of the most studied precursors in ToM.

Pretend play is supposed to share the same metarepresentational mechanism as ToM, in order to manage the real representation and the pretend one at the same time.

However, the sharing of this identical cognitive mechanism again raises the problem discussed earlier: Why does ToM not appear (perhaps at its elementary level) during the same period of development as pretend play? Lillard and Witherington (2004) explore this aspect in depth and criticize the meta representational nature of pretense, at least when it is performed in the developmental period that precedes the development of the ToM. In particular, they describe a developmental course of pretense that would take on a more complex and metarepresentational form only after the appearance of mentalistic ability. In this case, the new question concerns the nature of pretend play during the first four years of life. According to Lillard and Witherington (2004), the first instances of pretense would be very simple and almost totally based on the processing of behavioral cues, rather than on mentalistic operations. The authors show that activities performed in a pretense context by mothers and their eighteen-month-old children differ from the same activities performed in a real context for some specific behaviors, for example, faster, wider, and more stressed gestures and movements; more looking at the child by the mother; and more smiles. Lillard and colleagues (2007) confirm and extend these observations, by identifying the persistence of this phenomenon across different pretense scenarios as well as across different ages (fifteen-, eighteen-, and twenty-four-month-olds). The perspective by Lillard and colleagues does not solve all the problems briefly considered: The status of precursors and the specificity of the link between precursors and ToM are still open issues. However, the proposal to revise the concept of pretense and the new developmental trend that focuses on the gradual change of this competence in close relationship with the development of mentalistic abilities put new light on a field of research that is both significant and important and far from a clear and conclusive definition.

The second question at the basis of this short reflection concerns the educational value of relationships involving children in the age groups before ToM development. The literature underlines the presence of several types of behavior – in which children are engaged in different degrees of quality and intensity – that influence the timing and the developmental modalities of mentalistic ability. For instance, language rich in mentalistic references, the relationship between siblings, the quality of the attachment relationships, and other characteristics are variously predictive of ToM development.

If it is true that all these aspects of a relationship support the appearance of mentalistic ability, the question particularly concerns the relevance of those practices that are explicitly oriented to improving the predictive effect of these activities. Researchers have been investigating ToM for more than twenty-five years and are now studying the fascinating field of applied research in order to discover the applied potential of the recent discoveries on ToM development.

In this sense, Dyer, Shatz, and Wellman (2000) explored a wide range of children's books in order to check whether those materials that are commonly and frequently used may represent a valid source of mentalistic knowledge. Evidence shows how children's literature is rich in characters and situations, which are described using a considerable amount of terms referring to mentalistic activities. Moreover, they found that a discrete percentage of those situations present linguistic content of an ironic nature. Recently, Shatz and colleagues (2006) supported this claim from an intercultural perspective, by identifying specific differences (strongly related to cultural differences) in texts translated across different languages: The same mentalistic content is conveyed differently on the basis of specifics of the culture in which the original text was translated. Both the simple consideration of books as a mentalistic source and the more in-depth and analytic evaluation of the influence of culture on the process of acquisition stimulate reflection on the educational problem. ToM is a social competence – an ability that guarantees and supports the success of interpersonal exchanges. From this point of view, the sense of studying the development of this ability naturally develops into the study of its effects in reality, because ToM performs best in the vicissitudes of human beings.

THEORY OF MIND, IRONY, AND RELATIONAL CONTEXTS

Annalisa Valle

The links between ToM and language are evident from a narrative perspective, in which metarepresentational competences enable children to understand a story and a character's emotions (Massaro, Valle, & Marchetti 2013a). A more specific association between the two abilities is observable in many forms of figurative language, in which what is said does not coincide with its real meaning. One of these linguistic forms is irony, a particular mode of communication in which the speaker indirectly communicates to the listener his/her attitude concerning the object of conversation. Verbal irony is defined by a speaker when he/she remarks on a situation or a person to a listener, who is often the target of the comment. This is the case when, for example, a mother sees her son's messy bedroom and comments, "Your bedroom is really tidy!": In order to understand this statement the child has to discriminate between the literal (the room is tidy) and non-literal (the room is messy) meaning and to perceive the real intent, attitude, and emotional disposition of the mother. Attitude, intent, and emotions are examples of mental states, and their comprehension depends on ToM acquisition: This can explain children's difficulties in understanding ironic communication, although it occurs in many contexts, such as cartoons, films, books, and daily adult discourse. The first study concerning the association between irony and mentalistic abilities was undertaken in 1991, when Winner and Leekam investigated how children detect the stance behind ironic communication and distinguish it from the attitude conveyed by a white lie. According to the authors, a speaker uses utterances that are literally false to say something good and positive about a bad and negative situation in both irony and white lies. The two modes of communication differ from each other on two levels: First, regarding the speaker's intention and, second, concerning the nature of the speaker's attitude. As regards the first aspect, the speaker wants to convey false information in white lies, whereas in irony he/she wishes to share his/her attitude on the discourse content with the listener and create in his/her mind the same representation. The second difference surrounds the nature of the speaker's attitude, which in white lies is positive (the aim is to praise a person) and in irony is negative (the goal is to debase someone). Winner and Leekam studied five- to seven-year-old children and discovered that their ability to distinguish between the second-order intention of the liar and of the ironist (what he/she wants the listener to know) is a prerequisite in order to be able to distinguish an ironic from a deceptive attitude: Children are able to detect the critical attitude behind irony when they are able to make the distinction between the second-order intentions of an ironist as opposed to the intentions of a liar. In their conclusions, the authors hypothesized that understanding irony is more difficult than understanding the intentions of a liar: "Understanding the attitude behind irony may require a recognition of a third-order mental state.... Irony comprehension may also require the third-order judgement that the speaker wants (first-order) the listener to believe (second-order) that the speaker has a particular attitude (third-order)."

On the basis of these findings, more recent authors (cf. Creusere 1999) have proved that in order to understand an ironic utterance it is necessary and sufficient to pass the second-order false belief task; therefore, we can imagine using an irony task to establish children's metacognitive level within a communicative framework. But in ironic communication there are many elements that affect the mental state of an individual, such as the conversational context or the behavioral markers used during the conversation. In addition, Winner and Leekam, in order to provide a more in-depth investigation, introduced the feature of intonation of ironic utterances as a contextual and relational aspect, a role in processing irony. Although their initial results did not support this hypothesis, other authors have attempted to extend the study of irony to include different factors, in addition to mentalistic abilities, which could explain irony comprehension in children. Creusere (1999) states that throughout the history of irony research, different authors have been interested in a particular ironic tone of voice (piercing and frequency-modulated, with high intensity and slow rhythm), in facial expression of irony (the speaker seems to imitate the character he/she is mocking), in different contextual aspects in which ironic discourse takes place (discrepancy between the meaning of the utterance and the real situation). Therefore, it is clear that there are many different aspects of communication, interacting with the ToM, that enable children to understand irony in different contexts. In a recent piece of research (Massaro, Valle, & Marchetti 2013a) we studied the role of the speaker-listener relationship in the understanding of irony by children. The hypothesis is that children who have still not acquired second-order mentalistic abilities can be helped to understand irony by contextual indexes, for example, the relationship between characters. These relationships may be asymmetric or symmetric, as they may involve people with different statuses: An ironic asymmetric utterance is an utterance pronounced by an adult to a child, whereas an ironic symmetric communication is addressed by a child to another child. We tested the differences in irony comprehension under these two conditions in a sample of seventy-one children, attending the first, third, and fifth years of primary school. We used two irony understanding tasks, specifically devised for this piece of research, and two mentalistic tasks, which were first- and second-order false belief tasks. The results support the hypothesis: There is strong correlation in the entire sample between irony understanding and second-order false belief performances, confirming that children use progressive mentalistic abilities to process ironic communication. Moreover, asymmetric irony comprehension appears less difficult than symmetric comprehension at all ages; this confirms that the speaker interacts with ToM abilities and influences reasoning regarding the ironic statement. The fact that a particular relational context plays an important role in irony interpretation may be explained in two ways: The first way relates to the situational context. In this sense, children hear ironic language more often during interaction with adults than during interactions with peers, so they build a prototype, requiring the presence of an adult speaking ironically; the second way involves ToM abilities; it claims that children learn metacognitive competences for the first time by *reading* the caregiver's mind: Children understand the mental states of adults better than the mental states of their peers. In all situations, mentalistic reasoning interacts with contextual pointers to lead a child to a correct interpretation of irony, and as a consequence to an adequate relational skill. Regardless of the correct interpretation of the links between irony and ToM, the literature and the results of the present study highlight the complex multidimensional nature of irony understanding and invite us to continue to research all aspects of the interaction between ironic communication and metacognitive competences. In the future it will be important to extend ToM and language study to other relational or socio-contextual aspects of irony besides status difference (see for example Massaro, Valle & Marchetti, 2013b), in order to discover the numerous elements that bridge these two complex research areas.

LANGUAGE AND THEORY OF MIND: DEAFNESS AS A BENCHMARK

Serena Petrocchi

Several authors have hypothesized that language plays a significant causal role in ToM development, especially during the pre-school years, when children normally acquire first-order false belief understanding.

On the one hand, some researchers (e.g., Peterson & Siegal 2000) underline the importance that general language skills play in determining ToM abilities. According to these researchers, the broad cognitive and social function of language in general supports mentalistic development and explains the relationship between these two topics. For example, general language skills play a vital role, as children through conversations can establish mentalistic relationships with caregivers, siblings, and peers. The sociolinguistic hypothesis by Peterson and Siegal (1995) points out the role of conversations about mental topics in developing the ToM and understanding of the aims and intentions underlying the communication.

On the other hand, another position has focused on specific aspects of language in ToM development. De Villiers (2005), for example, pointed out the role of syntactic development for false belief understanding. In particular, children provide mentalistic interpretations of reality when they become able to produce sentences in which mentalistic verbs possess embedded phrases that children know to be referentially opaque.

The debate about the causal role of general versus specific aspects of language in ToM development is still open. Studies carried out on deaf children could provide a useful benchmark, in order to clarify the characteristics of this causal relationship. Indeed, deaf children are usually shown to have broad linguistic delays in acquisition; however, they have a similar degree of normal nonverbal intelligence to hearing children and do not lack any degree of sociability, as autistic children do (see paragraph ToM, Morality, and Pervasive Developmental Disorders). Furthermore, a large number of studies carried out by various researchers relate the difficulties in ToM understanding, as shown by deaf children, with the communicative characteristics of the context in which these children live. Indeed, authors throughout the literature usually distinguish three groups of deaf children, on the basis of the sensorial condition of their parents and the type of communication that they essentially use within their family (sign or spoken language).

The first group of deaf children are called "native signers." They are brought up in a family in which one or both parents are deaf, and they learn sign language from everyday life interactions, as this is the main way of communicating with their primary relational environment. By contrast, deaf children with hearing parents must learn sign or spoken language to communicate with others in formal education programs. In these cases, the authors distinguish, respectively, between "late signers" and the "oral deaf." Late signers are deaf children who do not learn sign language from their parents, because normal hearing people do not use sign language. They learn sign language from specific training programs at primary school or in some specialized centers. Oral deaf children learn spoken language through oral rehabilitation programs and with the help of technical hearing aids that amplify auditory residuals.

Given this classification, the sensorial condition of a parent appears to be an important factor to be considered, in order to understand the different performances of the three groups of deaf children in the ToM tasks described later. Moreover, studying these three different conditions also offers us the opportunity to explain the role played by language in ToM development in hearing children. Indeed, if language acquisition has a causal role in ToM development, then deaf children with delayed language acquisition should also have a delay in mentalistic understanding. By contrast, deaf children with deaf parents, who naturally learn sign language from birth, should develop ToM, through following the steps followed by normal hearing people.

In fact, a lot of studies showed more ToM difficulties in the group of late signers compared with hearing children and native signing deaf children (for a review see Peterson & Siegal 2000; De Villiers 2005). The question surrounding the mentalistic performance of the oral deaf children is more controversial (Peterson & Siegal 2000; De Villiers 2005). According to some research, ToM develops later in oral deaf children than in hearing and native children. According to other studies, the performance of oral deaf children could be compared to that of native signers and hearing children. The differences discovered between these studies could be linked to the different degrees of deafness: The moderately deaf child should have fewer mentalistic difficulties compared with the profoundly deaf child, because he/she may encounter fewer deprivations when taking part in daily conversation involving mental states.

In conclusion, from the studies briefly summarized here, it seems to emerge that language really plays a vital role in ToM development, as shown by the difficulties of the late signers and oral deaf children (except in one research study) compared with native signers and hearing children. It is not yet clear, however, whether general language skills, or specific aspects of language (i.e., syntactic skills), or a combination of both aspects are related to ToM development.

In this debate, there is another important topic that needs consideration: That is whether an environment of hearing caregivers can influence various aspects of the development of deaf children, and not only their communicative skills. For instance, some studies have shown that hearing mothers of deaf children spend less time interacting with their children, compared with control dyads. These mothers seem to be less flexible and more intrusive, and their children are, therefore, less creative and less active. Even when hearing parents are sensitive and well prepared for the problems to be faced, they most probably will encounter difficulties in affective interactions with their child. This remark underlines the important role of an adult in all aspects of the development of deaf children, and, furthermore, given the crucial role of affective relationships for ToM developmental in typical situations, it may be useful to analyze the role an adult plays in the mentalistic development of deaf children.

We are currently concerned with the role of affective relationships in the development of ToM in children (Marchetti, Liverta Sempio & Lecciso 2006). We are also interested in the role of a caregiver's mentalistic abilities in the development of ToM in children

(Lecciso, Petrocchi & Marchetti, 2013). Both studies focus on oral deaf children.

In the first study, the authors found that passing the ToM tasks appears to be closely related to the secure attachment of a child to both parents and teachers. This result is in line with those perspectives that consider ToM as a relational, intersubjective, and affective process.

In the second study, the results showed that both deaf children and their hearing mothers were less able to solve the ToM tasks than the hearing children and their hearing mothers. Since the mothers in this study were similar as regards socioeconomic status and IQ, the authors hypothesize that the unexpected birth of a deaf child in a hearing family may result in negative personal and familial dynamics. The reaction to the diagnosis may lead to narrow-minded behavior of a family toward a child's problems (see also Lecciso et al., 2013 as regards the link between the resolution of the diagnosis of autism, the maternal representation. of the child and child's attachment). Therefore, the authors suggest that the lower mentalistic abilities of mothers of deaf children may be due to lower time investment as a result of a relationship with a child who has difficulties in becoming an able communicative and relational mentalistic partner.

In conclusion, the results of this study show that maternal mentalistic abilities also predict the ToM performance of a child in hearing mother-deaf child dyads, not in controls. Perhaps this is due to the existence of an early sensitive developmental period within which the role of the adult takes place. It is possible that, in hearing children, the presence of an adult is more important in the years before the acquisition of first-order false beliefs, which are crucial for mentalistic development. In this window of opportunity, the mentalistic abilities of an adult are closely linked to comparable abilities in the child. The link may be lost later in life, as the child will have developed a ToM. By contrast, hearing parents of deaf children in the early years of a child's life who are caught up in the diagnosis process and are overfocused on deafness cannot draw any advantage from these crucial early opportunities and take longer to cover the normal steps.

Taken as a whole, research studies on deaf children support the importance of communicative, mentalistic, and affective context for the ToM development, as is also shown by studies on visually impaired children (Lecciso et al. 2005).

THEORY OF MIND, MORALITY, AND PERVASIVE DEVELOPMENTAL DISORDERS

Barbara Lucchini

In 1985, Frith, Baron-Cohen, and Leslie advanced the hypothesis that the central symptoms of autism (anomalies in social interaction, communication, and imagination) could be explained by a specific deficit of ToM, which involves the capacity to represent thoughts, beliefs, and desires of others mentally.

Autistic children show deficits in mind reading ability, joint attention, gaze monitoring, declarative gestures, and symbolic play and have particular difficulties with tasks requiring them to understand another person's beliefs.

Although they may have some rudimentary mind reading ability, there is indeed a small percentage of autistic children who succeed in the first-order false belief task, although this happens later than with normally developing children. They are unsuccessful, however, in more sophisticated mind reading tasks, such as the second-order false belief task, and they lack the full metarepresentational capacity that is fundamental for communication.

The number of successful performances on false belief tasks does not increase significantly with age: This leads to the conclusion that a central component of autism is a distinct deficit in mind reading ability, and not an impairment of general cognitive abilities.

Nevertheless, there is evidence that children with autism can represent some mental states, such as simple desire, simple emotions, and true beliefs, and can understand the intentions of other individuals on the basis of actions. Besides joint attention, gaze monitoring, and declarative gestures, intention is one of the earliest mental states to be understood by normally developing infants. The main differences between autistic children and children who have other developmental delays are to be found in communication, imitation, and joint attention; therefore, research in understanding the intentions of other individuals on the basis of mental states in autistic children is fundamental for understanding some of the symptoms of autism.

Children talk about beliefs and intentions in interpreting human actions and in evaluating the moral quality of these actions. Studies in moral development and ToM are also becoming more closely linked within the field of pathology, with attention given to individual developmental differences, social origins, and implications of ToM.

Moral development research has a long history of concern with children's moral reasoning and judgments of the actions of people, based on consideration of their mental states. Children in fact use information about intentions in evaluating the moral quality of the actions of others, and there are links between both understanding mental states and moral behavior.

Studies show that moral judgment is unimpaired in children who have autism. Indeed, autistic children showed some understanding of motives and were able to apply this understanding to social issues in an experimental setting. Autistic children judge culpability on the basis of motive and consider injury to people as more culpable than damage to property. Moreover, autistic children provided an appropriate verbal justification for their judgments. In addition, responsiveness to the distress of others is not impaired in autism, as is shown by their responses to the moral/convention distinction. This is, therefore, sufficient in order for children to make particular distinctions, however, not sufficient for them to make empathic behavioral responses.

Autistic children who failed both false belief tests presented to them possibly lack the ability to mentalize the moral/conventional distinction. As a result, the ability to mentalize is not a prerequisite for the development of the distinction.

A study by Lecciso, Lucchini, Liverta Sempio and Marchetti (2008) analyzed ToM and moral understanding in high-functioning autistic and normally developing children. The aim of the research was to investigate the value of intention of moral action and its link with mentalization ability. According to the literature, the research findings showed significant differences between the autistic children and two normally developing groups. They were matched in terms of chronological age and mental age and in ToM tasks, however, not in terms of moral understanding tasks. Autistic children showed difficulties in a first-order false belief task (unexpected transfer test) and a second-order false belief test (look-prediction task). The results support the wide body of evidence already present in the literature of a ToM deficit in autistic children, independent of cognitive abilities.

The ability to make moral judgments, however, is not impaired: Indeed autistic children have no difficulty with moral tasks or in the understanding of intentionality. Autistic children can evaluate differently identical actions depending on the motives of the subject. Development in understanding the intentions of other people on the basis of actions (*intention reading*) is largely intact in autistic children, who have marked deficits in ToM. However, *sharing intention* is impaired.

The literature regarding ToM in atypical development indicates that mentalizing may be partially developed, impaired, or totally inadequate in a wide range of clinical conditions. The most representative evidence of the severe impairment that a ToM deficit has on daily social interactions is from autism, with many studies confirming poor performances by autistic children on classical false belief tasks.

Furthermore, a study by Castelli, Lucchini, Antonietti, and Marchetti (2005) compared ToM understanding, through the use of a nonverbal false-belief task, in autistic children and girls with Rett syndrome – a genetic neurodegenerative disorder similar to autism. Despite the easiness of such nonverbal tasks and the better cognitive level of autistic children overall, they performed more poorly than girls who had Rett syndrome on the tasks. This result may lead to future research concerning ToM in atypical conditions, insofar as a basic level of mentalizing in a heavily impaired condition such as Rett syndrome is able to make these girls socially smarter than autistic children.

THEORY OF MIND IN MALTREATED CHILDREN

Eleonora Di Terlizzi

Investigating ToM development in children who have a history of maltreatment represents a relatively new line of research. Although a number of studies have been conducted in the field of child maltreatment that have aimed to provide a better understanding of its cognitive, emotional, and social sequelae, there are relatively few studies, to our knowledge, that explicitly explore the development of mentalization in maltreated children. Moreover, all of those studies have documented deficits in ToM abilities. A brief review will be given.

Cicchetti and colleagues (Cicchetti et al. 2003) examined false belief understanding in a large sample of three- to eight-year-old children. The sample included 203 low socioeconomic status (SES) maltreated children, 143 low SES nonmaltreated controls, and 172 middle SES nonmaltreated comparisons, all of whom lived at home with their biological parents. Children were administered two first-order false belief tasks and a language assessment. The results revealed that maltreated children were significantly less likely to exhibit false belief understanding than both nonmaltreated groups, when controlling for language and socioeconomic status.

A second piece of research carried out by Pears and Fisher (2005) supports the previous results. They investigated emotion understanding and ToM abilities among three- to five-year-old children. Data were collected from two groups: maltreated foster care children and a comparison group of nonmaltreated children of the same age, living at home with their biological families. Significant differences were recorded between the groups concerning emotion understanding and ToM, which were assessed by a first-order false belief task, a desire task, and a perception task. Additionally, maltreatment was negatively associated with these abilities even when age, IQ, and executive function were controlled. Moreover, the number of days spent in foster care and the number of transitions that a child experienced did not influence emotion understanding or ToM. Considering these findings, the experience of maltreatment appears to be the only variable that undermines emotion understanding and mentalization capacities.

Recently, a study (Liverta Sempio et al. 2007) was conducted that focused on the link between maltreatment and ToM in an institutional care[4] sample of maltreated children from 7.5 to 13 years of age and in a control group with similar features of age, gender, and IQ to the sample.

The ToM testing battery consisted of classical first-order and a second-order false belief task and a subtest of Strange Stories. This advanced test investigates several aspects of ToM, such as misunderstanding, irony, white lies, and mixed emotions. In order to pass the test, a child must be able to infer mental states and be able to understand that what the story's character feels or thinks may, however, be

---

[4] CAF, Help Centre for maltreated child and Family in crisis, Milan.

different from his/her outward appearance as described in the story. The stories represent real-life situations and, therefore, suggest social understanding. Considering the results, all the children in both groups passed the first-order false belief task. As regards the second-order false belief task and the Strange Stories there were significant differences between the two groups. In particular, the maltreated group was less successful than the nonmaltreated children in both tasks. In comparison to previous studies in which the ToM is investigated in younger children, these findings suggest that the gap in first-order false belief tasks is recovered with development. However, deficits are evident in second-order tasks and in tasks concerning social competences in maltreated children.

Why may the experience of maltreatment have an impact on the development of mentalization?

A great deal of research has shown that maltreated children exhibit a number of impairments in their psychological development, and there are several reasons to suppose that some of these could be associated with problems in mentalization. The link between maltreatment and deficits in mentalization could be explained through child-caregiver interaction. In the case of maltreatment, the cause of a distortion and deficit in acquisition of ToM would appear to be specifically a deprivation of social inputs (Fonagy, Gergely & Target 2007). Considerable research, for instance, has documented deficits in emotion recognition and understanding and in psychological problems characterized by emotion dysregulation. From a relational-affective point of view, these findings support the assumption that maltreated children are involved in poorer maternal emotion socialization processes than nonmaltreated children. In particular, maltreating mother-child dyads openly discuss emotion less frequently and make fewer references to internal states than nonmaltreating dyads (Shipman et al. 2007). In fact, within a maltreating environment, the children learn that it is unacceptable and dangerous to discuss their feelings and emotions, particularly the negative ones.

Consistent with this perspective, a trend of research points out the negative effects of power assertive parenting techniques (physical punishment, yelling, direct commands) on the understanding of false belief. In these situations, children do not engage in negotiations that would enable them to realize that people have different points of view. Considering maltreatment as an extreme form of assertive parenting style, the influence on mentalization might be similar.

Maltreatment is also associated with little coordination of social attention in caregiver-child interactions and several studies have shown that the child-caregiver relationship is characterized by insecure and disorganized attachment. These early social experiences might play an important role as regards the prediction of delayed mentalization.

Maltreating parents do not provide a supportive and responsive context. They are less likely to respond contingently and adequately to their infants and are more likely to show bias when reflecting on the mental states of a child.

The difficulty of maltreated children in understanding the mental states of their abusive parents might be understood by the abuser's attempts to mask his/her real thoughts, feelings, and intentions with the aim of justifying violent actions. The lack of clarity and ambiguous intentions make the parent's behavior unpredictable and provoke feelings of distress, fear, and helplessness in the child (Fonagy et al. 2002). Moreover, maltreating adults are unlikely to interact with their children, by talking to them with a "mind-minded" language, that is, namely, using internal-state terms to comment accurately on the states of mind and emotions of their children during interactions.

To sum up, a victim of maltreatment has fewer opportunities to explore the mind of the other individual; to find an image of himself/herself that is motivated by beliefs, feelings, and intentions; and to observe the difference between one's own perspective and the perspectives of others. Future research should focus on the maltreated condition and the context of everyday life in order to identify protective factors, in particular, in terms of affective quality in the child–professional caregiver relationship, in the educational and therapeutic settings that might moderate the negative effects of maltreatment on mentalization and on children's general development.

NEW FRONTIERS FOR THEORY OF MIND RESEARCH

Ilaria Castelli

After many years of rich and intense research in typical and atypical development, ToM has recently shifted to a life-span perspective, opening new lines of research that can be summed up as follows: (1) the development of ToM in old age, both in typical and atypical conditions – namely, dementia; (2) the neural basis of ToM investigated with brain-imaging methods – PET (positron emission tomography) and fMRI (functional magnetic resonance imaging); and (3) the possible links between ToM and other abilities that are important for adapting to social life situations, for example, decision making.

At the moment the debate concerning the development of ToM in old age (1) is still open, as some studies have found a ToM decline along with a general cognitive decline with advancing years, whereas few studies have found a preservation of ToM in old age. Interestingly, as was also the case in the research on children, researchers turned their attention, in the case of the elderly, to the boundary between typical and atypical development, insofar as the research on clinical conditions may provide useful insights in order to understand better what happens in typical development. Up to this point, various studies have been carried out on many forms of dementia (frontal variant frontotemporal dementia, Alzheimer's disease, Parkinson's disease, Huntington's disease), which show a ToM deficit in these clinical conditions. However, such a deficit is likely to assume different connotations, depending on the level of selectivity and impairment of the various kinds of dementia and on the kinds of tasks used to test the mentalistic competence (from simple tasks to complex ones). The Research Unit on ToM has devoted its attention to this topic[5] and has carried out research on ToM in patients with Alzheimer's disease and in old controls using a battery that covers all the aspects of Theory of Mind development (from precursors right through to classical false belief reasoning and advanced mentalistic reasoning). This research has shown a decline in clinical subjects at all levels of the ToM battery with the exception of a simple and acted out first-order false belief task (Castelli et al., 2011), thus opening up for the future some possible means of intervention, in order to face ToM deterioration in Alzheimer's disease in time and/or to support ToM reasoning while the disease progresses. This point is also connected with the second line of research, mentioned in point (2), that is, the discovery of the neural basis of mentalizing with brain-imaging methods, which we are now going to consider.

The newly developed field of neuroscience of ToM, which looks for the neural basis of mentalizing, has shown that ToM relies upon a precise brain circuit (Frith & Frith 2006) that comprises the following regions: the posterior end of the superior temporal sulcus (pSTS) and the adjacent temporoparietal junction (TPJ), the temporal pole (TP), the medial prefrontal cortex (mPFC), and the adjacent anterior paracingulate cortex. The discovery of this brain circuit has been possible thanks to a lot of research performed on typical and atypical conditions in adults; however, the neural basis of ToM from a life-span perspective is still to be explored, thus raising the question whether this set of brain regions undergoes any changes with advancing years and/or any deterioration with the beginning of clinical pathology. The Research Unit on Theory of Mind has tried

---

[5] In collaboration with the Unit of Rehabilitative Neurology at the Fondazione Don Carlo Gnocchi, I.R.C.C.S. Santa Maria Nascente in Milan.

to investigate such new topics[6] and has carried out research on the neural basis of mentalizing in successful aging (Castelli et al., 2010a) and in patients with mild cognitive impairment (MCI, a clinical condition that has a high probability to develop into Alzheimer's disease) compared with healthy old controls and healthy young controls (Baglio et al., 2012). The results of this research, which is still in progress, show that MCI patients face an initial decline in ToM at the neural level; however, such a decline is not necessarily mirrored by the behavioral level, thus opening possible insights for the prevention of the deterioration of ToM in MCI patients who are likely to develop Alzheimer's disease.

In conclusion, the idea that adults master full-fledged ToM ability as one of the tools of more general social competence has opened the way to the discovery of possible links between ToM and other abilities that are important in our social life, for example, decision making (3) and the use of brain-imaging methods. The discovery of such links has been facilitated by both ToM and decision-making research. ToM is starting to be considered as a component of the decision-making process, since the possession of good mind-reading abilities that can be explicitly or implicitly "embedded" into evaluating a situation may contribute to making proper decisions. This last point is supported by the recent discovery of common neural circuits for the resolution of ToM and of decision-making tasks in an economic context with *brain-imaging* methods. Rilling and colleagues (2004) found that two areas of the brain discovered for ToM – the anterior paracingulate cortex and the posterior superior temporal sulcus – were active when subjects believed that they were to be playing an interactive game with monetary offers with a human partner compared to a computer. The fact that mentalistic reasoning is implied in decision making through

---

[6] In collaboration with the Unit of Rehabilitative Neurology at the Fondazione Don Carlo Gnocchi, I.R.C.C.S. Santa Maria Nascente in Milan, and with the Unit of Functional Imaging of the San Raffaele Hospital in Milan.

the attribution of an *intentional stance* by the other individual may help us to shed some light on the various components of the decision-making process, which relies not only on deliberative components, but also on emotional-affective ones as well as mentalistic ones. This point is currently being investigated by the Research Unit on Theory of Mind[7] (Castelli et al., 2010b; Marchetti et al., 2011). The study of ToM involvement in decision making both in children and in adults may have educational implications, insofar as the ability to reflect upon the contents of one's own mind and the mind of another person may help manage all components involved in the decision-making process to formulate a good and adaptive decision.

REFERENCES

Astington, J. W., & Pelletier, J. (2005). *Theory of mind, language and learning in the early years: Developmental origins of school readiness.* In B. D. Homer & C. S. Tamis-LeMonda (Eds.) *The development of social cognition and communication* (pp. 205–230). Mahwah, NJ/London: Lawrence Erlbaum Associates.

Baglio, F., Castelli, I., Alberoni, M., Blasi, V., Griffanti, L., Falini, A., Nemni, R. & Marchetti, A. (2012). Theory of Mind in amnestic Mild Cognitive Impairment: an fMRI study. *Journal of Alzheimer's Desease*, 29,1, 25–37.

Baron-Cohen, S., Leslie, A. M., & Frith, U. (1985). Does the autistic child have a "theory of mind"? *Cognition*, 21, 37–46.

Bernath, M. S., & Feshbach, N. D. (1995). Children's trust: Theory, assessment, development, and research directions. *Applied and Preventative Psychology*, 4, 1–19.

Castelli, I., Lucchini, B., Antonietti, A., & Marchetti, A. (2005). *La teoria della mente nello sviluppo atipico. Un confronto tra autismo e sindrome di Rett.* In Riassunti delle comunicazioni del XIV Congresso Nazionale AIRIPA, Pisa, 21–22 ottobre, pp. 87.

Castelli, I., Baglio, F., Blasi, V., Alberoni, M., Falini, A., Liverta Sempio, O., Nemni, R. & Marchetti, A. (2010a). Effects of aging on mindreading ability through the eyes: An fMRI study. *Neuropsychologia*, 48, 2586–2594.

---

[7] In collaboration with the Neural Decision Science Laboratory directed by Professor Sanfey at the University of Arizona.

Castelli, I., Massaro, D., Sanfey, A. G. & Marchetti, A. (2010b). Fairness and intentionality in children's decision-making. *International review of Economics*, 57, 269–288.

Castelli, I., Pini, A., Alberoni, M., Liverta Sempio, O., Baglio, F., Massaro, D., Marchetti, A. & Nemni, R. (2011). Mapping levels of theory of mind in Alzheimer's disease: a preliminary study. *Aging & Mental Health*, 15(2), 157–168.

Castelli, I., Massaro, D., Sanfey, A. G. & Marchetti, A. (2013). "What is fair for you?" Judgments and decisions about fairness and Theory of Mind. *European Journal of Developmental Psychology*, 1–14. DOI: 10.1080/17405629.2013.806264.

Cavalli, G., & Liverta Sempio, O. (2007). *Capacità mentalistica, motivazione/amotivazione scolastica e somatizzazione.* XXI Congresso Nazionale AIP, sezione Psicologia dello Sviluppo, Bergamo, 20–22 September 2007.

Cicchetti, D., Rogosh, F., Maughan, A., Toth, S., & Bruce, J. (2003). False belief understanding in maltreated children. *Development and Psychopathology*, 15, 1067–1091.

Creusere, M. A. (1999). Theories of adults' understanding and use of irony and sarcasm: applications to and evidence from research with children. *Developmental Review*, 19, 213–262.

De Villiers, P., (2005). The role of language in theory-of-mind development: What deaf children tell us. In J. Astington & J. Baird (Eds.) *Why language matters for theory of mind.* Oxford: Oxford University Press.

Dyer, J. R., Shatz, M., & Wellman, H. M. (2000). Young children's storybooks as a source of mental state information. *Cognitive Development*, 15 (1), 17–37.

Fonagy, P., Gergely, G., Jurist, E. L., & Target, M. (2002). *Affect regulation, mentalization, and the development of the self.* New York: Other Press.

Fonagy, P., Gergely, G., & Target, M. (2007). The parent-infant dyad and the construction of the subjective self. *Journal of Child Psychology and Psychiatry*, 48(3–4), 288–328.

Fonagy, P., & Target, M. (1997). Attachment and reflective function: Their role in self-organization. *Development and Psychopathology*, 9, 679–700.

Frith, C. D., & Frith, U. (2006). The neural basis of mentalizing. *Neuron*, 50(4), 531–534.

Lecciso, F., Liverta Sempio, O., & Marchetti, A. (2004). Teacher-child relationship: A meeting of minds. *European Journal of School Psychology*, 2, 15–17.

Lecciso, F., Liverta Sempio, O., & Marchetti, A. (2005). *La teoria della mente a scuola.* In O. Liverta Sempio, A. Marchetti & F. Lecciso (Eds.) *Teoria della mente tra normalità e patologia* (pp. 85–114). Milano: Raffaello Cortina.

Lecciso, F., Liverta Sempio, O., Marchetti, A., & Pezzotta, C. (2005). Gli occhi della mente: Il caso dei soggetti ipovedenti e non-vedenti. In O. Liverta

Sempio, A. Marchetti & F. Lecciso (Eds) *Teoria della mente tra normalità e patologia*. Milano: Cortina Editore.

Lecciso, F., Lucchini, B., Liverta Sempio, O. & Marchetti, A. (2008), Giudizio morale e teoria della mente nell'autismo ad alto funzionamento, *Autismo e disturbi dello sviluppo*, 33, 179–211.

Lecciso, F., Petrocchi, S., Liverta Sempio, O. & Marchetti, A. (2011). Un contributo per un nuovo strumento di misura della fiducia tra affetti e mentalizzazione: la Trust Story. *Psicologia clinica dello sviluppo* 1, 63–94.

Lecciso, F., Petrocchi, S. & Marchetti, A. (2013). Hearing mothers and oral deaf children: an atypical relational context for theory of mind. *European Journal of Psychology of Education*, 28 (3), 903–922.

Lecciso, F., Petrocchi, S., Savazzi, F.A.M., Marchetti, A., Nobile, M. & Molteni, M. (2013). The association between maternal resolution of the diagnosis of autism, maternal mental representations of the relationship with the child, and children's attachment. *Life Span and Disability*, XVI, 21–38.

Lillard, A. S., Nishida, T., Massaro, D., Amrisha, V., Ma, L., & McRoberts, J. (2007). Signs of pretense across age and scenario. *Infancy*, 11(1), 1–30.

Lillard, A. S., & Witherington, D. C. (2004). Mothers' behavior modifications during pretense and their possible signal value for toddlers. *Developmental Psychology*, 40(1), 95–113.

Liverta Sempio, O. (2004). *L'interazione adulto-bambino secondo la psicologia culturale: Una risorsa dello sviluppo*. In B. Ligorio (a cura di) *Psicologia e cultura: Contesti, identità e interventi* (pp. 165–187). Roma: Carlo Amore.

Liverta Sempio, O., Bertetti, B., Di Terlizzi, E., & Marchetti, A. (2007). *La mentalizzazione in bambini vittime di maltrattamento*. IX Congresso Nazionale AIP- Sezione di Psicologia Clinica e Dinamica, Perugia, 28–30 settembre (pp. 232–233). Abstract Book.

Liverta Sempio, O., & Cavalli, G. (2007). *Theory of Mind, motivation to learn, and psychosocial risk in elementary school*. XIII European Conference on Developmental Psychology, Jena, 21–25 August 2007.

Marchetti, A., Liverta Sempio, O., & Lecciso, F. (2006). The silent understanding of the mind: The deaf child. In A. Antonietti, O. Liverta Sempio & A. Marchetti (Eds.) *Theory of Mind and language in different developmental contexts*. Plenum Series on Human Exceptionality. New York: Springer.

Marchetti, A., Castelli, I., Harlé, K. M &, Sanfey, A.G. (2011). Expectations and outcome: the role of proposer features in the Ultimatum Game. *Journal of Economic Psychology*, 32, 446–449.

Massaro, D., Valle, A., & Marchetti, A. (2013a). Irony and second-order false belief in children: What changes when mothers rather than siblings speak? *European Journal of Developmental Psychology*, 10(3), 301–317.

Massaro, D., Valle, a. & Marchetti, A. (2013b) Do social norms, false belief understanding, and metacognitive vocabulary influence irony comprehension? A study of five-and seven-year-old children. *European Journal of Developmental Psychology*, 10(3): 1–13, doi: 10.1080/17405629.2013.821407.

Meins, E. (1997). Security of attachment and maternal tutoring strategies: Interaction within the zone of proximal development. *British Journal of Developmental Psychology*, 15,129–144.

Meins, E., & Fernyhough, C. (1999). Linguistic acquisitional style and mentalising development: The role of maternal mind-mindedness. *Cognitive Development*, 14, 363–380.

Meins, E., Fernyhough, C., Wainwright, R., Clark-Cater, D., Das Gupta, M., Fradley, E., & Tuckey, M. (2003). Pathways to understanding mind: Construct validity and predictive validity of maternal mind-mindedness. *Child Development*, 74, 1194–1210.

Meins, E., Fernyhough, C., Wainwright, R., Das Gupta, M., Fradley, E., & Tuckey, M. (2002). Maternal mind-mindedness and attachment security as predictors of theory of mind understanding. *Child Development*,73, 1715–1726.

Olson, D. R., & Astington, J. W. (1995). *Pensare il pensiero: Imparare ad interpretare le affermazioni e a considerare le credenze*. In O. Liverta Sempio & A. Marchetti (a cura di) *Il pensiero dell'altro* (1995). Milano: Raffaello Cortina.

Pears, K., & Fisher, P. (2005). Emotion understanding and theory of mind among maltreated children in foster care: Evidence of deficits. *Development and Psychopathology*, 17, 47–65.

Peterson, C., & Siegal, M. (1995). Deafness, conversation and theory of mind. *Journal of Child Psychology and Psychiatry*, 3, 459–474.

(2000). Insights into theory of mind from deafness and autism. *Mind & Language*, 15, 123–145.

Pianta, R. C. (2001) *Enhancing relationships between children and teachers*, APA, Washington, D.C.

Rilling, J. K., Sanfey, A. G., Aronson, J. A., Nystrom, L. E., & Cohen, J. D. (2004). The neural correlates of theory of mind within interpersonal interactions. *Neuroimage*, 22(4), 1694–1703.

Shatz, M., Dyer, J. D., Marchetti, A., & Massaro, D. (2006). Mental language in storybooks for children. In A. Antonietti, O. Liverta Sempio & A. Marchetti (a cura di) *Theory of mind and language in different developmental contexts* (pp. 93–106). Plenum Series on Human Exceptionality New York: Springer.

Shipman, K., Schneider, R., Fitzgerald, M., Sims, C., Swisher, L., & Edwards, A. (2007). Maternal emotion socialization in maltreating and non-maltreating families: Implication for children's emotion regulation. *Social Development*, 16(2), 267–285.

Strauss, S., Ziv, M., & Stein, A. (2002). Teaching as a natural cognition and its relations to preschoolers' developing theory of mind. *Cognitive Development*, 17, 1473–1487.

Tomasello, M. (2001). Cultural transmission: A view from chimpanzees and human infants. *Journal of Cross-Cultural Psychology*, 32, 135–146.

Tomasello, M., Kruger, A. C., & Ratner, H. H. (1993). Cultural learning. *Behavioral and Brain Sciences*, 16, 495–511.

Winner, E., & Leekam, S. (1991). Distinguishing irony from deception: Understanding the speaker's second-order intention. *British Journal of Developmental Psychology*, 9, 257–270.

Ziv, M., & Frye D. (2004). Children's understanding of teaching: The role of knowledge and belief. *Cognitive Development*, 19, 457–477.

4

The Use of Metacognitive Language in Story Retelling: The Intersection between Theory of Mind and Story Comprehension

JANETTE PELLETIER, KATHLEEN HIPFNER-BOUCHER, AND ANTOINETTE DOYLE

The worlds of the child are replete with experiences that have come to be identified in the empirical literature as contributors to the child's emerging social understanding. Theory of Mind researchers have sought to understand the relationship between environmental factors and the general trajectory of Theory of Mind development in typically developing children. Findings gathered over the past twenty years highlight the important roles played by language, the family environment, pretend play, and culture in children's construction of social understanding (Antonietti & Iannello 2008; Cutting & Dunn 1999; Dunn et al., 1991; Jenkins et al., 2003; Symons, Fossum, & Collins 2006; Vinden & Astington 2000).

Researchers interested in emergent literacy, meanwhile, have focused their attention on the developmental precursors of conventional literacy. They have worked to identify the types of adult-child interactions that support the development of early literacy and to clarify the relationships between these interactions and reading and writing outcomes in school (Foy & Mann 2003; Fritjers, Barron, & Brunello 2000; Purcell-Gates 1996; Sénéchal & Lefevre 2002; Whitehurst & Lonigan 1998). Narrative competency, a component of emergent literacy generally measured in terms of storytelling ability, has been the subject of investigation by researchers attempting to elucidate the relationship between the preschooler's skill in interpreting and producing narrative accounts and later reading comprehension (Morrow 1985; Roth, Speece & Cooper 2002; Snow, Scarborough & Burns 1999).

In the past decade, Theory of Mind development and narrative comprehension, as intersecting processes, have become an area of increasing interest to researchers in both fields. In this chapter, the Theory of Mind achievements of typically developing kindergarten children will be considered in relation to the transactional processes of meaning making in storybook reading experiences. This chapter will demonstrate that four- to six-year-old children bring social understandings to storybook-based interactions in order to construct meaning actively from text, and that these understandings are manifested in their appropriate use of metacognitive language. The findings of a cross-sectional study aimed at investigating kindergarten children's production of mental state verbs in a story retell task are presented and discussed in terms of their relation to concurrent measures of narrative comprehension.

THEORY OF MIND ACHIEVEMENTS FOR SOCIAL UNDERSTANDING AND NARRATIVE COMPREHENSION

Social understanding is fostered by the dynamic interaction of elements in the child's physical, social-emotional, and cognitive worlds (Cutting & Dunn 1999; Jenkins et al. 2003, Meins et al. 2003; Perner 1999). The rich social-contextual experiences afforded children promote a burgeoning "Theory of Mind"; this emerging achievement then allows children to make meaning in all facets of their childhood experiences. In literate cultures one such experience is child engagement in storybook-based activities. What do children give to the storybook reading experience? What is the nature of this social understanding that contributes to story comprehension?

The Theory of Mind achievements a child contributes to social-contextual understanding, including story comprehension, are typically related to the age of the child. While it is not assumed that children systematically develop in lockstep fashion, as individual differences are widely reported in the literature, replications of Theory of Mind measures strongly support a developmental sequence through which all typically developing children progress. Understanding of intentionality, emotion attributions, beliefs about knowledge, belief-desire-action relationships, and perspective taking are all facets of social understanding that impact upon the degree to which the child can give meaning to narrative.

The three-year-old child typically brings to text the understanding of intentionality in human behavior, an achievement attributed to children as early as the end of the first year of life (Meltzoff 2002) or by eighteen months of age (Moore 2006). Repacholi and Gopnik (1997) report that by eighteen months, children attribute desires to others on the basis of people's facial expressions and vocalizations. Astington (2001) states that by the age of two, children see people as intentional agents from their observations of a person's behavior of "trying." She notes that by age three, children's acknowledgment of intention is strongly associated with a successful outcome, whereas by age five, children understand that intention is not dependent on goal achievement: The achievement of five-year-olds, then, may lie in their appreciation of intention and action as important mediators between desire and outcome. In my view it is the metarepresentational ability to see intentions as representational states causing actions that allows for an understanding of this mediation (p. 98).

Perner (1999) suggests that by the age of four, children understand that emotional states are dependent upon goal achievement. Over the early childhood years, then, children progress from the ability to recognize intention, to developing an understanding that goal achievement is not guaranteed by desire and intention, but that emotional states are dependent on the match or mismatch among these.

Children's language reflects their growing understanding of their own and others' mental states. Two-year-olds increasingly talk about feelings and desires. By the age of three children begin to talk more frequently about believing and knowing, and do so with increasing accuracy. Moore and Furrow (1991) report that at about the age of four children begin to distinguish effectively between the terms "think" and "know," while the mastery of distinctions between other terms, such as "think" and "guess," is achieved much later. Perner (1991, 1999) suggests that three-year-olds possess a behavior-based theory of knowledge whereby "knowing" is dependent upon success of an action. He cites O'Neill and Astington's work in children's understanding of aspectuality in which improvement is noted between the ages of four and five, signaling a shift from a behavior-based theory of knowledge to an understanding that perceptual access to sufficient and reliable information is necessary for knowledge (O'Neill, Astington & Flavell 1992). False belief understanding has been widely researched and reported, and a distinction is noted between implicit and explicit understanding of the concept (Perner 1999). While there is disagreement regarding the age at which children demonstrate false belief understanding, Wellman, Cross, and Watson's (2001) metaanalysis suggests that although task conditions may ease or inhibit success on false belief measures, it is generally accepted that children achieve false belief understanding at the age of four.

Beyond the age of four when children achieve false belief understanding, social understanding continues to develop. Children's attribution of belief-based emotion understanding is typically not achieved until a significantly later time, between the ages of six and seven years (de Rosnay et al. 2004). Second-order false beliefs are reported by Perner (1988) to be achieved between the ages of six and nine. Development of an interpretive Theory of Mind by which children come to understand that knowledge is interpretively constructed continues to emerge into middle childhood and adolescence (Chandler & Lalonde 1996). Similarly, Kuhn (2000) argues that children's epistemological understandings of belief states evolve over time. In her view a progression from viewing knowledge as located externally with certainty, to realizing the subjective component of knowledge, to potentially arriving at an evaluative understanding of knowledge whereby the multiplicity of interpretations is recognized, but one is held to be true, is a life-span Theory of Mind achievement – one that some may even fail to accomplish.

While the brevity of this sketch cannot capture the complexities of children's achievements in social understanding, it highlights the "minds" that children bring to constructing meaning from text. The Theory of Mind achievements of a three-year-old and a seven-year-old will differ significantly and impact upon the child's comprehension of narrative text, as these texts are not merely renderings of actions constituting a plot, but are richly woven with mental references that give meaning to action. How well the child then can construct meaning from text involves not only how well equipped the Theory of Mind "tool kit" that they take to the task is, but also the nature of the transactions among the child, the adult, and the text. The storybook reading experience has, therefore, the potential to contribute to the growth of children's social understanding.

THE CONTRIBUTION OF STORYBOOK EXPERIENCES TO THEORY OF MIND GROWTH IN CHILDREN

There is ample evidence that shared reading experiences in the home can serve to promote children's understanding of the mind (Le Sourn-Bessaoui & Deleau 2001; Ratner & Olver 1998; Symons et al. 2005). For example, Adrian et al. (2005) found a significant association between the frequency of storybook reading at home, mothers' use of mental state terms in a picture-book reading task, and child success on a series of false belief tasks. In a longitudinal study conducted two years later with children between three and seven years of age, Adrian, Clemente, and Villanueva (2007) examined the frequency with which mothers used cognitive verbs in reading-based discourse, as well as the pragmatic features of verb use. They distinguished between maternal references to their own or their child's mental states during the shared story experience and references to storybook characters' thoughts and actions expressed largely in "think" terms. The former were found to predict performance on both concurrent and delayed tasks of Theory of Mind, while the latter predicted performance on delayed tasks only. The authors also found that these pragmatic features of mothers' meta-cognitive language were more sensitive than frequency measures for capturing the association with children's understanding of mental states. Symons et al. (2006) conducted a study examining social inter-change following storybook reading using a book premised on the theme of mistaken identity. They found that children whose mothers chose to engage in a discussion about the false identity feature of the book after its initial reading were more than twice as likely to exhibit near-mastery on Theory of Mind tasks compared with children whose mothers did not engage them in such a discussion.

Taken together, these findings suggest that storybook sharing holds the potential for further enhancement of the child's Theory of Mind when a knowledgeable adult, acting as the mediator, is purposeful in his/her interaction with the child. For such purposeful interaction to occur there must first be recognition by the adult that the child may not fully comprehend the mental world embedded within the plot. Cassidy et al. (1998) report that a high proportion of books purchased by families for three- to six-year-old children contained mental state references, and more than one-third of these books contained false beliefs. By design, storybooks often rely heavily upon illustration to convey meaning. Yet Szarkowicz (2000) notes that not all children's book illustrations make emotional states equally salient. Adult medi-ation, therefore, is essential in helping the young child to understand and to integrate the mental states of characters with the plot in order truly to construct meaning from the storybook experience. Mediation is widely reported as essential for helping children to comprehend nar-rative (Tough 1983; Wells 1985; Teale & Sulzby 1999).

Mediation in this context involves teaching children both the lan-guage they will need to talk about language (metalanguage) and the language they will need to talk about mental states (metacognitive language). Astington (2000) argues that both language and metalanguage are needed to code perceptual reality, and that acquisition of these skills "helps the child to conceptualize the contrast between the world and the mind" (p.281). Olson (1982) states that exposure to adult talk about language teaches children to use metalanguage to negotiate meaning in day-to-day conversations with others and in conversations that arise during storybook interactions. Heath (1986) documents how children's orientation to language has an impact upon their success in taking meaning from print: Children who have not been exposed to a metalinguistic orientation to language in the preschool years typically encounter significant difficulty with story comprehension in school. Adult metalinguistic input in the context of storybook interactions has been shown to benefit children in other ways as well. Findings from a study by Deckner, Adamson, and Baker (2006) point to a strong association between the rate of maternal metalingual utterances during shared reading, such as prompts and recasts, and interest in reading in very young children. The important role of motivation to read in promoting literacy is well documented (Sonnenschein & Munsterman 2002).

With respect to metacognitive language, Astington (1998) suggests that helping children to develop their understanding of mentalistic language allows them to talk about their own and others' thoughts – that using language about thinking "brings cognition into consciousness" (p. 48). In their study of children's retelling of stories, Pelletier and Astington (2004) report that teachers' use of metacognitive language and discussions of mental states may impact upon children's story comprehension by helping them to make connections between the storybook characters' thoughts, beliefs, desires and intentions (the landscape of consciousness) and their behaviors (the landscape of action). Peskin and Astington (2004) found that exposing children to metacognitive vocabulary in storytelling resulted in significantly more metacognitive verb production in subsequent retellings but no improvement in metacognitive language comprehension. Comprehension, they argue, results when adults actively engage children in the construction of mentalistic interpretations based on illustrations and text that implicitly draw attention to mental states. Similarly, Tager-Flusberg and Sullivan's (1995) study of the mental state references of typically developing, mentally handicapped, and autistic children concludes that it is not just the frequency of mental state usage but the child's ability to explain mental states that is important for children's story understanding. Taken together, these studies highlight the importance of adult mediation in modeling, monitoring, and scaffolding children's understanding and usage of metacognitive language. Story sharing provides an excellent medium in which this mediation can occur.

THE CONTRIBUTION OF STORYBOOK EXPERIENCES TO NARRATIVE COMPETENCE IN CHILDREN

The language of storytelling, be it oral or written, is highly decontextualized; it is talk about people, places, things, and events that are situated beyond the here and now. It stands in contrast to the contextualized language of face-to-face conversation in which speakers and listeners draw upon gesture, expression and intonation, interactive negotiation, and so on, to facilitate mutual comprehension. The language used in the context of storytelling has particular features through which meaning is conveyed in the absence of the real world cues that support comprehension in contextualized discourse, such as explicit reference to the characters' mental states. These literate language features have been shown to occur at measurable rates in the unprompted stories generated by three- to five-year-old children, supporting the claim that decontextualized language skill has its origins in the preschool years (Curenton & Justice 2004). Facility with decontextualized language has been shown to increase with age (Ukrainetz et al. 2005).

Research suggests that preschool children's sensitivity to the distinct registers of contextualized and decontextualized language is predictive of reading and writing achievement in the school years (Roth, Speece, & Cooper 2002; Snow 1991). Limited ability to produce and comprehend narratives is one of the characteristics that distinguish language-impaired children from their typically developing counterparts (Greenhalgh & Strong 2001; Kaderavek & Sulzby 2000). Given the preponderance of decontextualized language use in the classroom setting, children who experience difficulty in mastering this particular form of discourse are generally viewed as being at risk for academic failure (Feagans & Short 1984; John, Lui & Tannock 2003).

Storybook-reading practices are important influences on the development of decontextualized language. Teale and Sulzby (1999) propose that reading aloud with children serves to bridge the gap between contextualized and decontextualized language, making the complex, formalized discourse of narrative, also known as story language, accessible to children. Sulzby (1985) posited that the talk that parents use during storybook reading interactions allows children to experience the differences between registers because it is a hybrid of the spoken and literary forms: In parent-child storybook interactions, characteristics of oral language permeate the parents' rendering of the written text. Wells (1985) suggested that helping preschool children understand the differences between the two registers is essential for their later success in school literacy. Over repeated readings of stories, he argues, children come to internalize story language and gradually begin to use it in their own narrative productions.

The child's developing sense of story structure or schema is also supported through shared storybook experiences. A story schema, or mental model of a story, provides the child with a mechanism for meaning making; it serves as a backdrop against which comprehension can be monitored as the reader progresses through a text (Heath 1986). A sense of story schema is not innate in children but must be developed. Morrow (2001) found that through hearing many well-written stories, children develop understandings about story structure such as setting, theme, plot, and resolution. As a result, they have more success in constructing their own oral and written stories. Through interaction with stories read at home, young children develop understandings of the structure of individual stories that may eventually allow them to make intertextual links across stories (Sipe 2001). Sulzby's (1985) research on children's emerging sense of story through repeated readings indicated progressive development of control over story language and structure over time. Brown and Briggs (1991) have reported similar gains as children are increasingly exposed to familiar stories.

In discussing the findings of their metaanalytical review of the effects of storybook reading on children's literacy and language development, Bus et al.'s (1995) conclusion may best summarize the findings with respect to the influence of shared storybook experiences on the development of narrative competence. They argued that through storybook reading experiences, children are confronted with the literary language register – the grammatical forms and discourse rules governing narrative – in ways that conversation typically does not allow, and this, they concluded, is a prerequisite for reading comprehension.

The everyday life experiences of children, therefore, provide numerous and varied opportunities to develop social understanding. Children take to the shared story reading experience a wealth of achievements in "Theory of Mind" development. These accomplishments provide an orientation for approaching the construction of meaning from the literacy event. Because it facilitates rich language interaction in considering mental states and multiple character perspectives, mediated storybook reading provides a powerful medium for growth in children's understandings of self and others. At the same time, it exposes children to the literate language register, thereby supporting the development of narrative competence. Through their interaction during storybook reading, Theory of Mind and narrative competence promote and enhance one another.

Research clearly demonstrates the contribution made by early developments in narrative competence – supported by advances in social understanding – to reading comprehension in the elementary school grades. The antecedents of reading comprehension itself, however, have been largely overlooked in studies of emergent literacy development (Lynch et al. 2008) as work in that field tends to focus on the foundational skills on which word decoding builds, such as phonological and phonemic awareness, letter identification, and letter-sound knowledge (Whitehurst & Lonigan 1998). Working within the framework presented in the literature, we attempted to assess the contribution of children's Theory of Mind achievements to narrative comprehension during the kindergarten years. More specifically, we conducted an experiment to examine whether or not preschool children's ability to recall story elements occurring at the level of consciousness predicts performance on a concurrent measure of text comprehension requiring the children to infer characters' mental states.

In order to examine this question of the contribution of "consciousness" understanding to overall reading ability in kindergarten, we used wordless picture books depicting thoughts, beliefs, and intentions of story characters derived from an earlier methodology (see Pelletier & Astington 2004), a measure of narrative productivity, as well as standardized measures of vocabulary and early reading ability. In employing this methodology, we were able to extract children's "mentalistic" understanding of stories and to relate that to narrative productivity and to their story comprehension. That is, we examined how children's "production" of Theory of Mind language as evidenced in metacognitive vocabulary contributed to their early reading comprehension, particularly their comprehension of the dual landscapes of action and consciousness.

Method

The data reported in the present chapter are taken from a larger study on parent involvement in kindergarten. All children were recruited for a randomized controlled trial of a family literacy intervention; families who consented to participate were assigned to either the fall (experimental) or spring (control) group. Data were collected at three time points during the kindergarten year: October/November, February/ March, and May/June. The analyses reported in this chapter are based only on the May/June data collection period after all children had participated in the same study. Nevertheless, approximately one-third of children and their parents had consented to participate in the intervention program but did not attend. One reason for this attrition was that parents had hoped to be placed in one time slot but because of the randomization of the methods, the time they were given was not convenient. A comparison of means showed that there were no significant differences in maternal education levels or in standard vocabulary scores among children who participated in the fall, in the spring, or not at all.

Participants

One hundred and fifty-three (153) Junior and Senior Kindergarten children (mean age 58.4 months in the fall of kindergarten) from eight publicly funded schools in the Greater Toronto Area were recruited for the study. Demographic data could not be obtained from all parents. For those for whom there were demographic data, 66 children were in Junior Kindergarten and 71 children were in Senior Kindergarten. There were 63 girls and 74 boys. The participant school board combines Junior and Senior Kindergarten age groups into one two-year program, known in Ontario as "The Kindergarten Program." The participant school populations were reflective of the vast multicultural and multilingual complexity of the larger population of Toronto and its surround, with a high influx of recent immigrants to Canada. Sixty-one percent (61 percent) of the families of participant children spoke a language other than English at home. The most common language groups other than English included but were not limited to Arabic, Cantonese, Gujarati, Hindi, Mandarin, Punjabi, Tamil, Urdu, and Vietnamese. Participant children understood and spoke English at a high enough level of competence to take part in the research tasks.

Procedures

After informed consent was obtained from parents, and verbal assent was obtained from the children themselves, researchers withdrew children from their kindergarten classes to a quiet nearby room and administered the research tasks individually. Task administration time varied from child to child, with an average time of approximately forty minutes. Children were administered a battery of measures for the larger study. All language measures as well as maternal education were used in the present chapter to describe the findings related to metacognitive language and reading in the kindergarten year.

Measures

1. *Maternal Education.* Mothers' education levels ranged from 0 to 6 (0 = no high school, 1 = some high school, 2 = completed high school, 3 = some college, 4 = completed college, 5 = completed university, 6 = graduate/professional degree). The mean maternal education level was 4.27.

2. *Vocabulary.* The Peabody Picture Vocabulary Test – III (Revised) (Dunn & Dunn 1997). This task was administered according to standardized procedures. Children were asked to look at plates of four drawings and to point to the drawing that represented the word spoken by the examiner. Standard scores were used in the analyses.

3. *Early Reading.* The Test of Early Reading Ability – III (Reid, Hresko & Hammill 2001) was administered according to standardized procedures. This measure provides raw and standard scores in each of three early reading concepts: alphabet knowledge, conventions of print, and meaning, as well as a total standard score (reading quotient). The standard scores for the meaning subtest and the total reading quotient were employed in the analyses for this chapter.

4. *Metacognitive Language.* A wordless picture book, entitled "Caterpillar, Bluejay and Fox," was used to elicit children's story retelling with the aim to coordinate action and consciousness using metacognitive language (Pelletier & Astington 2004). The story has a parallel structure to stories reported in earlier research; it included drawings that contained thought bubbles designed to link the action of the character with the thoughts he/she held. The researcher narrated a script using thirteen metacognitive terms (as well as emotion terms, not reported here). The children were then asked to retell the story they had heard. A score of 1 was given for each use of a metacognitive term. The following is the script used by the researchers while showing each page of the book (• marks new page):

- Caterpillar is *happy* because he is *thinking* about eating a tasty leaf.
- Bluejay is *hiding* behind the tree. Caterpillar does not *know* that Bluejay is there.
- Bluejay *imagines* that she catches Caterpillar.
- Bluejay *hopes* to catch Caterpillar so she *decides* to *play a trick.* Bluejay puts some leaves under the tree. She *knows* that Caterpillar will come to get the leaves.
- Caterpillar sees the leaves. He is *happy* because he *had been wondering* how he would get some leaves to eat.
- Then Caterpillar looks up and sees Bluejay sitting on the tree branch. Caterpillar is *afraid.* He *thinks* that Bluejay will catch him.
- So Caterpillar *decides* to *play a trick.* He *decides* to call his friend Fox who lives in a nearby foxhole.
- Ah-wooo! Fox howls. Bluejay is *afraid* of Fox and she flies away. Caterpillar is *glad* because he *knows* that Bluejay will not bother him anymore.
- Fox and Caterpillar have a delicious picnic under the tree.

5. *Narrative Productivity.* After the researcher told the story to the child using the wordless picture book, the child retold the story to the researcher. The child's story retelling was recorded verbatim. The story recall was supported by the storybook illustrations to alleviate memory load. A total word count was used to calculate narrative "productivity."

6. *Story Comprehension.* Children were asked three questions about the content of the story that was told to them. Questions tapped children's understanding of story characters' thoughts and intentions. As one example, the researcher turns to the page when Caterpillar is thinking of calling Fox.

Researcher asks child, *Why is Caterpillar thinking of calling Fox?*

Scoring

0 = incorrect fact (e.g., because he doesn't have any other friends)

.5 = correct fact (because Fox is his friend; because Fox lives nearby in a foxhole)

1 = understanding *that* Fox will help him (e.g., because Fox can help him)

1.5 = understanding *how* Fox will help him (e.g., because Fox will scare away Bluejay. Bluejays are afraid of foxes)

2 = reference to mental state/trick (e.g., because then he can play a trick on Bluejay; he knows that Fox will scare Bluejay)

Scores for the three comprehension questions were totaled.

Results

Descriptive analyses were carried out on all of the variables and are reported in Table 4.1.

The next set of analyses employed multivariate analyses of variance to examine group differences (JK/SK x EFL/ELL x gender) on

TABLE 4.1 *Means and standard deviations*

Name of Measure	JK or SK	English Language Learner	Gender	N	Mean	(SD)
Mothers' education	JK	EFL	Boy	7	4.1	(.9)
			Girl	10	3.0	(1.6)
		ESL	Boy	12	4.4	(1.4)
			Girl	13	4.5	(1.8)
	SK	EFL	Boy	15	4.5	(1.5)
			Girl	10	4.1	(1.7)
		ESL	Boy	13	4.6	(2.1)
			Girl	9	4.4	(1.2)
PPVT (standard)	JK	EFL	Boy	14	104.4	(10.3)
			Girl	13	111.5	(10.4)
		ESL	Boy	15	92.3	(16.3)
			Girl	16	101.3	(10.4)
	SK	EFL	Boy	15	113.0	(10.1)
			Girl	11	112.1	(13.6)
		ESL	Boy	15	94.1	(17.3)
			Girl	12	88.0	(13.6)
TERA meaning (standard)	JK	EFL	Boy	14	11.1	(2.1)
			Girl	13	11.5	(2.4)
		ESL	Boy	15	9.1	(3.0)
			Girl	16	10.4	(2.4)
	SK	EFL	Boy	15	108.4	108.4
			Girl	11	9.7	(2.2)
		ESL	Boy	15	9.1	(3.7)
			Girl	12	7.5	(3.4)
TERA RQ (reading quotient)	JK	EFL	Boy	14	108.4	(15.5)
			Girl	16	111.2	(14.8)

		ESL	Boy	15	106.0 (15.5)
			Girl	16	113.6 (18.0)
	SK	EFL	Boy	15	108.7 (19.6)
			Girl	11	107.1 (12.1)
		ESL	Boy	15	100.5 (16.7)
			Girl	12	99.9 (18.6)
Narrative productivity (total words)	JK	EFL	Boy	14	75.9 (20.1)
			Girl	13	92.7 (37.6)
		ESL	Boy	15	65.3 (22.6)
			Girl	16	88.3 (13.0)
	SK	EFL	Boy	15	79.5 (22.3)
			Girl	11	98.5 (18.6)
		ESL	Boy	15	75.3 (23.9)
			Girl	12	92.9 (16.2)
Metacognitive language	JK	EFL	Boy	14	2.7 (1.4)
			Girl	13	2.5 (1.2)
		ESL	Boy	15	1.9 (1.1)
			Girl	16	3.5 (1.7)
	SK	EFL	Boy	15	3.3 (1.8)
			Girl	11	3.5 (1.7)
		ESL	Boy	15	2.6 (1.7)
			Girl	12	2.4 (1.2)
Story comprehension (total score)	JK	EFL	Boy	14	3.3 (1.1)
			Girl	13	3.7 (.94)
		ESL	Boy	15	2.5 (1.5)
			Girl	16	3.5 (.91)
	SK	EFL	Boy	15	3.4 (.84)
			Girl	11	3.9 (.51)
		ESL	Boy	15	3.2 (1.5)
			Girl	12	2.9 (1.4)

all of the variables. There were main effects of language group (EFL x ELL) on standardized vocabulary: English Language Learners (ELL) (M = 94.3) scored significantly lower than their English First Language (EFL) peers (M = 110.2) (p< .001). Similarly ELL children (M = 9.1) scored significantly lower than EFL children (M = 10.4) on the meaning subtest of the Test of Early Reading Ability (p < .05) and on the comprehension of the story (ELL M = 3.1; EFL M = 3.5, p < .05). There were gender differences on the narrative production task; girls (M = 92.6) used significantly more words than boys (M = 74.) in retelling the story (p < .001). Finally there were grade effects on the meaning subtest of the Test of Early Reading Ability – III. SK (five-year-old) children scored significantly higher on the meaning component; however, overall JK (four-year-old) children scored higher on overall reading quotient, which included alphabet knowledge and conventions of print understanding. Although mean scores were higher for SK children, when age was taken into account through the standardization procedure, JK children (M = 109.8) performed better than SK children (M = 104.1) although the difference only approached significance (p = .07).

There were interaction effects of grade and language, as well as grade and gender. Specifically, SK English Language Learners and JK boys scored significantly below other children on the standardized vocabulary measure (p < .05).

We were interested to know what the patterns of relations were among the variables, specifically whether children's metacognitive language use was related to their story comprehension and to their scores on the meaning subtest of the standardized early reading measure. Therefore, the next set of analyses employed correlations to examine the degree to which the variables were related. Table 4.2 presents the first correlation matrix.

As can be seen from Table 4.2, children's vocabulary scores were strongly correlated with all of the variables – reading, narrative productivity, use of metacognitive terms, and story comprehension

TABLE 4.2 *Intercorrelations among the variables*

	1	2	3	4	5	6
1. PPVT (standard)		.55***	.51***	.35***	.44***	.48***
2. TERA (early reading) Meaning			.77***	.16	.29**	.36***
3. TERA (early reading) Reading quotient				.16	.26**	.34***
4. Narrative productivity					.55***	.42***
5. Metacognitive language						.45***
6. Story comprehension						

** $p < .005$; *** $p < .001$

Note: Based on data from 120 children.

($p < .001$). Children's use of metacognitive language was related to total number of words used in retelling the story and to their understanding of the story as well as to the standardized reading measure. Because of the strong relation of vocabulary to all other variables, a partial correlation controlling for children's standardized vocabulary score was carried out (see Table 4.3). The strong relation between children's metacognitive language use and their understanding of the story held ($r = .30$, $p < .001$). Not surprisingly a strong link remained between metacognitive language use and narrative productivity ($r = .48$, $p < .001$) (see Table 4.3).

In order to examine the relative contribution of metacognitive language to story comprehension, a stepwise hierarchical linear regression analysis was carried out on the dependent variable. Vocabulary was entered into the equation since much of the variability would be explained in this way. Nevertheless we wanted to know whether children's metacognitive language use would explain additional variance in the equation. In addition to vocabulary and metacognitive language, children's overall reading quotient from the Test of Early Reading Ability – III was entered into the regression analysis. This

TABLE 4.3 *Partial correlations controlling for vocabulary*

	1	2	3	4	5
1. TERA (early reading) Meaning		.69***	–.01	.64***	.15
2. TERA (early reading) Reading quotient			–.01	.03	.11
3. Narrative productivity				.48***	.31**
4. Metacognitive language					.30***
5. Story comprehension					

** $p < .005$; *** $p < .001$
Note: Based on data from 116 children.

measure includes alphabet knowledge, conventions of print (such as book handling skills), and meaning. Maternal education was also entered as a predictor variable. Results of the regression analyses revealed that in addition to general vocabulary knowledge, which contributed to 23 percent of the variance, children's use of metacognitive language contributed an additional 29 percent of the variance in children's story comprehension. Two other regression analyses were carried out on the dependent variables of the meaning subtest of the standardized reading measure (TERA – III) and on the measure as a whole, using the reading quotient. Both of these analyses revealed that vocabulary and maternal education contributed to most of the variance in standardized reading (although not to the story comprehension).

In summary, the results showed that children's understanding and use of metacognitive language were strongly related to other language and literacy factors such as vocabulary, narrative productivity, and reading comprehension. In our analyses, metacognitive language played the greatest role in explaining performance in story comprehension.

Discussion

The purpose of the present study was to assess the contribution of pre-school children's social understanding to narrative comprehension. In order to do so, we elicited retellings of a narrative supported by a word-less picture book that depicted the thoughts, beliefs, and intentions of the story characters. We examined how children's "production" of Theory of Mind language as evidenced in metacognitive vocabulary contributed to their early reading comprehension, particularly their comprehension of the dual landscapes of action and consciousness.

Multivariate analyses were conducted to determine potential group differences (age, language status, gender). Of particular interest were differences in performance on three measures of narrative competence: narrative productivity, story comprehension, and meta-cognitive language use. With respect to age, we found surprisingly few effects. Contrary to our expectations, no significant differences were found on any of the narrative measures. Closer examination of the data revealed why this was so. We found that the remarkably strong performance of the four-year old ELL (English Language Learner) girls masked potential grade-related differences. For example, on the measure of metacognitive language use, the ELL girls in Junior Kindergarten were found to outperform all children except the EFL (English First Language) Senior Kindergarten girls, whose perfor-mance they matched. A similar pattern of results was found on the story comprehension measure: The performance of the JK ELL girls was surpassed only by the performance of the SK EFL girls. The results of the JK ELL girls on the productivity measure were somewhat less striking but nonetheless attest to the relative strength of this subgroup of children.

Main effects for language group (EFL/ELL) were found on the story comprehension measure only. No language effects were found on the measures of productivity and metacognitive language use, in part because of the unexpectedly strong performance of the JK ELL girls. Overall, students identified as native speakers of English scored significantly higher than their nonnative counterparts on the comprehension questions following the initial storytelling and story retell. This result was expected. Whereas the productivity and metacognitive language measure required children to "give back" language they were exposed to by the researcher during the storytelling, the comprehension task required a self-generated response, making it more linguistically challenging. As a result, the measure may have been more sensitive to the gaps in vocabulary between the native and nonnative speakers than either the productivity or metacognitive language tasks, gaps we know to exist on the basis of the results of the test of receptive language. These findings suggest that comprehension measures that tap children's ability to generate, rather than reiterate, language may be particularly useful to educators in evaluating the linguistic/narrative competence of their students. This is particularly important to keep in mind when working in a multilingual school environment.

To investigate differences in performance due to linguistic status further, we examined performance patterns within groups. The data reveal that the range of scores on the comprehension task among ELLs was between 0 and 5.5 out of a possible 6; the range of scores among EFLs was between 2 and 5.5. While the number of ELL children scoring between 3 and 5.5 closely matches the number of EFL children scoring within the same range (40 vs. 43), the number of ELL children scoring in the lower range – one-third of the total ELL population – is more than twice the number of EFL children scoring in the same range (21 vs. 10). Clearly, differences in overall performance are attributable to the relatively small proportion of ELL children who were in the early stages of English language acquisition. On the basis of our overall results, we conclude that for the most part, ELL children were able to perform on par with their EFL counterparts on the majority of narrative tasks. It may very well be that the familiarity and level of comfort with storybook-based interactions – an integral feature of kindergarten programming in Ontario's schools – served to support the ELL children's performance. Our results argue favorably for the extensive use of storybook-based instructional practices in the early years classroom as an effective means of developing narrative skill.

Finally, a main effect for gender was found for the narrative production measure only. Across age and linguistic groups, girls produced narratives that were significantly longer than the narratives produced by boys. In our review of the research literature, we found only one study that investigated gender differences in narrative competence. Our findings corroborate those of Kaderavek et al. (2004), who found significant differences favoring girls on a standardized measure of narrative production. This area holds potential promise for future research.

The results of the regression analyses are particularly informative when considering the contribution of Theory of Mind development to narrative comprehension, the primary goal of the present study. Results showed that the frequency with which children used metacognitive words "know," "think," "hope," "decide" – in their story retells was highly predictive of their success on the story comprehension measure. In fact, metacognitive language use played the greatest role in explaining performance in story comprehension, accounting for 29 percent of the variance in scores over and above the variance attributed to vocabulary (23 percent).

The story scripts told to children by the researchers were peppered with metacognitive terms, a relatively small number of which the children included in their retells. It is difficult to evaluate the extent to which children's use of these terms in their retells reflects a genuine understanding of mind, rather than an artifact of the task. The comprehension questions, on the other hand, required the children to generate answers based on two factors: their personal interpretations of the internal states of the characters (the landscape of consciousness constructed by the child) and their ability to coordinate that self-made mental landscape with the landscape of action provided them by the narrator. In order to score full points in the sample question given previously, for example, the child must infer that Caterpillar knows that Bluejay is afraid of Fox since that information is not made explicit in the script. The subsequent action (the phone call, Bluejay's reaction to Fox's appearance) can only be explained if one understands, and integrates, the plotlines occurring at the levels of the mental and physical worlds. The more successful children were in making explicit reference to inferred states of mind and establishing causal links between them and the events that followed – coordinating the landscapes of consciousness and action – the higher their score on the comprehension measure.

IMPLICATIONS FOR EDUCATORS AND PARENTS

The magnitude of the contribution of Theory of Mind development to narrative understanding found in this study strongly suggests that adult mediation be directed toward children's metalinguistic knowledge and mentalistic language development. Although typically developing children take to the storybook reading experience a wealth of social understanding fostered by the richness of the numerous social-contextual influences in their daily lives, adult support and mediation through the medium of storybook reading may further support children's social understanding. Of course, Theory of Mind achievement is not an all-or-none phenomenon. Although the acquisition of false belief understanding is considered an important hallmark in understanding the representational mind, children acquire Theory of Mind by degree, and as Kuhn (2000) and others suggest, it should be viewed as a life-span process. Focusing even within early childhood, the differing achievements among typical three- and five-year-olds suggest that the level of comprehension of narrative will vary considerably.

Children's storybooks may be a particularly effective medium through which metalinguistic and mentalistic language can be presented to children, and practiced by them, to develop their understanding of self and others. Three ways that storybook reading experiences present unique opportunities for exploring mental states can be considered: through examination of textual elements and discussion routines, through illustrations, and through literature response experiences.

In a storybook, the text provides opportunity for metalinguistic and mentalistic exploration. In fact, text may well be unrivaled in its ability to make explicit the causal relationship between mental states (the beliefs, desires, and intentions of the characters) and physical events (dialogue and action). If the child fails to make the association between the mental and physical levels of the story line on her/his own, the adult can pause the reading interaction and review these textual elements with the child. Benson (1997) argues that it is by beginning to understand this psychological causation embedded in the plot that children start to gain a fuller understanding of the story.

Contextually meaningful consideration of false belief and belief-based emotion attribution is also naturally supported within the storybook reading episode. Adults reading to children frequently engage the child's sense of anticipation about what will happen by pausing from the reading of the text to ask the child to speculate about the response of a character to a future situation that the readers are aware of, but the character in the story is not. Again, the ability to pause the "event" and consider the implications of what a character expects versus what the reader knows will happen is a rich opportunity for the adult, who is scaffolding the child's understanding, to help the child to make the connections among desire, belief, action, and the emotion that will result from the character's false belief intersecting with reality.

Repeated readings of texts permit a revisiting of the familiar, while allowing for a mining for deeper understanding. Ratner and Olver (1998) report that in repeated readings of stories, children's talk increasingly focuses on the mental states of characters as they relate to understanding cause and effect. They suggest that this may assist the child in acquiring an understanding of representation. Nelson, Plesa, and Henseler (1998) suggest that although "the landscape of consciousness" begins to emerge at age two, the connection between action and consciousness remains unclear to children for an extended period. They suggest that, like adults, children work from an experiential and interpretive knowledge base in making sense of the social world, and to make sense of Theory of Mind itself "it needs to be surrounded by the complexities of context, motivations, institutions, power relations, prior knowledge, and so on" (p. 22). Story text helps to provide this context and knowledge base to allow the child's interpretive schemas to develop.

Storybook illustrations also provide a context for exploring desire, belief, and emotion. Wordless books, because of their reliance on illustration to convey meaning, tend to be excellent in their capacity to represent both action and consciousness. In the hands of a skilled mediator, the illustrations can serve as a rich resource for exploring mental states. As the story proceeds, the adult, referring to the depictions of expression, can draw the child's attention to the unfolding story from a mental state perspective as well as from an action stance. Similarly, a review of the story can be approached through picture, a common technique for use with young children. The retelling, however, through the illustrations of expression and what they mean for plot, rather than the usual story retelling where action is the focus, can make salient for the child that mental states give direction to plot, rather than the reverse.

Wellman, Hollander, and Schult's (1996) examination of wordless books with thought bubbles reported that while most children were not familiar with thought bubbles, they were quick to learn their function and representational nature. This suggests that although such books do not represent a high proportion of the books young children read, they can be purposefully selected to illuminate to children the mental underpinnings that shape story. It also suggests that in addition to the unparalleled value of wordless books to elicit language and contribute to oral language growth in young children, well documented in reading literature as essential for eventual independent print literacy mastery (Dickenson & Tabors 1991; Snow 1993; Davidson & Snow 1995), wordless books, with or without thought bubbles, can be an excellent resource for connecting the landscapes of action and consciousness. Tomie de Paola's (1978) wordless children's book *Pancakes for Breakfast* is an excellent example of the primacy of desire in shaping plot, through use of the thought bubble technique.

Finally, storybook reading can influence growth in children's social understanding through the culturally normative practices (in Western education) of literature response. Although widely varied across grade level and story genre, literature response activities invite deeper reflection on both the action and consciousness levels, helping the child to advance across what Bloom (1956) categorized as the taxonomy of learning. Curriculum manuals and professional literature for educators provide suggestions for developing and capturing children's understanding of the consciousness level of story through such literature response forms as writing, debating, and artistic representation (Emery 1996; Kuhn, Shaw & Felton 1997; Shanahan & Shanahan 1997). Programs for developing early childhood literacy at home also provide suggestions for literature response (Morrow, Tracey, & Maxwell 1995; Thomas 1998) and thus can further the opportunities for developing children's social understanding. Rall and Harris's (2000) claim that children adopt a spatial orientation to the protagonist's point of view provides evidence of the extent to which children psychologically immerse themselves in text. By reflecting upon text through response activities, children's understanding of themselves and others in the real world can be further developed through the imagined world of the storybook.

REFERENCES

Adrian, J. E., Clemente, R. A., & Villanueva, L. (2007). Mothers' use of cognitive state verbs in picture-book reading and the development of children's understanding of mind: A longitudinal study. *Child Development, 78,* 1052–1067.

Adrian, J. E., Clemente, R. A., Villanueva, L., & Rieffe, C. (2005). Parent-child picture-book reading, mothers' mental state language and children's theory of mind. *Journal of Child Language, 32,* 673–686.

Antonietti, A., & Iannello, P. (2008). *Representing the mind: A collection of instruments to assess naïve psychological conceptions.* Milano: Polimetrica International Scientific.

Astington, J. W. (1998). Theory of mind goes to school. *Educational Leadership,* 56(3), 46–48.

Astington, J. W. (2000). Language and metalanguage in children's understanding of mind. In J. W. Astington (Ed.) *Minds in the making: Essays in honor of David R. Olson* (pp. 267–284). Oxford: Basil Blackwell.

Astington, J. W. (2001). The paradox of intention: Assessing children's metarepresentational understanding. In B. F. Malle, L. J. Moses & D. A. Baldwin (Eds.) *Intentions and intentionality: Foundations of social cognition.* Cambridge, MA: MIT Press, (pp. 85–103).

Benson, M. (1997). Psychological causation and goal-based episodes: Low-income children's emerging narrative skills. *Early Childhood Research Quarterly, 12,* 439–457.

Bloom, B. (1956). *Taxonomy of educational objectives: The classification of educational goals.* Handbook 1: *Cognitive domain.* Ann Arbor, MI: David McKay.

Brown, D., & Briggs, L. D. (1991). Becoming literate: The acquisition of story discourse. *Reading Horizons,32,* 139–153.

Bus, A., Van IJzendoorn, M. H. & Pellegrini, A. (1995). Joint book reading makes for success in learning to read: A meta-analysis on intergenerational transmission of literacy. *Review of Educational Research,* 65(1), 1–21.

Cassidy, K., Ball, L., Rourke, R., Werner, R., Feeney, N., Chu, J., Lutz, D., & Perkins, A. (1998). Theory of mind concepts in children's literature. *Applied Psycholinguistics,* 19(3), 463–470.

Chandler, M., & Lalonde, C. (1996). Shifting to an interpretive theory of mind: 5-to-7-year olds' changing conceptions of mental life. In A. J. Sameroff & M. M. Haith (Eds.) *The five to seven year shift: The age of reason and responsibility* (pp. 301–326). Chicago: University of Chicago.

Curenton, S. M., & Justice, L. (2004). African American and Caucasian preschoolers' use of decontextualized language: Use of literate language features in oral narratives. *Language, Speech, and Hearing Services in the Schools, 35,* 240–253.

Cutting, A., & Dunn, J. (1999). Theory of mind, emotion understanding, language, and family background: Individual differences and interrelations. *Child Development, 70*(4), 853–865.

Davidson, R. G., & Snow C. (1995). The linguistic environment of early readers. *Journal of Research in Childhood Education, 10*(1), 5–21.

Deckner, D. F., Adams, L. B., & Bakeman, R. (2006). Child and maternal contributions to shared reading: Effects on language and literacy development. *Applied Developmental Psychology, 27,* 31–41.

dePaola, T. (1978). *Pancakes for breakfast.* New York: Harcourt, Brace, Jovanovich.

de Rosnay, M., Pons, F., Harris, P. L., & Morrell, J. M. B. (2004). A lag between understanding false belief and emotion attribution in young children: Relationships with linguistic ability and mothers' mental-state language. *British Journal of Developmental Psychology, 22,* 197–218.

Dickenson, D., & Tabors. P. (1991). Early literacy: Linkages between home, school, and literacy achievement at age five. *Journal of Research in Childhood Education, 6*(1) 30–46.

Dunn, J., Brown, J., Slomkowski, C., Teals, C., & Youngblade, L. (1991). Young children's understanding of other people's feelings and beliefs: Individual differences and their antecedents. *Child Development, 62,* 1352–1366.

Dunn, L. M., & Dunn, D. M. (1997). *Peabody Picture Vocabulary Test 3-Revised.* Bloomington, MN: Pearson Assessments.

Dyer, J., Shatz, M., & Wellman, H. (2000). Young children's storybooks as a source of mental state information. *Cognitive Development, 15,* 17–37.

Emery, D. (1996). Helping readers comprehend stories from the characters' perspectives. *Reading Teacher, 49*(7), 534–541.

Feagans, L., & Short, E. (1984). Developmental differences in the comprehension and production of narratives by reading-disabled and normally achieving children. *Child Development, 55,* 1727–1736.

Foy, J., & Mann, V. (2003). Home literacy environment and phonological awareness in preschool children: Differential effects for rhyme and phoneme awareness. *Applied Psycholinguistics, 24,* 59–88.

Fritjers, J., Barron, R., & Brunello, M. (2000). Direct and mediated influences of homeliteracy and literacy interest on prereaders' oral vocabulary and early written language skill. *Journal of Educational Psychology, 92,* 466–477.

Greenhalgh, K., & Strong, C. (2001). Literate language features in spoken narrative of children with typical language and children with language impairments. *Language, Speech & Hearing Services in Schools, 32,* 114–125.

Heath, S. B. (1986). What no bedtime story means: Narrative skills at home and school. In B. Schieffelin & E. Ochs (Eds.) *Language socialization across cultures* (pp. 97–124). Cambridge: Cambridge University Press.

Jenkins, J. M., Turrell, S. L., Kogushi, Y., Lollis, S., & Ross, H. S. (2003). A longitudinal investigation of the dynamics of mental state talk in families. *Child Development, 74,* 905–920.

John, S. F., Lui, M., & Tannock, R. (2003). Children's story retelling and comprehension using a new narrative resource. *Canadian Journal of School Psychology, 18,* 91–113.

Kaderavek, J., Gillam, R., Ukrainetz, T., Justice, L., & Eisenberg, S. (2004). School-age children's self-assessment of oral narrative production. *Communication Disorders Quarterly, 26*(1), 37–48.

Kaderavek, J. & Sulzby, E. (2000). Narrative production by children with and without specific language impairment: Oral narratives and emergent readings. *Journal of Speech, Language, and Hearing Research, 43,* 34–49.

Kuhn, D. (2000). Theory of mind, metacognition, and reasoning: A life-span perspective. In P. Mitchell & K. Riggs (Eds.) *Children's reasoning and the mind* (pp. 301–326). Hove, UK: Psychology Press.

Kuhn, D., Shaw, V., & Felton, M. (1997). Effects of dyadic interaction on argumentative reasoning. *Cognition and Instruction, 15*(3), 287–315.

Le Sourn-Bissaoui, S., & Deleau, M. (2001) Discours maternel et compréhension des états mentaux émotionnels et cognitifs à 3 ans. *Enfance, 53,* 329–348.

Lynch, J. S., van den Broek, P., Kremer, K. E., Kendeou, P., White, M. J., & Lorch, E. P. (2008). The development of narrative comprehension and its relation to other early reading skills. *Reading Psychology, 29,* 327–365.

Meins, E., Fernyhough, C., Wainwright, R., Clark-Carter, D., Gupta, M. D., Fradley, E., & Tuckey, M. (2003). Pathways to understanding mind: Construct validity and predictive validity of maternal mind-mindedness. *Child Development, 74,* 1194–1211.

Meltzoff, A. N. (2002). Imitation as a mechanism of social cognition: Origins of empathy, theory of mind, and the representation of action. In U. Goswami (Ed.) *Blackwell handbook of childhood cognitive development* (pp. 6–25). Malden, MA: Blackwell.

Moore, C. (2006). *The development of commonsense psychology in the first five years.* Mahwah, NJ: Lawrence Erlbaum Associates.

Moore, C., & Furrow, D. (1991). The development of the language of belief. In D. Frye & C. Moore (Eds.) *Children's theories of mind: Mental states and social understanding* (pp. 173–193). Hillsdale, NJ: Lawrence Erlbaum Associates.

Morrow, L. (1985). Retelling stories: A strategy for improving young children's comprehension, concept of story structure, and oral language complexity. *Elementary School Journal*, 85, 646–661.

Morrow, L. M. (2001). *Literacy development in the early years: Helping children read and write*. Boston: Allyn & Bacon.

Morrow, L. M., Tracey, D., & Maxwell, C. (1995). *A survey of family literacy in the United States*. Newark, DE: International Reading Association.

Nelson, K., Plesa, D., & Henseler, S. (1998). Children's theory of mind: An experiential interpretation. *Human Development*, 41, 7–29.

Olson, D. (1982). See! Jumping!: Some oral language antecedents of literacy. In H. Goelman, A. Oberg & F. Smith (Eds.) *Awakening to literacy* (pp. 185–192). Exeter, NH: Heinemann.

O'Neill, D. K., Astington, J. W., & Flavell, J. H. (1992). Young children's understanding of the role that sensory experiences play in knowledge acquisition. *Child Development*, 63, 474–490.

Pelletier, J., & Astington, J. W. (2004). Action, consciousness and theory of mind: Children's ability to coordinate story characters' actions and thoughts. *Early Education and Development*, 15(1), 5–22.

Perner, J. (1988). Developing semantics for theories of mind: From propositional attitudes to mental representation. In J. W. Astington, P. L. Harris & D. R. Olson (Eds.) *Developing theories of mind* (pp. 141–172). New York: Cambridge University Press.

Perner, J. (1991). *Understanding the representational mind*. Cambridge, MA: MIT Press.

Perner, J. (1999). Theory of mind. In M. Bennett (Ed.) *Developmental psychology: Achievements and prospects* (pp. 205–230). Philadelphia: Psychology Press/Taylor & Francis.

Purcell-Gates, V. (1996). Stories, coupons, and the *TV Guide*: Relationships between home literacy experiences and emergent literacy knowledge. *Reading Research Quarterly*, 31, 406–428.

Peskin, J., & Astington, J. W. (2004). The effects of adding metacognitive language to story texts. *Cognitive Development*, 19(2), 253–273.

Rall, J., & Harris, P. L. (2000). In Cinderella's slippers? Story comprehension from the protagonist's point of view. *Developmental Psychology*, 36(2), 202–208.

Ratner, N., & Oliver, R. (1998). Reading a tale of deception, learning a theory of mind? *Early Childhood Research Quarterly*, 13(2), 219–239.

Reid, D. K., Hresko, W. P., & Hammill, D. D. (2001). *The test of early reading ability*, 3rd ed. Austin, TX: PRO-ED.

Repacholi, B., & Gopnik, A. (1997). Early reasoning about desires: Evidence from 14- and 18-month olds. *Developmental Psychology*, 33(1), 12–21.

Roth, F., Speece, D., & Cooper, D. (2002). A longitudinal analysis of the connection between oral language and early reading. *Journal of Educational Research, 95*, 259–272.

Sénéchal, M., & LeFevre, J. (2002). Parental involvement in the development of children's reading skill: A five-year longitudinal study. *Child Development, 73*, 445–460.

Shannahan, T., & Shannahan, S. (1997). Character perspective charting: Helping children to develop a more complete conception of story. *Reading Teacher, 50*(8), 668–677.

Sipe, L. (2001). A palimpsest of stories: young children's construction of intertextual links among fairytale variants. *Reading Research and Instruction, 40*, 333–352.

Snow, C. (1991). The theoretical basis for relationships between language and literacy in development. *Journal of Research in Childhood Education, 6*(1), 5–10.

Snow, C. E. (1993). Families as social contexts for literacy development. *New Directions for Child Development, 61*, 11–24.

Snow, C., Scarborough, H. S., & Burns, M. S. (1999). What speech-language pathologists need to know about early reading. *Topics in Language Disorders, 20*, 48–58.

Sonnenschein, S., & Munsterman, K. (2002). The influence of home-based reading interventions on 5-year olds' reading motivations and early literacy development. *Early Childhood Research Quarterly, 17*, 318–337.

Sulzby, E. (1985). Children's emergent reading of favourite storybooks: A developmental study. *Reading Research Quarterly, 20*(4), 458–481.

Symons, D. K., Fossum, K. M., & Collins, T. B. K. (2006). A longitudinal study of belief and desire state discourse during mother-child play and later false belief understanding. *Social Development, 15*, 676–691.

Symons, D. K., Peterson, C. C., Slaughter, V., Roche, J., & Doyle, E. (2005). Theory of mind and mental state discourse during book reading and story-telling tasks. *British Journal of Developmental Psychology, 23*, 81–102.

Szarkowicz, D. (2000). "When they wash him they'll know he'll be Harry": Young children's thinking about thinking within a story context. *International Journal of Early Years Education, 8*(1), 71–81.

Tager-Flusberg, H., & Sullivan, K. (1995). Attributing mental states to story characters: A comparison of narratives produced by autistic and mentally retarded individuals. *Applied Psycholinguistics, 16*, 241–256.

Teale, W., & Sulzby, E. (1999). Literacy acquisition in early childhood: The role of access and mediation in storybook reading. In D. Wagner (Ed.)

The Future of Literacy in a Changing World (pp. 131–150). Cresskill, NJ: Hampton Press,

Thomas, A. (1998). *Family literacy in Canada: Profiles in effective practices.* Welland, ON: Soleil Press.

Tough, J. (1983). Children's use of language and learning to read. In R. Parker & F. Davis (Eds.) *Developing literacy: Young children's use of language* (pp. 55–67). Newark, DE: International Reading Association.

Ukrainetz, T. A., Justice, L. M., Kaderavek, J. N., & Eisenberg, S. L. (2005). The development of expressive elaboration in fictional narratives. *Journal of Speech, Language, and Hearing Research, 48,* 1363–1377.

Vinden, P. G., & Astington, J. W. (2000). Culture and understanding other minds. In S. Baron-Cohen, H. Tager-Flusberg & D. J. Cohen (Eds.) *Understanding other minds: Perspectives from developmental cognitive neuroscience* (pp. 503–519). Oxford: Oxford University Press.

Wellman, H., Cross, D., & Watson, J. (2001). Meta-analysis of theory of mind development: The truth about false-belief. *Child Development, 72*(3), 655–684.

Wellman, H., Hollander, M., & Schult, C. A. (1996). Young children's understanding of thought bubbles and of thoughts. *Child Development, 67,* 768–788.

Wells, G. (1985). Pre-school literacy related activities and success in school. In D. Olson, N. Torrance & A. Hildyard (Eds.) *Literacy, language, and learning* (pp. 229–255). New York: Cambridge University Press.

Whitehurst, G., & Lonigan, C. (1998). Child development and early literacy. *Child Development, 69,* 848–872.

5

Language Access and Theory of Mind Reasoning: Evidence from Deaf Children in Bilingual and Oralist Environments

MAREK MERISTO, KERSTIN W. FALKMAN, ERLAND HJELMQUIST, MARIANTONIA TEDOLDI, LUCA SURIAN, AND MICHAEL SIEGAL

INTRODUCTION

Possession of a "Theory of Mind" (ToM) is a core aspect of cognitive development. ToM reasoning involves the ability to understand mental states – the beliefs, desires, and intentions of others – and to appreciate how these differ from our own. It is fundamental for communication and social relationships, especially in understanding irony, jokes, and deception (Siegal & Peterson 2008).

A key issue for how children learn to express ToM reasoning concerns the effect of language input (Courtin & Melot 2005; Milligan, Astington, & Dack 2007; Peterson & Siegal 1999, 2000; Schick, De

This chapter has been adapted with permission of the American Psychological Association from an article that appeared in *Developmental Psychology*, 43, 1156–1169 (2007). The research reported here was supported by grant 2001–1112 to Erland Hjelmquist from the Swedish Council for Social Research and a Leverhulme Trust Research Interchange Grant, a Fondazione Benefica Kathleen Foreman-Casali Grant, and an EU Marie Curie Chair to Michael Siegal. It has benefited from discussions at the AHRC Culture and the Mind Workshop in Sheffield, UK, October 2006. Some of the results were presented at the Language Acquisition and Bilingualism Conference, Toronto, Canada, May 2006, and the 8th Tokyo Conference on Psycholinguistics, Tokyo, Japan, March 2007. Thanks are due to Bencie Woll for her advice and guidance, and to all participating children and their families, teachers, and school administrators.

Villiers, De Villiers, & Hoffmeister 2007; Remmel, in press; Siegal & Peterson 2008; Siegal & Varley 2002). Specifically, to what extent is an expression of ToM dependent on the timing at which children gain access to language? In what manner does it reflect early access and exposure to conversations that concern beliefs and other mental states? In this regard, a critical test results from comparisons of native signing deaf children raised by signing deaf parents with late signing deaf children raised by hearing parents.

In a study designed to address this issue (Woolfe, Want, & Siegal 2002), hearing and deaf children aged four to nine years in nine locations in England were given "thought picture" measures of ToM that minimize verbal task performance requirements. The aim was to determine whether differences would exist between hearing and deaf children in understanding others' false beliefs and whether native signing children (who from birth have had access to a sign language used by deaf family members) would outperform late signing deaf children (who have hearing parents and have gained access to a signed language later in school) owing to their early proficiency in a sign language. The native signers were younger than the late signers and less proficient in British Sign Language (BSL). However, compared to the late signers, they excelled in their ToM performance and did not differ in this respect from hearing children. Similar findings involving children using American Sign Language have recently been reported by Schick et al. (2007).

These results demonstrate that the advantage shown by native signers on ToM stories normally used to test hearing children extends even to tasks that minimize the need for verbal comprehension skills. Performance on measures of language ability such as knowledge of vocabulary and aspects of syntax correlates with success on ToM false belief tasks in both hearing and deaf children (Schick et al. 2007; Slade & Ruffman 2005; Woolfe et al. 2002). However, deaf late signers still show deficits in ToM reasoning relative to deaf native signers or hearing controls even after factors such as syntax ability as well as nonverbal mental age and executive functioning are controlled (Siegal & Peterson 2008). The difficulties of late signing children on ToM tasks do not appear to generalize to causal reasoning in the physical and biological domains (Peterson & Siegal 1997) and are specific to reasoning about mental representations such as beliefs rather than representations generally. Although delayed in ToM reasoning, late signers are adept at understanding photographs in terms of true or false representations of physical reality (Peterson & Siegal 1998; Woolfe et al. 2002).

Whether or not intensive input from hearing parents who have learned a sign language to communicate with their deaf children and from learning environments in which a sign language is a medium for instruction serves to overcome persistent ToM false belief deficits requires further investigation. On the one hand, in a Swedish longitudinal study (Falkman, Roos, & Hjelmquist 2007), deaf children aged seven to nine years of age from hearing families who had been exposed to a sign language as early as two years of age still displayed specific protracted ToM difficulties. On the other hand, Moeller and Schick (2006) studied the mothers of a group of American late signing deaf children aged seven to ten years, many of whom wore hearing aids or had received cochlear implants, who attended schools where both sign and spoken English were encouraged. The mothers, who had acquired advanced signing skills through access to continuous sign instruction and early intervention programs, had children who scored well on ToM tasks that hearing children often pass by the age of four years. These mothers were observed to direct more communication about mental states to their children than did mothers with less advanced sign language skills whose late signing children did not score well.

This pattern of findings can be seen to point to the powerful impact of early access to conversation on ToM performance (see Harris 1996; Peterson 2004; Siegal & Varley 2002), supported by research indicating that mothers' "mind-mindedness" talk that focuses on mental states directed at infants that takes place even at the age of six months is predictive of mentalizing skills at forty-eight months of age (Meins et al. 2002). In contrast to late signing deaf children, children who are native signers have early opportunities for exposure to conversations about others' beliefs and to formulate an understanding of how these can be false. On this account, the increase with age in performance on ToM reasoning tasks in both typically developing hearing children and native signing deaf children reflects resources gained through very early exposure to conversations about mental states. These resources enable children to attend to others' mental states and to facilitate the expression of ToM.

A conversational account of ToM performance based on access to language is consistent with findings from other groups of children, for example, children with visual impairments (Hobson & Bishop 2003; Peterson, Peterson, & Webb 2000) and nonvocal children with cerebral palsy (Dahlgren, Dahlgren Sandberg, & Hjelmquist 2003; Falkman, Dahlgren Sandberg, & Hjelmquist 2005) – groups who have early difficulty in engaging in conversations about beliefs and other mental states and who also have specific difficulties on ToM tasks. It is also in keeping with the effects of early access to language on second language learning. Children spontaneously gain from early language exposure in that, for example, those who become deaf after having acquired spoken English appear to be more proficient in learning a sign language than those born profoundly deaf with little linguistic experience before exposure to a sign language at school; conversely, the deaf who are exposed early to a sign language are able to learn English better than those who have been exposed late (Mayberry, Lock, & Kazmi 2002).

In previous studies of ToM reasoning that have examined false belief understanding, native signing deaf children normally attended bilingual schools where there was access to a sign language as the medium of instruction. In such schools, there is access to both a sign and a spoken language with the aim of preparing deaf children to live and work as bilingual individuals in society. However, in many parts of the world, deaf children who have gained early proficiency in a sign language nevertheless have no choice but to attend classes in an oralist environment. The aim of oralism is mainly to facilitate the integration of deaf children with the hearing community and to prepare students in the hearing society without the need for sign language interpretation. Because access to communication in a sign language is not readily available in an oralist environment, children are instead required to follow instruction through lipreading. In the research reported here, the purpose was to compare the performance on ToM measures of deaf children who differ in their language environment at school but share similar home language environments. Specifically, we sought to determine whether this lack of access to a sign language as a medium for instruction influences performance on ToM tasks both in native signers and in late signers.

In Italy, for example deaf children are provided with instruction in several different ways (Maragna 2000; Pizzuto 2002; Pizzuto et al. 2002). Some attend mainstream government schools along with hearing children in which instruction is given in spoken Italian. Occasionally oral instruction is supplemented by individual explanations in Italian Sign Language (LIS – Lingua Italiana dei Segni) or in Sign Supported Italian (SSI) from a teaching assistant, although this was not the case for the deaf children instructed in an oralist environment in the study reported here. In the case of the late signing children who are users of LIS but attend oralist schools, they had acquired LIS through interactions with other deaf schoolmates and sometimes also through contact with adults outside their family who had proficiency in LIS. Research such as that in the Nicaraguan deaf community has shown that children can spontaneously create a sign language in conversations with their schoolmates (Senghas & Coppola 2001; Senghas, Kita, & Ozyurek 2004).

Other children in Italy attend schools that provide instruction using "bimodal/bilingual" (B/B) communication methods in LIS or SSI and spoken Italian. The teachers use SSI that relies on spoken Italian words simultaneously accompanied by the corresponding LIS signs, or there is a LIS interpreter who simultaneously translates the teacher's messages into LIS. In such schools, LIS grammar and vocabulary are taught as subjects (from a minimum of one hour a week to a maximum of six hours a week) as LIS is considered to be the children's native language. Conversations between deaf children and teachers in the schools are based on LIS, SSI, or a combination, and those among the deaf children are in LIS. In this instructional environment, deaf children, whether native or late signers, are constantly exposed to an LIS language community, and they can often communicate spontaneously in their native language environment – an environment in which they would be constantly alerted to the possibility that beliefs can differ from one's own and from reality.

Given the contrast between the two types of schools in providing access to a sign language during school instruction, we sought to determine whether deaf children with sign language access would outperform children without sign language access on ToM measures. Therefore, in Experiment 1, we carried out a comparison of the ToM reasoning performance of native and late signing deaf children in Italy who were enrolled either in oralist classes in which only spoken Italian was used or in B/B classes involving the use of both LIS/SSI and spoken Italian.

EXPERIMENT 1

Method

Participants
These were ninety-seven profoundly deaf children, aged 4 to 12 years, of whom forty-one were late signers (M = 10 years 1 month, range = 6 years 5 months to 12 years 9 months) and fifty-six were native signers (M = 8 years 7 months, range = 4 years 6 months to 12 years 8 months). They were healthy and had no additional disabilities such as cerebral palsy, autism, mental retardation, or visual impairment. Sixteen other

deaf children were initially tested and excluded. There were six children who did not understand the procedure for the LIS Test: four late signers (two 3-year-olds, one 5-year-old, and one 6-year-old) and two native signing 3-year-olds. Ten other children did not understand the thought bubbles in the pretest for the ToM tasks: seven late signers aged 6 to 9 years and three native signers aged 4, 7, and 11 years.

The native signers who participated in Experiment 1 had at least one signing deaf parent who was proficient in LIS, whereas late signers had hearing parents who were not proficient. The children were recruited from schools in mainly middle-class districts of eight cities located throughout Italy. Of the forty-one late signers, twenty-three children attended oralist schools and eighteen children attended B/B schools. For the fifty-six native signers, comparative figures were twenty and thirty-six, respectively.

In addition to the deaf children, 105 hearing children were recruited as controls from schools located in urban areas of northeastern Italy. They were divided into four age groups: 3- to 4-year-olds ($N = 26$, $M = 4$ years 3 months, range = 3 years 5 months to 4 years 10 months), 5- to 6-year-olds ($N = 25$, $M = 6$ years 7 months, range = 5 years 1 month to 6 years 11 months), 7- to 8-year-olds ($N = 36$, $M = 7$ years 9 months, range = 7 years 0 months to 8 years 8 months), and 9- to 10-year-olds ($N = 18$, $M = 9$ years 10 months, range = 9 years 0 months to 10 years 8 months). Both the deaf and hearing children were of white Italian background and had been raised in urban areas.

Procedure

A professional LIS interpreter who was also hearing tested the deaf children following the procedure used by Woolfe et al. (2002). All deaf children were first given a test for proficiency in LIS based on the BSL Receptive Skills Test (Herman, Holmes, & Woll 1999). Each of the forty sentences in the original BSL test was translated into LIS and recorded on a DVD as a test of proficiency in LIS. The translations used LIS constructions common to Italian signers despite regional variations.

Before the test was administered, the children were given a vocabulary check involving signs for items (book, pencil, table, car). As in the BSL test, the LIS test evaluated the understanding of grammatical features such as spatial verb morphology, number/distribution, size/shape specifiers, noun/verb distinctions, and handling classifiers. Performance was recorded out of a maximum score of 40. The mean scores of the children in the various groups tested ranged from 23.7 to 27.9 and were nearly identical to those in Woolfe et al. Teacher ratings of children's abilities in LIS were available for all ninety-seven children. As in Peterson and Siegal's (1999) study, teachers rated each child on scales of expressive language skill, comprehension, and vocabulary size. Ratings ranged from 1 (both "below average" and "inadequate for effective communication"), through 3 ("average"), to a high of 5 (both "highly competent" and "well above the average for signing children of the same age"). The overall score for each child was created by averaging ratings on the three scales. The mean score for the ninety-seven children was 3.80 ($SD = .98$). The correlation between scores on the LIS test and the teacher ratings was .68, $p < .01$, providing evidence for validation of the LIS adaptation of the BSL test. We used LIS scores rather than teacher ratings as a language measure as LIS test scores provide a constant measure of language proficiency across schools. The teachers were also asked to provide information on the home language environment of the native signing children in terms of whether deaf parents, siblings, and other relatives used only LIS or both LIS and oral Italian to communicate to their child. There was diversity in the children's home language environment with twenty-nine of the thirty-six B/B instructed native signers and nine of the twenty native signers instructed in oralist schools receiving only LIS at home and the others receiving both LIS and Italian. For late signing children from hearing families in Italy, the home language environment of late signing children is complex and variable (Caselli, Maragna, & Volterra 2006; Russo Cardona & Volterra 2007). Although details of the home environment for the late signing children who participated in Experiment

1 were not available, these children received little or no LIS compared to the home environment of native signers.

After the language assessment, both the deaf and hearing children's understanding of "thought bubbles" was examined. As in the procedure used by Wellman, Hollander, and Schult (1996) and Woolfe et al. (2002), two pictures were shown: one depicting a boy thinking about a dog (a boy with an attached thought bubble containing a dog) and the other depicting a boy with a real dog (a boy with a dog on a lead). The deaf children were asked in LIS (and the hearing in spoken Italian) to point to the picture showing a boy thinking about a dog. The children were then shown four ToM "thought pictures" (adapted from a procedure used by Custer 1996): two in a False Belief condition (FB), and the other two in a True Belief condition (TB). The four thought pictures were 1) a boy fishing thinks he has caught a fish (TB = fish / FB = boot); 2) a girl thinks she sees a tall boy over a fence (TB = a tall boy / FB = a small boy standing on a box); 3) a man thinks he is reaching into a cupboard for a drink (TB = a drink / FB = a mouse); and 4) a man thinks he sees a fish in the sea (TB = a fish / FB = a mermaid). The content of the items of FB and TB tasks was randomized across children. For each task, children were asked a belief and a reality question. They were scored as having passed the task if they answered both questions correctly. Each child therefore received an FB score from 0 to 2 and a TB score from 0 to 2.

Finally, all children were given the colored version of Raven's Progressive Matrices as a measure of nonverbal mental age (Raven 1962).

Results

The children's mean ages, FB and TB scores, LIS, and nonverbal MA scores are shown in Table 5.1. For the deaf children, a series of 2 (sign language status: native vs. late signing) X 2 (instructional format: oralist vs. B/B) analyses of variance were carried out on age, LIS, and

TABLE 5.1 *Means (with SDs in parentheses) for age, nonverbal mental age, false belief, true belief, Italian Sign Language (LIS) measures in Experiment 1*

Group and language access	N	Mean age (months)	Nonverbal mental age (months)	False belief	True belief	LIS test
Native signers						
Bimodal/Bilingual	36	108.1 (29.7)	105.4 (35.0)	1.11 (0.82)	1.42 (.65)	27.6 (6.0)
Oralist	20	95.0 (22.6)	100.3 (29.5)	0.55 (0.76)	1.55 (.61)	27.9 (3.1)
Late signers						
Bimodal/Bilingual	18	123.6 (18.8)	117.2 (27.3)	0.83 (0.86)	1.22 (.81)	27.9 (6.3)
Oralist	23	118.4 (16.8)	108.0 (23.8)	0.43 (0.66)	1.52 (.73)	23.7 (4.1)
Hearing children						
3 to 4 yr	26	50.9 (5.2)	52.4 (10.9)	1.15 (.78)	1.35 (.71)	–
5 to 6 yr	25	67.1 (6.6)	68.8 (24.9)	1.56 (.71)	1.32 (.75)	–
7 to 8 yr	36	92.6 (7.5)	102.3(28.2)	1.75 (.55)	1.31 (.71)	–
9 to 10 yr	18	117.9 (6.3)	126.5 (16.4)	1.89 (.32)	1.17 (.71)	–

nonverbal MA. On age, the sign language status main effect was significant, $F(1, 93) = 15.09$, $p < .001$, $\eta^2 = .14$, indicating that the late signers were significantly older than the native signers. On LIS, there was a significant sign language status X instructional format interaction, $F(1, 93) = 4.27$, $p < .05$, $\eta^2 = .04$. The late signers instructed in an oralist environment were significantly less proficient in LIS than were the B/B instructed native signers, $t(57) = 2.76$, $p < .01$, $\eta^2 = .12$; the B/B late signers, $t(39) = 2.55$, $p < .02$, $\eta^2 = .14$; and the native signers instructed in an oralist environment, $t(41) = 3.65$, $p < .001$, $\eta^2 = .24$. On nonverbal MA, there were no significant main or interaction effects, F's$(1, 93) < 1$.

To compare the scores of the groups of deaf and hearing children, we carried out an 8 (group: B/B native signing, oralist native signing, B/B late signing, oralist late signing, hearing 3–4, 5–6, 7–8, and 9–10-year-olds) X 2 (belief measure: FB vs. TB) ANOVA. There were significant main effects for both group, $F(7, 194) = 5.79$, $p < .001$, $\eta^2 = 17$, and belief measure, $F(7, 194) = 6.20$, $p < .02$, $\eta^2 = .03$, as well as a significant group X belief interaction effect, $F(7, 194) = 8.16$, $p < .001$, $\eta^2 = .23$. Bonferroni multiple comparisons at the $p < .05$ level of significance indicated that the hearing 3- to 4-year-olds outperformed the orally instructed late signers, that the hearing 5- to 6-year-olds outperformed all the deaf groups except for the native signing instructed in a B/B environment, and that the hearing 7- to 8-, and 9- to 10-year-olds outperformed all the deaf groups. There were no significant differences on TB measures between any of the groups. We also compared the scores of the 18 youngest of the 36 B/B instructed native signers ($M_{age} = 82.5$ months; $SD = 15.6$) with those of the two youngest groups of hearing children. A 3 (group: young B/B native signing, vs. hearing 3–4 vs. 5–6-year-olds) X 2 (belief measure: FB vs. TB) ANOVA revealed no significant main effects, F's < 1.90, p's $> .15$, but did yield a significant group X belief measure interaction effect, $F(2, 66) = 3.34$, $p < .05$, $\eta^2 = .09$. On the FB tasks, the hearing 5- to 6-year-olds, but not the hearing 3- to 4-year-olds, significantly outperformed younger B/B native signers, $t(41) = 2.55$, $p < .05$, $\eta^2 = .11$, and $t(42) = .83$, $p > .20$, respectively.

Discussion

Overall, deaf children in B/B schools outperformed those with oralist instruction on the FB tasks, even after age, nonverbal intelligence, and level of sign language were partialed out. The importance of the instructional environment is underscored by the finding that there were no significant differences between the responses of native signers with a home language environment in which either LIS alone or LIS plus Italian was used. Those who had B/B instruction displayed a significant advantage over those with oralist instruction irrespective of whether they were exposed to LIS alone or LIS plus Italian (and thus would have had a lower proportion of their communication at home solely in LIS).

There was no significant difference in performance as shown by responses on FB tasks between the B/B instructed native signers and a sample of hearing children aged three to six years. However, the hearing three- to six-year-olds significantly outperformed the native signers instructed in an oralist environment as well as the late signers with either oralist or B/B instruction. When just the youngest B/B instructed native signers were considered, they were outperformed by the hearing five- to six-year-olds.

As the Italian deaf children were older than the English children in Woolfe et al.'s (2002) study, their performance should have been superior. The B/B instructed Italian late signers, who were mostly nine- to eleven-year-olds, did have a 42 percent success rate compared to 17 percent for their English late signing counterparts, who were mostly six- to eight-year-olds. However, the B/B instructed native signing Italian children, who were mostly eight- and nine-year-olds, produced 56 percent correct responses on the ToM tasks compared to 71 percent correct for the English native signing children, who were mostly six- and seven-year-olds.

Unlike for those schools attended by the children in the Woolfe et al. study, there are many B/B schools in which instructors and interpreters may not have full competence in using a sign language to communicate with children (Schick, Williams, & Kupermintz 2006; Singleton & Morgan 2005). The B/B schools in Italy were certainly not as well placed to deliver instruction in LIS as were the schools that used BSL continually as the medium for instruction in the Woolfe et al. (2002) study, and often teachers relied on SSI rather than LIS in their communication. Although teacher ratings enabled comparisons across children in different instructional environments, many of the teachers in the oralist schools had knowledge of LIS vocabulary but not of LIS syntax. When LIS signs were used, these followed the order in Italian syntax (subject-verb-object, e.g., "Io vado a casa" or "I go home") rather than that used in LIS (subject-object-verb, "Io casa vado"). As their own proficiency in LIS was limited, teacher ratings of the children's LIS proficiency need to be considered with caution. We did not have data on the quality and effectiveness of LIS used in communication within the actual home language environment, but clearly the deaf parents of Italian deaf children themselves were variable in their LIS proficiency and have limited access to education and employment. Moreover, much of the educational environment in the Italian bimodal/bilingual schools was based on SSI or LIS translation rather than the instructor's direct use of LIS. We were restricted in being unable to determine the extent to which the mode of instruction in such schools was directly in LIS, in LIS translation, or in SSI. Nevertheless, given that often there is a lack of direct instruction in LIS, even Italian native signing children in B/B schools might still not have full opportunity in a sign language to monitor input about mental states continually. This situation may contribute to a lower level of performance on ToM tasks compared to that of native signers in previous studies.

EXPERIMENT 2

Experiment 1 was limited to the responses of deaf and hearing Italian children on one set of thought picture ToM measures. Experiment 2 was designed to examine the responses of children on a wide variety of measures of ToM or "mentalizing" and to provide a basis for comparing the pattern of performance of deaf children in Estonia and Sweden in northern Europe with those in Italy. Presently, in both Estonia and Sweden, there is substantial expertise in deaf education that, in comparison to that in Italy, focuses on bilingual instruction without the use of sign supported methods. In this environment, ToM performance should be enhanced as there is greater direct access to a sign language than is the case in a B/B instructional environment.

Deaf education in Estonia has historically followed the oralist tradition in which children are taught to talk and lip-read mostly by hearing teachers, and sign language is avoided as much as possible (Laiapea et al. 2003). However, in 1994, a school with a bilingual approach was established in which students are educated by teachers, most of whom are deaf themselves, in Estonian Sign Language (ESL). A few lessons are also held in spoken Estonian with an interpreter simultaneously interpreting into ESL the communication between the teacher and the students. Unlike in Italy, sign supported methods are not used. From fifth grade, Estonian is taught once a day as a second language in reading and writing.

Education for the hearing impaired in Sweden is coordinated by the National Agency for Special Schools for the Deaf and Hard of Hearing (SPM-Specialskolemyndigheten; see http://www.spm.se/in english.4.b32ed4f816633f9b7fff1265.html). To fulfill the ultimate aim of preparing deaf children to live and work as bilingual individuals in society, both Swedish Sign Language (SSL) and Swedish are used in instruction rather than oralist instructional methods. Again, unlike in Italy, sign supported methods are not used. In classes for deaf children in which both SSL and Swedish are used, SSL is taught twice a week and Swedish four times a week. The schools also provide instruction in SSL for siblings who have unimpaired hearing and for hearing children whose parents are deaf. There is also a 240-hour training program in SSL for parents of deaf children that is validated by the Swedish

National Agency for Education. This program is designed to provide parents with functional sign language skills so that they can interact with their children and thus support their development. All hearing parents of the late signing Swedish children in Experiment 2 had taken the SSL course, except in one case, in which it was not completed. In practice, the 240 hours is a minimum figure since, apart from the main curriculum based course, parents attend introductory and follow-up sessions. The program in SSL is designed to provide hearing parents of deaf children with functional sign language skills to interact with their children effectively and support their development. The parents all did use SSL when communicating with their children, although data on the quality of their sign language skills or how sign language was combined with spoken Swedish or other communicative modalities were unavailable. However, given the tradition of SSL as an official language in Sweden since 1981 and the participation of the hearing parents in the SSL course, the signing skills of the Swedish hearing parents can be assumed to be generally more advanced than those of either their Estonian or Italian counterparts.

Method

Participants

These were sixty-one deaf children, ranging in age from 7 years 4 months to 16 years 1 month, of whom twenty-four were native signers from deaf families in which a sign language was used at home (M = 12 years 3 months, range = 7 years 4 months to 16 years 1 month) and thirty-seven were late signers from hearing families (M = 12 years 3 months, range = 8 years 0 months to 15 years 11 months). The native signers attended schools in Estonia: eleven attended a bilingual school (M = 12 years 10 months, range = 7 years 4 months to 16 years 1 month) and thirteen attended an oralist school (M = 11 years 9 months, range = 7 years 10 months to 15 years 6 months). Of the thirty-seven late signers, sixteen attended a bilingual school in Estonia (M = 12 years

1 month, range = 8 years 0 months to 15 years 11 months) and twenty-one attended a bilingual school in Sweden (M = 12 years 4 months, range = 9 years 0 months to 15 years 10 month). Regardless of whether the native signers attended a bilingual or an oralist school, they had a similar home language environment. In either case, save for one exception, only ESL was used at home. All the children were prelingually deaf and none of them had any additional disabilities such as cerebral palsy, autism, mental retardation, or visual impairment. Seven other deaf children (five in Sweden and two in Estonia) were excluded for these reasons.

All native signers lived together with two deaf parents except for one boy in each of the bilingual and oralist groups, who had hearing parents but had an older brother who was five to six years older. These boys were considered to be native signers since they had access to another speaker of sign language in their immediate household throughout childhood (Peterson & Siegal 2000, p. 131). According to teachers, the older brothers were in both cases very good signers and used only sign language in communication with their younger brothers. The two younger brothers who were included in the current study scored within one standard deviation of the group means in their total mentalizing scores. Also according to teachers, deaf parents used ESL proficiently in communicating with their children even though, since the bilingual school has existed only in the last ten years, the parents had been instructed in oral language themselves.

Although the lack of a formal test of proficiency in either Estonian or Swedish Sign Language precluded an assessment of level of language skills, all deaf children used either ESL or SSL as their primary and preferred means for communication and all had been judged by their teachers to have sign language fluency. In addition to the deaf children, twenty-six hearing children, aged from 6 years 1 month to 15 years 4 months (M = 10 years 9 months), were recruited as controls from schools located in Estonia. We did not include a group of late signing Estonian children from hearing families with oralist instruction

because none of the children could be identified as comparatively fluent in ESL and all preferred to communicate in spoken Estonian.

Procedure

Each child was tested individually in a quiet room at school. An
assistant who knew the children well carried out the testing. At the
bilingual deaf school in Estonia, the assistant was deaf herself and
communicated in ESL. The hearing assistant who tested the Estonian
deaf children in ESL at the oralist school was fluent in both ESL and
spoken Estonian as she had been raised in Estonia by a deaf parent.
Similarly, the hearing assistant who tested the Swedish deaf children in
SSL was fluent in both SSL and spoken Swedish as she had been raised
in Sweden by a deaf parent.

Test sessions did not last longer than approximately twenty minutes
in order to prevent fatigue. These were video recorded with two cam-
eras, one directed at the child and the other at the assistant who carried
out the testing. Before the testing began, all assistants were carefully
briefed on how to administer the tasks. As certain lexical terminology
in the test situation can influence responses on ToM measures (Lee,
Olson, & Torrance 1999; Maridaki-Kassotaki, Lewis, & Freeman 2003;
Shatz et al. 2003), the exact formulation of the language used for the
tasks and questions was developed in consultation with the deaf assistant and an interpreter at the sign language school in Estonia, and in
consultation with a hearing interpreter and two deaf native speakers
of SSL in Sweden. We also consulted a professor of English born in
Sweden of Estonian parents concerning semantic fields of epistemic
verbs in English, Swedish, and Estonian such as *think* and *believe*.

Materials

All children received eight mentalizing tasks: (1) *Second-Order False-
Belief Task* (Hughes et al. 2000), (2) *"Faux Pas"* task (Baron-Cohen
et al. 1999); (3) *Belief-Desire Based Emotion Reasoning Task* (Harris et al.
1989); (4) and (5) two *Emotion Recognition Cartoon Tasks* following

Howlin, Baron-Cohen, and Hadwin (1999); (6) *Unexpected Location Task* (Hughes et al. 2000), (7) *"Strange Story"* task (Happé 1994), and (8) *Unexpected Contents Task* (Perner, Leekam, & Wimmer 1987). The children were given two other measures. As in Experiment 1, they received Raven's matrices as a test of nonverbal intelligence. Following Zaitchik (1990), a test of nonmental representation was also included in order to make sure that possible difficulties in performance of false belief tasks were due to problems specifically with mental representation and not representation in general. All children passed the non-mental representation task.

Results and Discussion

Responses on the eight tasks were scored on a 0–8 scale. Mean scores of the five groups, together with details of the children's chronological and nonverbal mental ages, are shown in Table 5.2. The children performed well across the corresponding control questions with a success rate of 92 percent. As shown in a one-way ANOVA, there was a significant difference between the groups in mentalizing scores, $F(4,81) = 5.46, p < .001, \eta^2 = .21$. Planned contrasts indicated that the hearing children outperformed the late signing Estonian bilingual deaf children, $t(81) = 3.49, p < .001, \eta^2 = .13$, and the late signing Swedish bilingual children, $t(81) = 2.82, p < .01, \eta^2 = .09$, as well as the native signing Estonian oralist children, $t(81) = 3.23, p < .005, \eta^2 = .11$. However, the native signing bilingually instructed children performed at the same level – 82 percent correct – as did the hearing children, $t(81) = -0.05$, $p > .95$. They significantly outperformed the bilingually instructed Estonian late signers, $t(81) = 2.89, p < .005, \eta^2 = .09$; the bilingually instructed Swedish late signers, $t(81) = 2.28, p < .05, \eta^2 = .06$; and the oralist instructed native signers, $t(81) = 2.74, p < .01, \eta^2 = .09$. Further, there were no significant differences in mentalizing abilities between bilingually educated late signers in Estonia and Sweden, $t(81) = 0.85$, $p > .35$.

TABLE 5.2 *Means (with SDs in parentheses) in Experiment 2 for chronological age (CA), nonverbal mental age (MA), and "mentalizing" theory of mind (ToM) scores with percentage correct on ToM*

	n	CA (months)	Nonverbal MA (months)	ToM scores	ToM%
Native signers					
Bilingual	11	153.5 (29.2)	152.2 (38.1)	6.59 (1.93)	82
Oralist	13	141.5 (26.5)	137.8 (32.6)	4.46 (1.90)	56
Late signers					
Bilingual (Estonia)	16	144.9 (28.3)	122.8 (32.5)	4.44 (2.28)	56
Bilingual (Sweden)	21	148.3 (27.2)	138.6 (39.7)	4.98 (2.11)	62
Hearing children	26	128.6 (36.4)	130.7 (40.1)	6.56 (1.36)	82

We reanalyzed the data to exclude responses on individual questions on which children answered the corresponding control questions incorrectly. On the proportion of correct overall responses for each child on items where the control questions were answered correctly, the pattern of significant results was unchanged. Since the eleven native signing bilinguals were on average two years older than their twenty-six hearing counterparts, we examined in an age-matched analysis whether their mean scores differed significantly from those of the eleven oldest hearing children (M = 13.45 yr; SD = 1.14) who were comparable in age to the native signing bilinguals (M = 12.79 yrs; SD = 2.43). There were again no significant differences, $t(20)$ = 1.33, p > .15.

Although there were no significant overall differences among the five groups in chronological age, $F(4, 82)$ = 1.89, p > .10, or nonverbal mental age, $F(4, 82)$ = 1.13, p > .30, scores on the mentalizing tasks for the deaf sample as a whole did correlate significantly with both chronological age, r = .69, p < .001, and nonverbal mental age, r = .46, p < .001. Similarly, for the hearing children, there was a significant correlation between mentalizing scores and chronological age, r = .61, p < .001, and between mentalizing scores and mental age, r = .48, p < .02.

We carried out an analysis of covariance to determine whether the differences among the five groups in performance on the mentalizing tasks would remain once chronological and mental age were partialed out as covariates. These differences remained significant, $F(4, 79) = 13.23$, $p < .001$, $\eta^2 = .40$, and planned contrasts confirmed that the hearing children significantly outperformed all groups of deaf children, p's $< .001$, η^2's $> .26$, except for the bilingually instructed native signers. The difference between the bilingually instructed native signers and each of the three other deaf groups of children also remained significant, p's $< .012$, η^2's $> .08$.

Overall, on a wide-ranging index of ToM reasoning, the bilingually instructed native signing children in Experiment 2 performed at a high level. They significantly outscored bilingually instructed late signers and oralist instructed native signers. Unlike other deaf children, the bilingually instructed native signers answered correctly to the extent that the level of their performance did not differ from that of an age-matched group of hearing children. All children in Experiment 2 passed the non-mental representation task indicating that variations in performance on the ToM reasoning measures cannot easily be attributed to variations in understanding representation generally. Rather, differences in the level of performance of the bilingually instructed native signers in Experiment 2 may be seen in terms of the intensive and continuous sign language environment that is present for bilingually instructed deaf children in Estonia. Together with the results of Experiment 1, this pattern suggests that early "total immersion" in a sign language is important specifically for the typical development of mentalizing skills where language facilitates joint attention and social interaction that provides opportunities to focus on mental states in a "mind-minded" way.

GENERAL DISCUSSION

In contrast to deaf children of hearing parents who normally acquire a sign language late in their development, deaf children of deaf parents for whom sign is their native language have early opportunities to converse about the beliefs of others and to formulate an understanding of how these can be false. On this account, development in the expression of ToM reasoning of typically developing hearing children, as well as native signing deaf children, on the tasks often used to test ToM understanding can be viewed to reflect a cumulative and constant exposure to conversation. This early and continuous access, together with a rich innate competence that permits metarepresentation (Leslie 1987), promotes the development of resources that facilitate the expression of ToM reasoning. The present findings from deaf children in Estonia, Italy, and Sweden add to those from previous studies based on children and adolescents from Scotland (Russell et al. 1998) and children, adolescents, and adults in Nicaragua (Morgan & Kegl 2006). These indicate that the expression of ToM reasoning in late signers at a level shown by hearing children is not inevitable – even by the onset of adolescence or later. Particular groups of late signing deaf children remain an exception to an otherwise culturally universal timetable of performance on ToM tasks that has been documented to date (Callaghan et al. 2005; Sabbagh et al. 2006). This, of course, is not to conclude that groups such as late signing deaf children are totally without the ability to attribute mental states (Marschark et al. 2000; Morgan & Kegl 2006), only that correct responses on certain FB measures are not expressed to the same degree as in hearing children or native signing deaf children.

However, the results from the present investigation suggest for the first time that the expression of ToM in native signing deaf children may also depend on children's continuing exposure to opportunities for monitoring the nature of conversational input about mental states and its implications for evaluating beliefs and other mental states as true or false. With similar home language environments, bilingually or B/B instructed native signers in both experiments outperformed those instructed in oralist schools, and, as shown in Experiment 2, the performance of those provided with bilingual instruction did not differ from that of similar aged hearing children. Though there appear to be no differences between native and late signers on general measures of executive functioning (Remmel, Bettger, & Weinberg 2001; Woolfe et al. 2002), the expression of ToM in native signers may be maintained through practice and automatization specifically in an environment where they have access to their native language both at home and in school. Given intensive intervention, there are indications that such an environment can also be advantageous for deaf children from hearing families for whom a sign language is their first, preferred language (Moeller & Schick 2006). By contrast, impairment in the expression of ToM reasoning appears to occur under conditions when this environment is degraded such as is the case for native signers enrolled in oralist schools in which conversation is centered on a spoken language or even, as shown in Experiment 1, in B/B schools in which there is sign supported instruction or instruction through a translator.

If the language environment is one that constantly demands that children work in a "foreign" mode of communication such as is the case in an oralist school or even in a bimodal/bilingual school in which a sign language is not always used as a direct medium for instruction, their expression of a ToM could be impaired even if the tasks and test questions are presented in their native language. By contrast, in a bilingual environment in which both spoken and sign languages are used directly as the medium for instruction, deaf children – including possibly even many signing children who have received implants – can better monitor and attend to others' mental states. They gain full access to a conversational environment in their native language that supports the expression of ToM reasoning on various mentalizing tasks. For hearing bilinguals, the mechanisms that prompt success on ToM tasks may differ in that, as noted previously, children may gain an advantage in aspects of executive functioning and metalinguistic understanding.

It is well established that children's proficiency in the syntax, semantics, and morphology of sign and spoken languages is correlated with their performance on measures of ToM (Milligan et al. 2007). This pattern is consistent with the significant relation between performance on the LIS test and ToM found in Experiment 1. In particular, Schick et al. have reported that children's understanding of sentence complementation – a specific skill not examined in our investigation – predicts performance on ToM tasks. This understanding requires the possession of syntactic structures such as those that permit the embedding of false propositions within true statements ("Mary knows that John (falsely) thinks chocolates are in the cupboard"). Although our data do not address this hypothesis, it has yet to be shown that differences in FB understanding in groups of either deaf or hearing children disappear when these groups are equated on sentence complementation skills (Tardif, So, & Kaciroti 2007).

Although a certain level of linguistic skill may be necessary for children to succeed on particular ToM tasks, many children do achieve proficiency in formal aspects of language understanding but still do not answer correctly. This result points to a substantial independence between aspects of language development and ToM performance (Harris, de Rosnay, & Pons 2005; Meins et al. 2006; Siegal & Peterson 2008). A language test was not available for the children in Experiment 2. However, the assessment in Experiment 1 indicated, as in Woolfe et al., that differences in ToM performance between native and late signers, or between children instructed either in B/B or oralist schools, cannot be accounted for solely by language skill differences, bearing in mind that our language assessment was limited and did not involve, for example, sentence complementation. Indeed, although an issue for intense debate (Perner & Ruffman 2005), the attentional patterns of preverbal thirteen- to fifteen-month-olds (Onishi & Baillargeon 2005; Surian, Caldi, & Sperber, 2007), as well as two-year-olds (Southgate, Senju, & Csibra 2007), suggest that FB understanding is present in typically developing hearing children even before onset of the syntax of sentence complementation. Therefore, as suggested by our findings, the expression of ToM reasoning, at least for deaf children, appears to be strengthened in two ways: first, through very early access to a sign language in the form of conversational interactions that may occur even before language emerges in the child or shortly thereafter and, second, through continuing access to a sign language as a medium for instruction. This ongoing access may permit the child to monitor others' mental states and to express ToM reasoning based on insight into their beliefs, emotions, and overall viewpoints.

In closing, we highlight several issues for further investigation that arise from this study. First, it may be that many deaf children can actually be proficient at ToM reasoning but that this proficiency requires that further steps be taken to clarify the nature of the tasks and to provide training (Bloom & German 2000; Yazdi et al. 2006). Alternatively, some deaf children, such as many late signers instructed in an oralist environment, may have a delay or deficit in performance on FB tasks that is resistant to steps taken to clarify the tasks or to training procedures. Therefore, one avenue for research concerns the need for studies that involve language comprehension and training. As a priority, this work would extend to investigations of quality of the language input, particularly in the context of the conversational opportunities afforded by parents as well as by the siblings of different groups of native and late signing children (Slaughter, Peterson, & Macintosh 2007; Woolfe, Want, & Siegal 2003). Additional study is also needed to determine whether native signing children with bilingual or oralist instruction display individual differences on executive functioning tasks that are associated with ToM performance in typically developing children (Carlson & Moses 2001) as well as flexibility in reasoning (Deák & Narasimham 2003).

Finally, the present investigation was limited mainly to ToM reasoning in terms of false belief understanding and various measures of mentalizing. Other work is necessary to examine a broader range of ToM-related attributes such as deaf children's ability to understand and to produce mental state verbs, to infer intentionality and access to knowledge in speakers' language and behavior, and to socialize with others (Bat-Chava, Martin, & Kosciw 2005). In particular, as ToM is a cornerstone of effective communication, there is a pressing need to investigate whether differences between groups of deaf children extend to measures of conversational understanding that concern the recognition of messages as sincere, relevant, and free of ambiguity (Siegal & Surian 2007; Sperber & Wilson 2002).

REFERENCES

Baron-Cohen, S., O'Riordan, M., Stone, V., Jones, R., & Plaisted, K. (1999). Recognition of faux pas by normally developing children and children with Asperger syndrome or high-functioning autism. *Journal of Autism and Developmental Disorders*, 29, 407–418.

Bat-Chava, Y., Martin, D., & Kosciw, J. G. (2005). Longitudinal improvements in communication and socialization of deaf children with cochlear implants and hearing aids: Evidence from parental reports. *Journal of Child Psychology and Psychiatry*, 46, 1287–1296.

Bloom, P., & German, T. P. (2000). Two reasons to abandon the false belief task as a test of theory of mind. *Cognition*, 77, B25–B31.

Callaghan, T. C., Rochat, P., Lillard, A., Claux, M. L., Odden, H., Itakura, S., Tapanya, S., & Singh, S. (2005). Synchrony in the onset of mental-state reasoning. *Psychological Science*, 16, 378–384.

Carlson, S. M., & Moses, L. J. (2001). Individual differences in inhibitory control and children's theory of mind. *Child Development*, 72, 1032–1053.

Caselli, M. C., Maragna, S., & Volterra, V. (2006). *Linguaggio e sordità: Gesti, segni e parole nello sviluppo e nell'educazione*. Bologna: Il Mulino.

Courtin, C., & Melot, A-M. (2005). Metacognitive development of deaf children: Lessons from the appearance-reality and false belief tasks. *Developmental Science*, 8, 16–25.

Custer, W. L. (1996). A comparison of young children's understanding of contradictory representations in pretense, memory, and belief. *Child Development*, 67, 678–688.

Dahlgren, S. O., Dahlgren Sandberg, A., & Hjelmquist, E. (2003). The non-specificity of theory of mind deficits: Evidence from children with communicative disabilities. *European Journal of Cognitive Psychology*, 15, 129–155.

Deák, G. O., & Narasimham, G. (2003). Is perseveration caused by inhibition failure? Evidence from preschool children's inferences about word meanings. *Journal of Experimental Child Psychology*, 86, 194–222.

Falkman, K. W., Dahlgren Sandberg A., & Hjelmquist, E. (2005). Theory of mind in children with severe speech and physical impairment (SSPI): A longitudinal study. *International Journal of Disability, Development and Education, 52,* 139–157.

Falkman, K., Roos, C., & Hjelmquist, E. (2007). Mentalizing skills of non-native, early signers: A longitudinal perspective. *European Journal of Developmental Psychology, 4,* 178–197.

Happé, F. G. E. (1994). An advanced test of theory of mind: Understanding of story characters' thoughts and feelings by able autistic, mentally handicapped, and normal children and adults. *Journal of Autism and Developmental Disorders, 24,* 129–154.

Harris, P. L. (1996). Desires, beliefs, and language. In P. Carruthers & P. K. Smith (Eds.) *Theories of Theory of Mind* (pp. 200–220). New York: Cambridge University Press.

Harris, P. L., de Rosnay, M., & Pons, F. (2005). Language and children's understanding of mental states. *Current Directions in Psychological Science, 14,* 69–73.

Harris, P. L., Johnson, C. N., Hutton, D., Andrews, G., & Cooke, T. (1989). Young children's theory of mind and emotion. *Cognition and Emotion, 3,* 379–400.

Herman, R., Holmes, S., & Woll, B. (1999). *Assessing BSL development: Receptive Skills Test.* London: Forest Books.

Hobson, R. P., & Bishop, M. (2003). The pathogenesis of autism: Insights from congenital blindness. *Philosophical Transactions of the Royal Society, Series B358,* 335–344

Howlin, P., Baron-Cohen, S., & Hadwin, J. (1999). *Teaching children with autism to mind-read. A practical guide for teachers and parents.* Chichester: Wiley.

Hughes, C., Adlam, A., Happé, F., Jackson, J., Taylor, A., & Caspi, A. (2000). Good test-retest reliability for standard and advanced false-belief tasks across a wide range of abilities. *Journal of Child Psychology and Psychiatry, 41,* 483–490.

Laiapea, V., Miljan, M., Sutrop, U., & Toom, R. (2003). *Eesti viipekeel.* Tallinn: Eesti Keele Sihtasutus.

Lee, K., Olson, D., & Torrance, N. (1999). Chinese children's understanding of false beliefs: The effect of language. *Journal of Child Language, 26,* 1–21.

Leslie, A. M. (1987). Pretense and representation: The origins of "theory of mind." *Psychological Review, 94,* 412–426.

Maragna, S. (2000). *La sordità: Educazione, scuola, lavoro e integrazione sociale.* Milan: Hoepli.

Maridaki-Kassotaki, K., Lewis, C., & Freeman, N. H. (2003). Lexical choice can lead to problems: What false belief tests tell us about Greek alternative verbs of agency. *Journal of Child Language, 30,* 1–20.

Marschark, M., Green, V., Hindmarsh, G., & Walker, S. (2000). Understanding theory of mind in children who are deaf. *Journal of Child Psychology and Psychiatry, 41,* 1067–1073.

Mayberry, R. I., Lock, I., & Kazmi, H. (2002). Language ability and linguistic exposure. *Nature, 417,* 38.

Meins, E., Fernyhough, C., Johnson, F., & Lidstone, J. (2006). Mind-mindedness in children: Individual differences in internal-state talk in middle childhood. *British Journal of Developmental Psychology, 24,* 181–196.

Meins, E., Fernyhough, C., Wainwright, R., Gupta, M., Fradley, E., & Tuckey, M. (2002). Maternal mind-mindedness and attachment security as predictors of theory of mind understanding. *Child Development, 73,* 1715–1726.

Milligan, K., Astington, J. W., & Dack, L. A. (2007). Language and theory of mind: Meta-analysis of the relation between language ability and false-belief understanding. *Child Development, 78,* 622–646.

Moeller, M. P., & Schick, B. (2006). Relations between maternal input and theory of mind understanding in deaf children. *Child Development, 77,* 751–766.

Morgan, G., & Kegl, J. (2006). Nicaraguan sign language and theory of mind: The issue of critical periods and abilities. *Journal of Child Psychology and Psychiatry, 47,* 811–819.

Onishi, K. H., & Baillargeon, R. (2005). Do 15-month-old infants understand false beliefs? *Science, 308,* 255–258.

Perner, J., Leekam, S., & Wimmer, H. (1987). Three-year-olds difficulty with false belief: The case for a conceptual deficit. *British Journal of Developmental Psychology, 5,* 125–137.

Perner, J., & Ruffman, T. (2005). Infants' insight into the mind: How deep? *Science, 308,* 214–216.

Peterson, C. C. (2004). Theory of mind development in oral deaf children with cochlear implants or conventional hearing aids. *Journal of Child Psychology and Psychiatry, 45,* 1096–1106.

Peterson, C. C., Peterson, J. L., & Webb, J. (2000). Factors influencing the development of a theory of mind in blind children. *British Journal of Developmental Psychology, 18,* 431–447.

Peterson, C. C., & Siegal, M. (1997). Psychological, biological and physical thinking in normal, autistic, and deaf children. In H. M. Wellman & K.

Inagaki (Eds.) *The emergence of core domains of thought*. San Francisco: Jossey-Bass.

Peterson, C. C., & Siegal, M. (1998). Changing focus on the representational mind: Deaf, autistic and normal children's concepts of false photos, false drawings and false beliefs. *British Journal of Developmental Psychology*, 16, 301–320.

(1999). Representing inner worlds: Theory of mind in autistic, deaf, and normal hearing children. *Psychological Science*, 10, 126–129.

(2000). Insights into theory of mind from deafness and autism. *Mind and Language*, 15, 123–145.

Pizzuto, E. (2002). The development of Italian Sign Language (LIS) in deaf preschoolers. In G. Morgan & B. Woll (Eds.) *Directions in sign language acquisition*. Philadelphia: John Benjamins.

Pizzuto, E., Ardito, B., Caselli, M. C., & Volterra, V. (2002). Cognition and language in Italian deaf preschoolers of deaf and hearing families. In M. Marschark, D. Clark & M. Karchmer (Eds.) *Cognition, context, and deafness*. Washington, DC: Gallaudet University Press.

Raven, J. C. (1962). *Coloured progressive matrices*. London: H. K. Lewis.

Remmel, E., Bettger, J. G., & Weinberg, A. M. (2001). Theory of mind development in deaf children. In M. D. Clark, M. Marschark & M. Karchmer (Eds.) *Context, cognition, and deafness* (pp. 113–134). Washington, DC: Gallaudet University Press.

Remmel, E., & Peters, K. (2009). Theory of Mind and language in children with cochlear implants. *Journal of Deaf Studies and Deaf Education*, 14(2), 218–236.

Russell, P. A., Hosie, J. A., Gray, C. D., Scott, C., Hunter, N., Banks, J. S., & Macaulay, M. C. (1998). The development of theory of mind in deaf children. *Journal of Child Psychology and Psychiatry*, 39, 903–910.

Russo Cardona, T., & Volterra, V. (2007) *Le lingue dei segni: Soria e semiotica*. Rome: Carocci.

Sabbagh, M. A., Xu, F., Carlson, S. M., Moses, L. J., & Lee, K. (2006). Executive functioning and theory of mind in preschool children from Beijing, China: Comparisons with U.S. preschoolers. *Psychological Science*, 17, 74–81.

Schick, B., De Villiers, P., De Villiers, J., & Hoffmeister, R. (2007). Language and theory of mind: A study of deaf children. *Child Development*, 78, 376–396.

Schick, B., Williams, K., & Kupermintz, H (2006). Look who's being left behind: Educational interpreters and access to education for deaf and hard-of-hearing students. *Journal of Deaf Studies and Deaf Education*, 11, 3–20.

Senghas, A., & Coppola, M. (2001). Children creating language: How Nicaraguan Sign Language acquired a spatial grammar. *Psychological Science*, 12, 323–328.

Senghas, A., Kita, S., & Ozyurek, A. (2004). Children creating core properties of language: Evidence from an emerging sign language in Nicaragua. *Science*, 305, 1779–1782.

Shatz, M., Diesendruck, G., Martinez-Beck, & Akar, D. (2003). The influence of language and socioeconomic status on children's understanding of false belief. *Developmental Psychology*, 39, 717–729.

Siegal, M., & Peterson, C. C. (2008). Language and theory of mind in atypical children: Evidence from studies of deafness, blindness, and autism. In C. Sharp, P. Fonagy & I. Goodyer (Eds.) *Social cognition and developmental psychopathology* (pp. 79–110). New York: Oxford University Press.

Siegal, M., & Surian, L. (2007). Conversational understanding in young children. In E. Hoff & M. Shatz (Eds.) *Handbook of language development* (pp. 304–323). Malden, MA: Blackwell.

Siegal, M., & Varley, R. (2002). Neural systems involved in "theory of mind." *Nature Reviews Neuroscience*, 3, 463–471.

Singleton, J. L., & Morgan, G. (2005). Natural signed language acquisition within the social context of the classroom. In B. Schick, M. Marschark & P. Spencer (Eds.) *Advances in the sign language development of deaf and hard-of-hearing children* (pp. 344–373). New York: Oxford University Press.

Slade, L., & Ruffman, T. (2005). How language does (and does not) relate to theory of mind: A longitudinal study of syntax, semantics, working memory and false belief. *British Journal of Developmental Psychology*, 23, 117–141.

Slaughter, V., Peterson, C. C., & Macintosh, E. (2007). Mind what mother says: Narrative input and theory of mind in typical children and those on the autism spectrum. *Child Development*, 78, 839–858.

Southgate, V., Senju, A., & Csibra, G. (2007). Action attribution through anticipation of false beliefs by two-year-olds. *Psychological Science*, 18, 587–592.

Sperber, D., & Wilson, D. (2002). Pragmatics, modularity and mindreading. *Mind and Language*, 17, 3–23.

Surian, L., Caldi, S., & Sperber, D. (2007). Attribution of beliefs by 13-month-old infants. *Psychological Science*, 18, 580–586.

Tardif, T., So, C. W. C., & Kaciroti, N. (2007). Language and false belief: Evidence for general, not specific, effects in Cantonese-speaking pre-schoolers. *Developmental Psychology*, 43, 318–340.

Wellman, H. M., Hollander, M., & Schult, C. A. (1996). Young children's understanding of thought bubbles and of thoughts. *Child Development, 67,* 768–788.

Woolfe, T., Want, S. C., & Siegal, M. (2002). Signposts to development: Theory of mind in deaf children. *Child Development, 73,* 768–778.

(2003). Siblings and theory of mind in deaf native signing children. *Journal of Deaf Studies and Deaf Education, 8,* 340–347.

Yazdi, A. A., German, T. P., Defeyer, M., & Siegal, M. (2006). Competence and contributions to performance in belief-desire reasoning: The truth, the whole truth, and nothing but the truth about false belief? *Cognition, 100,* 343–368.

Zaitchik, D. (1990). When representations conflict with reality: The preschooler's problem with false beliefs and "false" photographs. *Cognition, 35,* 41–68.

6

Commentary: Aspects and Perspectives of Research into Metarepresentative Thought

PIERGIORGIO BATTISTELLI

The chapters by Carugati and Selleri, Antonietti and Colombo, Marchetti et al., Pelletier, Hipfner-Boucher, and Doyle, and by Meristo et al. outline a vast and significant picture of the area of research that has been developing around the central theme first known as children's Theory of Mind in development psychology circles. The term was, as we know, first coined in the field of ethological observation but soon became used everywhere to refer to a subject associated with an ingenious research paradigm for the understanding of false belief. Development of the ability to understand thought, representing one's own and others' mental representations and taking into account mental states as ultimate determiners of peoples' behavior, was thus to become one of the most important stages in research in the area of cognitive development. Nevertheless, initially a certain resistance could be noted in some branches of psychology or at least a certain delay in recognizing the full importance that this theme objectively might have for general psychology of thought, social development, personal relations, and practical applications, for example, in the field of education. Possibly the strictly cognitive background from which the research pattern originated was in this sense detrimental to it; the connotation "cognitive," with its reductive and individualistic implications, may in the early years have excited some puzzlement and doubts in those areas of research most concerned with the social and cultural framework of thought development. What is more, *"children's Theory of Mind"* was soon reformulated in strictly modular terms and tested in this form as a model for determining pathologies of autism. This aspect too may have contributed to provoking reservations and resistance. In other words, the artificial barriers and constraints that so often separate scholars of different persuasions were up in force once again.

However, the importance and heuristic relevance of the question did ultimately attract the attention of scholars of varying interests and persuasions, sometimes even outside strictly psychological circles. In an excellent popular work written recently by an Italian scholar of natural evolution (Boncinelli 2009, p. 192) the appearance of Theory of Mind is seen as a fundamental stage in the development of the human species. Another important sign is the appearance of our subject in a few recent manuals of general psychology and the psychology of communication, as well as in those of the psychology of development, of course. Today the subject first known as "children's Theory of Mind" has acquired all the importance and complexity that it objectively deserves in the field of human sciences, and the essays in this volume are the proof. Bearing in mind that the name itself, however appropriate, still has somewhat reductive associations today, in this brief essay I have preferred to use the expression *metarepresentative thought* (MT).

The essay by Carugati and Selleri recommends including the theme of MT in an important tradition of research and theoretical formalization in European social psychology. This is the classic theory of social representation, which, as you know, started in French, Italian, and Swiss psychology circles; branched out in various directions; and was developed in many different research centers, intertwining with other traditions based on English research into groups and identity. Carugati and Selleri's contribution aims to show that MT originates within the dynamic interaction of personal relations and the *in-group*. The conceptual tools for evaluating such processes are, on one hand, the distinction between the *operative system* assigned to categorizing, inferring, and so on, and the *metasystem*, which works out the results of the former in the light of social rules and normative values. From another point of view, within the genesis of social representations, one can identify *sociogenesis*, in which shared representations in the context of groups and social institutions are generated; then *ontogeny*, in which the individual, and not only during the age of development, processes and reconstructs representations shared in his "thinking environment," at the same time constructing his social identity; and finally, *microgenesis*, that is, the set of processes that take place in the course of everyday interaction and interpersonal negotiation.

The areas of knowledge in which this theoretical position has encountered resonance and stimuli for research are well known; Carugati and Selleri illustrate a few of them: the building of gender identity and understanding of certain economic and social processes such as the "distributive justice" and social disparity. The study of the development of childhood representations in these areas of knowledge shows clearly that it is the shared representations in specific social contexts that provide anchorage for individual evaluation and interpretation produced by the child. Also, the important concept of *interpretive reproduction* underlines the active, creative contribution by the individual, not only as a child, to forming social representations in the course of concrete routines in daily life.

The application of the general principles of a social construction of knowledge to the question we are interested in has been tested in a series of studies on the concept of intelligence, especially in a school environment. It can be seen clearly how school culture governs pupils' progressive interpretation of the concept of intelligence and how, in turn, these representations influence pupils' behavior and ultimately their everyday school lives. Carugati and Selleri's contribution is part of an extremely significant area of research: What are the levels of comprehension and representation of school events and dynamics from the point of view of the pupils? In spite of some excellent studies (as well as those mentioned by Carugati & Selleri, we should remember Dweeck's research (1999) conducted on older secondary school children), it is surprising that such an approach, which you would think obvious and essential in any study of educational processes, should be so relatively little developed.

Yet over and above the aspect of the applications, the study of social representation of the mental dimension constitutes a virtually unprecedented approach to the study of naive psychology. It is well known that Heider (1958) was the first to start a systematic study of naive psychology; in addition to the phenomenological framework he wished to give his analysis, he was well aware of the social merits of the subject (the title of the volume was *Psychology of Interpersonal Relations*), but the theory of social representation had yet to be formulated. Moreover, the study of naive psychology from this latter point of view should be the framework within which attempts to study cultural representations of the mental dimension will find their natural collocation.

Carugati and Selleri's work also poses another problem: The experimental paradigm of false belief, apart from its supposedly reductive "cognitivist" attribute, proves, among other things, that the representation of mental states also implies the development of specific skills and competence in certain rules of logic, that is, "mentalistic reasoning." This is hardly surprising if we remember that the first analyses of recursive thought and of the "intentional propositions" were conducted by important scholars of logic (Frege, Carnap, Quine, etc.). Thus we find ourselves facing a significant problem: The metarepresentation of representations and, more generally speaking, of mental states is made possible both by competence in specific rules of thought and by the acquisition, as a result of negotiation and conversational practices, of a system of socially constructed and shared knowledge; but what is the relative contribution of these processes and most of all, how are they integrated? Does the child predict that Sally will go and look for her ball in the basket because he is able to realize that her mind does not possess the information that he has or because he has experienced and assimilated, directly or in everyday negotiation, the script according to which people usually look for things where they left them? Either representation leads him to the right solution, but which develops first?

The script evidently has an internal logic compatible, if not coinciding, with that of false belief, but which does the child acquire first? And moreover, which explanation will the child be able to provide for his response? The two perspectives are not alternatives, and we cannot say that if one is true, the other is false. Both seem completely true; we learn to reason according to the logic of metarepresentative thought (by decoupling the representation from the real object with consequent "referential opacity" of the metarepresentation, decentralizing from our own representation, and considering access to perceptual information, etc.) just as we learn to think other people's thoughts and our own by interacting and negotiating our representations in our relations with other people and through these mediations, by assimilating cultural representations of the mind.

On this subject, we might also remember another important contribution to the study of cognitive development made by a specific branch of social psychology (closely linked to the theory of social representations) in the 1960s and 1970s: A series of important research studies on cognitive social conflict showed that the mental operations that Piaget's theory considered fundamental to operational thought were activated in adequate social and relationship contexts and that the child's judgment was strongly governed by the meaning that the situation and problems set assumed in his eyes. In this case, too, though with a number of differences, the child, on one hand, discovers the rules of logical thought; on the other, he is a subject and in a way an actor in the construction of shared representations and judgments.

A similar dilemma is at the basis of Nisbett and Ross's work (1980) on human inference, which is considered one of the founding texts of social cognitivism. The two authors note that biases to be found in human reasoning may be studied both as logical information-processing errors and as a result of needs, expectations, and values of the people processing the information. The former are known as "cold," the latter as "warm" cognition. With great intellectual honesty, the two authors recognized that both viewpoints are legitimate and that they simply preferred the former.

It seems to me that in studying "children's Theory of Mind" we find ourselves at a similar junction between processing information and working out representations in the context of interpersonal and affective relations. None can argue for the predominance of either one or the other interpretation; if anything, one could point out the important prospect for psychology of integrating the empirical knowledge provided by the two approaches in a comprehensive theoretical framework. And this volume in fact constitutes an important contribution in that direction.

Antonietti and Colombo's essay reviews a rich vein of research on metacognition, based on the principle that metacognitive competence is decisive in the learning process using multimedia tools. The effectiveness of such tools depends to a large extent on learners' competence in using them to their full potential, and within this competence, the skill with the preeminent role is without doubt that of metacognitive expertise. As we know, metacognition has been tackled from many points of view that have illuminated diverse aspects and stages of the process, from the most elementary knowledge to beliefs and conscious cognitive strategies, to monitoring the learning process (metacomprehension) online. Essentially, we are talking about the awareness of what goes on in our minds when we are engaged in a learning task, and it is inevitable that that awareness will influence our way of using multimedia tools. The literature on this subject is surprisingly abundant, and for this reason, too, Antonietti and Colombo's work is a valuable contribution to our knowledge and to a critical review of material that can be unwieldy. The authors deal with the complexity of the subject matter from three points of view: (1) the artifact as a tool to promote metacognition, (2) the artifact as a tool to scaffold metacognition and learning, (3) metacognition and artifact together to promote learning. In this way, they are able to give an account of the knowledge acquired in this field, but they also do not fail to point out many critical and problematic aspects emerging in areas where you would expect to find simple and unambiguous relationships among multimedia tools, metacognitive knowledge (or monitoring), and learning. Evidently, the empirical data that research is providing contradict the apparently schematic nature of the subject matter. This fact reminds us that in reality metacognition is a part of awareness; it is an awareness applied to knowledge. A few references to scholars such as James and Searle should suffice to remind us of the complexities and difficulty of capturing such themes at an empirical level.

Antonietti and Colombo correctly note the appearance in metacognition of variables connected to the image of self, self-esteem, and experience(s) connected to these personality dimensions, which we may consider "warm (meta)cognition" and whose integration into a system of metarepresentative thought is a necessity that emerges from a reading of this part of the book.

The essay by Marchetti et al. represents a valuable synthesis of the extremely wide research carried out over the last two decades by the Theory of Mind Research Unit of the Catholic University of the Sacred Heart in Milan. To my mind, the wealth of results and the systematic quality of the work carried out by this center, to whose foundation and guidance Professor Olga Liverta Sempio has contributed greatly, are unique in Italian research about MT.

The fundamental approach is that of contextualism and recognizes Vygotski as its first historical reference. The basic thesis is well known: Children's thought and knowledge develop in the context of interpersonal relations, along with their linguistic determiners and their affective values, in the context of cultural models and values. This principle is developed in several specific themes. First, the family context with its primary affective dynamics, well illustrated in the light of the psychoanalytical theories of Fonagy et al. (2002), Meins (1997) and Meins and Fernyhough (1999). The empirical contribution, summarized by Flavia Lecciso, enables us to specify, in a development of Theory of Mind, the role of the child's secure attachment to and trust of the caregiver. The school context also systematically uses and works with mentalistic concepts such as mental skills, effort and commitment, intentions and objectives, knowledge and ignorance. The various research studies reviewed by Giulia Cavalli show how school presupposes a certain mental competence in the child and at the same time sets itself up as one of the most important sources for the acquisition of metacognitive skills; the school context is also the one in which the child experiences that same knowledge as well as the differences between individuals in comparison with the teacher and with his peers. What also emerges from this piece of research is the need for schools to develop adequate procedures for testing and stimulating these metacognitive skills in pupils. This aspect is evidently closely linked to Carugati and Selleri's contribution; perhaps integrating the different perspectives could lead to setting up a school psychology on the pupil's side, that is, a systematic study of the pupil's subjectivity. What does the pupil think of school? Has this banal question ever found an exhaustive answer? Davide Massaro points to another source of stimulation of the representation of mental states: children's literature, with its wealth of characters and references to their thoughts and emotions. This can be fictional literature, which links back to the game of pretense, one of the most famously debated hypothetical precursors of Theory of Mind. As we know, according to Leslie (1987) the game of pretense is based on the same mechanism as Theory of Mind, and therefore the problem arises of how to explain the lack of synchronism in their development. Various studies suggest that in reality there are different levels of cognitive organization and that the whole question of the precursors of Theory of Mind (apart from pretense, understanding of intentions, shared attention, etc.) still appears very problematic. Equally complex is the question of understanding irony, discussed by Annalisa Valle; development of the ability to perceive irony must take place at school age, at the time of second-level mentalistic understanding. Research on this topic offers a significant suggestion to the questions we considered before: Contextual markers interact with the development of mentalistic reasoning skills (in this case, for example, the respective status of two interlocutors in an ironic exchange). Logical variables interact with extralogical variables, one would have said in the years when Piaget's theory was being discussed. Serena Petrocchi tells of various research studies conducted on deaf children, which confirm that the development of an adequate Theory of Mind depends crucially on relations of secure attachment to parents and teachers, so as to suggest the perspective of considering Theory of Mind as "affective, inter-subjective and relationship-based." In fact, this research perspective also seems to pick up on important family dynamics, such as depression, which can have a negative influence on the level of metarepresentative thought, for the child and the parents. So we are back to documenting from this angle the intersection between MT development and affective dynamics as conjectured and documented by Fonagy and Meins's approach.

I would like to emphasize that psychoanalysis, if supported by research, can meet empirical research on cognitive development and become a very significant contribution to research into metarepresentative thought. Barbara Lucchini deals with an area of research in which the understanding of what from many points of view is a particularly important mental state such as intention was considered a variable crucial for moral judgment for many years (Piaget 1932): The child manages to formulate a moral judgment correctly only when he considers the intentional, or unintentional, aspect of human actions. The research cited by Lucchini provides a somewhat unexpected insight: Autistic children, compared to normal children, show cognitive deficits on the classic Theory of Mind, tests but they do not exhibit any difference in assessing intention implicit in an action to be evaluated from a moral point of view. These data may be indicators of the significance of the implicit or explicit nature of the task assigned. Indications of this kind have already been provided by Clements and Perner's work (1994), and the need to consider different degrees of awareness in representations in the course of development was stressed in the work of Karmiloff Smith (1992). Generally speaking, these references all point to a close connection between metarepresentative thought and awareness (Battacchi, Battistelli, & Celani 1998), but this is only rarely explored, no doubt because of the difficulties encountered when tackling the theme of awareness on a conceptual plane and even more so on an empirical level.

Finally, Eleonora Di Terlizzi points once more, in her review of research on abused children, to the importance of the quality of affective relationships to the development of children's Theory of Mind. Even when abused children are able to recover to the stage of first-level metarepresentation, they still show significant deficits at second-level tasks. These results must be interpreted in the context of deprived or distorted processes of recognition and verbalization of emotions that can be recorded in families that abuse their children: I believe it is important to stress that this case too deals with the process of awareness. The results being gathered in this field have drawn the attention of research fellows and field researchers to parental style(s) that can affect the capacity to mentalize. At the end of this dense review, Ilaria Castelli calls attention to three research projects that the Research Unit on Theory of Mind Milan is currently engaged in: (1) research into the deterioration of metarepresentative thought in old age and as a consequence of pathologies such as Alzheimer's disease; (2) research on "neuroscience and Theory of Mind," that is, research on neural bases for MT; (3) the connection of MT with the decision-making process (we shall return to this point further on).

To conclude our reading of this contribution, I merely wish to point out how far the science of psychology has progressed in this field since two ethologists started to ask themselves whether a chimpanzee's gaze was directed at the mind of the warden and since other imaginative researchers enabled us to see the ingenious paradigm of false belief in a box of chocolates. In 2000 and even more recently (2004), Flavell took stock of developments in research into Theory of Mind, yet already today, from the contributions gathered together in this part of the volume, we are bound to register a further extension and enrichment of our knowledge.

We shall now examine the essay by Janette Pelletier, Kathleen Hipfner-Boucher, and Antoinette Doyle of the University of Toronto, on the relationship between development of Theory of Mind and understanding of stories. This is a classic theme that emerges from the more general relation between Theory of Mind (or metarepresentative thought) and narrative thought already highlighted many years ago in contributions by Jerome Bruner (1990). The main thesis of this work is that comprehension of narrative text is based on the understanding of mental states that lend meaning to the characters' actions. In the theoretical introduction to the essay there is also a very interesting reference, in my opinion, to the research on Theory of Mind in relation to life span. In my view this theme constitutes a new and very important line of research, but also one very little developed to date; we have few data on what the mind comprehends in adolescence and little information too for old age (cf. Castelli et al. 2001, 2010; Baglio et al. 2012). Few studies are concerned with mentalistic reasoning in adulthood: For example, how do adults apply the logic of false belief? When and how often do people rely more on naive realism in daily life or maintain constant awareness of the mental perspectives of other people? In the context of heuristics and evaluating decisions, recently various studies have recorded interesting biases that lead us to suppose that a vast number of erroneous inferences are made in everyday thought as a result of "mistakes" in mentalistic reasoning (e.g., Keiser, Lin, & Barr 2003; Bernstein et al. 2007, 2011; Birch & Bloom 2003, 2004; Pohl 2007; some studies are currently in progress at the Research Unit on Theory of Mind in Milan).

We should also remember "outcome bias" and "hindsight," which may be considered the effect of "wisdom after the event" and have been repeatedly documented (e.g., Fischhoff 1975; Baron & Hershey 1988; Mazzocco & Cherubini 2010) and picked up again recently, too, by Massaro, Giudici, and Marchetti (2011) and Massaro, Castelli, Giudici, and Marchetti (2011) (cf. also Massaro et al. submitted). Outcome bias consists in making an assessment based on today's known outcome of a decision made previously, when one obviously could not have known what the outcome would be. Evidently the cause of this error lies in not being able to represent to oneself correctly the representation that gave rise to the decision. Hindsight bias consists in considering predictable something that actually took place, while ignoring the uncertainties of the initial situation. These studies are also noteworthy for their practical implications, but the picture that emerges places us face to face with the limited rationality of everyday thought. The mind is evidently capable of following rigorously logical algorithms, even with mentalistic reasoning, but in everyday real life, it often trips up on simple and sometimes deceptive heuristics. In this specific case, what is hard to give due consideration to is the state of not-knowing of an individual; so what is problematic is the representation and understanding of ignorance. This would be a good research topic on the naive Theory of Mind, to be developed in a life-span perspective.

From a more general point of view, we face a situation that has occurred repeatedly in psychological research. The authors cited previously, in summarizing the history of research on heuristics, note that compared with theories on the logic of decision making and probabilistic reasoning, people are actually much less rigorous and infallible in their reasoning, but probably more "economical," making do with "reasonably" effective thought. A similar situation occurred when empirical research attempted to test the consistency of Piaget's theories on concrete and formal operational thought; as readers will remember, many psychological studies showed that in reality the formal operational thought, expected by the epistemological model to constitute the completion of intellectual development, was mastered or regularly used only by a percentage, and not even a very high one, of young people and adults. It is interesting to note that the same situation perhaps is also emerging in the field of metarepresentative thought.

With regard to children, an important source of stimulation to mental understanding and metacognitive language acquisition lies in those storybooks in which information on the protagonists' mental states systematically accompanies the narrative of their actions: The landscape of consciousness always goes hand in hand with the landscape of action, as Pellettier et al. indicate. The results of this research show that in Canadian children attending kindergarten, competence in metacognitive language predominantly explained the ability to understand stories. But another particularly interesting fact, to my mind, emerges from the paper: The group of children who, not belonging to English language groups, were assigned to a specific program to learn the English language, were those with better performance than other peer groups and performance equal to that of a higher age group. Presumably this was a category of children exposed to bilingual stimuli and they themselves are, or are about to become, bilingual.

The importance of language in the development of metarepresentative thought also inspired the research conducted by Meristo, Falkman, Hjelmquist, Tedoldi, Surian, and Siegal on deaf children between four and twelve years in Italy and between seven and sixteen years in Sweden and Estonia. Both studies are rather complex in the number of variables and instruments used and provide us with highly interesting data on the effects of different programs and teaching methods on deaf children compared to children with normal hearing. But one fact that emerges clearly above all others is that the deaf children who were native signers, who had therefore received teaching in two languages, that of signing and the spoken language and could thus also be considered virtually bilingual, performed far better on the false belief task than all the other groups of their age and in some cases better than older children who had normal hearing. The authors attribute this result to the fact that the deaf children, who could be considered native signers but had also been trained in oral communication, had from a very early age had more opportunities to take part in conversations focusing, among other things, on the mental dimension. The results of this research substantially tally with those of Pellettier et al.; what appears to favor performance in metarepresentative thought in both is mastery of a kind of double code: two languages, the native language and English in the Canadian group, the signing and speech in the deaf Italian, Swedish, and Estonian children. Yet how can two codes help one to understand better what is going through other people's minds?

In the last few years various other studies have confirmed that bilingual children perform better in the false belief task; there are several different possible explanations for this (often executive functions and those of control are involved or the effect of acquisition and mastery of a dual code), but the positive effect of bilingualism on understanding of the mind may be due to frequent contact with people with a different language and presumably a different culture, which should be the usual condition of life for bilinguals. This situation may in particular stimulate the inferring of another's thoughts as well as operations of cognitive decentralization based on the assumption of another person's point of view. Thus the experience of diversity could be the crucial variable. Starting from similar reflections, Benelli, Carelli, and Arnold (1995) did some research on twin brothers living in a situation where the difference between self and the other is reduced to a minimum and they found that compared to siblings of different ages, the twins' performance on the false belief task was inferior. This almost seems counterevidence to the deduction made about bilingualism: When the privileged interlocutor (the twin brother) is too similar, metarepresentative thought becomes deprived of stimuli and experience. In other words, similarity could damage the development of Theory of Mind while diversity might favor it. This general principle obviously needs developing and requires adequate confirmation, but it does appear loaded with significance. We have already referred to research work on sociocognitive conflict: When a child experiences the difference between his own representation and that of his interlocutor (and is prevented from solving the conflict, passively accepting the other's opinion), he oftendraws the right conclusion about the problem, provides the solution (even if his friend's opinion was equally wrong), and apparently stably acquires the logical principle thus discovered. In such situations of discrepancy, the experience of difference again gives a decisive kick to cognitive development. If in biology the diversity of living species is considered a fundamental condition for natural evolution and a balanced environment, might we not discover the fundamental function of this principle in psychology as well?

One of the most important recent achievements in neuropsychological research is the discovery of the famous mirror neurons, neurons that are activated both when the subject performs a given action and when he sees another person performing that action. This datum is important for two reasons. First of all, these neurons evidently have both a function of perception and a motor function and thus are a kind of bridge between the two functions. Therefore, these neurons provide the explanation, hitherto somewhat problematic, of certain precocious skills and processes, for example, the ability of a baby to imitate gestures made by an adult. In general, the function of mirror neurons is even more emphasized in empathy and recognition of mental states in other people. These mirror neurons are considered the neural basis of the ability to become close to other people and identify with them, and the Theory of Mind is often cited in this context. This is not the place to enter further into the merits of these theses, but I should like to add that in the task of understanding false belief the subject shows he has the right representation of another's mental state when he notices and takes into account the difference between his own representation and that of the other; in fact, if the child is unable to make this distinction and lets himself be induced into attributing his own representation to the other, he will certainly fail the test. To exemplify this mistake, can we remember the old concept of "egocentricity" (Mounoud 1996):

A wise old man warned people of the danger of mistaking mirrors for windows: To recognize what is different outside ourselves and be aware of other people's minds, safe from false projections and attribution,; do we need windows rather than mirrors? A mirror reflection shows us the representation of what there is in common or what is similar between me and the other, but to comprehend fully what is "other" than me in its specific qualities and irreducible diversity, I need to arm myself with more sophisticated cognitive tools. Yet we saw earlier that perhaps the experience of diversity itself could be the important stimulus for developing these tools of more advanced thought. We are well aware that the subject of diversity and differences (between individuals, groups, and cultures) takes on a significance that goes far beyond psychological research; it is, in fact, subject-matter of vast proportions that is at present dominating the fields of sociology and pedagogy but also perhaps those of ethics and politics. This is of course hardly the place to tackle such arguments, but it is certainly important to remember that it is precisely the systems of moral values and political passions (in the very broadest sense) that provide a meaning to our daily lives and our very work as psychology researchers.

REFERENCES

Baglio, F., Castelli, I., Alberoni, M., Blasi, V., Grifanti, L., Falini, A., Nemni, R., & Marchetti, A. (2012). The mindreading ability through the eyes in amnestic mild cognitive impairment: An fMRI study. *Journal of Alzheimer's Disease*, 29(1), 25–37.

Baron, J., & Hershey, J. C. (1988). Outcome bias in decision evaluation. *Journal of Personality and Social Psychology*, 54(4), 569–579.

Battacchi, M. W., Battistelli, & P. Celani, G. (1998). *Lo sviluppo del pensiero meta rappresentativo e della coscienza*. Milano: F. Angeli.

Benelli B., Carelli, M. G., & Arnold, S. (1995). Effetti del tipo relazione interpersonale sul decentramento e sulla competenza meta cognitiva: la teoria della mente in gemelli, fratelli e figli unici. *Giornale Italiano di Psicologia*, 22, 107–135.

Bernstein, D. M., Atance, C., Meltzoff, A. N., & Loftus, G. R. (2007). Hindsight bias and developing theories of mind. *Child Development*, 78(4), 1374–1394.

Bernstein, D. M., Erdfelder, E., Meltzoff, A. N., Peria, W., & Loftus, G. R. (2011). Hindsight bias from 3 to 95 years of age. *Journal of Experimental Psychology: Learning, Memory & Cognition*, 37(2), 378–391.

Birch, S. A. J., & Bloom, P. (2003). Children are cursed: An asymmetric bias in mental-state attribution. *Psychological Science*, 3, 283–286.

(2004). Understanding children's and adults' limitations in mental state reasoning. *Trends in Cognitive Sciences*, 8(6), 255–260.

Boncinelli, E. (2009). *Perché non possiamo non dirci darwinisti*. Milano: Rizzoli.

Bruner, J. (1990). *Acts of meaning*. Cambridge, MA: Harvard University Press.

Castelli, I., Baglio, F., Blasi, V., Alberoni, M., Falini, A., Liverta Sempio, O., Nemni, R., & Marchetti, A. (2010). Effects of aging on mindreading ability through the eyes: An fMRI study. *Neuropsychologia*, 48, 2586–2594.

Castelli, I., Baglio, F., Blasi, V., Alberoni, M., Falini, A., Liverta Sempio, O., & Marchetti, A. (2010). Effects of aging on mindreading ability through the eyes: An fMRI study. *Neuropsychologia*, 48, 2586–2594.

Castelli, I. Pini, A., Alberoni, M., Liverta Sempio, O., Baglio, F., Massaro, D., Marchetti, A., & Nemni, R. (2001). Mapping levels of theory of mind in Alzheimer's disease: A preliminary study, *Aging and Mental Health*, 2, 157–168.

Clements, W. A., & Perner J. (1994). Implicit understanding of belief. *Cognitive Development*. 9, 377–395.

Dweeck, C. S. (1999). *Self theories: Their role in motivation, personality and development*. Philadelphia: Psychology Press.

Fischhoff, B. (1975). Hindsight is not equal to foresight: The effect of outcome knowledge on judgment under uncertainty. *Journal of Experimental Psychology: Human Perception and Performance*, 1(3), 288–299.

Flavell, J. (2004). Theory of mind development: Retrospect and prospect. *Merill-Palmer Quarterly*, 50, 274–290.

Fonagy, P., & Target, M. (1997). Attachment and reflective function: Their role in self-organization. *Development and Psychopathology*,9, 679–700.

Fonagy, P., Gergely, G., Jurist, E. L., & Target, M. (2002). *Affect regulation, mentalization, and the development of the self*. New York: Other Press.

Heider, F. (1958). *Psychology of interpersonal relations*. New York: Wiley.

James, W. (1890). *Principles of psychology*. New York: Holt.

Karmiloff-Smith, A. (1992, reprinted 1995). *Beyond modularity: A development perspective on cognitive science*. Cambridge, MA: MIT.

Keysar, B., Lin, S., and Barr, D. J. (2003). Limits on theory of mind use in adults. *Cognition*, 89, 25–41.

Leslie, A. M. (1987). Pretense and representation: The origins of "theory of mind." *Psychological Review*, 94, 412–426.

Massaro, D., Castelli, I., Giudici, F., & Marchetti, A. (2011). Basta che funzioni: Le decisioni tra teoria della mente ed emozioni. In G. Bellelli & R. D. Schiena (Eds.) *Decisioni ed emozioni: Come la scienza psicologica spiega il conflitto tra ragione e sentimento*. Bologna: Il Mulino.

Massaro, D., Castelli, I., Sanvito, L., & Marchetti, A. (submitted). "I knew-it-all-along": The contribution of second-order Theory of Mind in preventing hindsight and outcome biases in primary school children. *Learning and Instruction*.

Massaro, D., Giudici, F., & Marchetti, A. (2011). Errori nella valutazione delle decisioni e Teoria della Mente. In A. Iannaccone, L. Tateo & G. Storti (Eds.), *Decisa-mente: Teorie, processi e contesti di decision making* (pp. 51–59). Roma: ARACNE.

Mazzocco, K., & Cherubini, P. (2010). The effect of outcome information on health professionals spontaneous learning. *Medical Education*, 10, 962–968.

Meins, E. (1997). Security of attachment and maternal tutoring strategies: Interaction within the zone of proximal development. *British Journal of Developmental Psychology*, 15, 129–144.

Meins, E., & Fernyhough, C. (1999). Linguistic acquisitional style and mentalising development: The role of maternal mind-mindedness. *Cognitive Development*, 14, 363–380.

Mounoud, P. (1996) Perspective taking and belief attribution: From Piaget's theory to children's theory of mind. *Swiss Journal of Psychology*, 55, 93–103.

Nisbett, R. E., & Ross, L. (1980). *Human inference: Strategies and shortcoming of social judgement*. Englewood Cliffs, NJ: Prentice-Hall.

Piaget, J. (1932). *Le jugement moral chez l'enfant*. Paris: PUF.

Pohl, R. F. (2007). Ways to assess hindsight bias. *Social Cognition*, 25, 14–31.

PART II

NARRATIVES

7

Narrative, Culture, and Psychology

JEROME BRUNER

In the deepest sense, psychology seeks to understand the human condition. But the human condition, given its multiple nature, is not easily understood. Or perhaps it would be better to say that it can be understood in many ways, ways that may seem incompatible with each other. For in some deep sense, the human condition is shaped both by the biological constraints inherent in our nature as a species living in a particular physical environment, and at the same time by the symbolically rich cultures that we humans construct and in terms of which we live our lives communally.

Indeed, we uniquely as a species are both limited biologically in our human condition, and at the same time liberated from that condition by our striking capacity to go beyond it by our ability to imagine and create "possible worlds" that transcend that condition. In a word we are both constrained by our biology and liberated from it by the cultures we create to actualize those possible worlds. There is no species on the face of the earth so marked by such a duality. Our human lives, as it were, are a never-ending dialectic between inherited constraints and the possibilities generated and realized by cultural means.

And besides, as we well know, our realization of the possible, far-reaching though it may be, is also limited by what we might call the intrinsic constraints of culture. For in their very nature, cultures are also constraining on those who live within their bounds. By their nature, cultures too limit the freedom of those who live in them. Cultures too are constraining in their ways, for they are institutionalized to maintain stability and order, whether by custom or by legal systems designed to punish impermissible departures from the customary.

Even when we ignore biological constraints, the human condition, viewed culturally, is an endless dialectic between the already Established and what we imagine to be Possible, between convention and temptation, as it were. Yet, it is in our very nature to shape a way of life for ourselves that makes it feasible to do so – though, alas, we sometimes pay a high price in uncertainty and anxiety for it.

It is this often conflicted form of life, this perpetual compromise between the already Established and the imaginatively Possible, that both generates our human troubles and, at the same time, provokes human creativity. Living life in full conformity to the Established creates boredom and banality. Living with a view only to the Possible is a pretty sure way of ending up in prison! Indeed, the challenge of life is to find a viable compromise between the Established and the Possible.

And it is this challenge that I want to address. Indeed, it is this challenge that shapes how psychology goes about or should go about its business in researching the nature of man and his condition. Yet, let me confess that I did not reach this conclusion only speculatively. I was virtually forced into it by trying to make sense of my own research findings. So let me begin by telling you briefly how this came about.

Indeed, it started with my early effort to clarify what constitutes perception, how we make sense of what impinges on our senses. How lengthy an input of a stimulus, for example, is needed for it to be correctly recognized? My research instrument was a tachistoscope, a gadget that varies the length of exposure of a display. I'd begin by showing each subject a thousandth or so of a second of input of a picture or design of some sort, then increasing the exposure time to see how lengthy an exposure it would take for a subject to recognize the display correctly. Simple enough.

What I very soon discovered bwas that my subjects, no matter what the stimulus and no matter how brief the exposure, were never passively waiting for a long enough exposure to see what was being displayed in my fancy tachistoscope. Rather, they were brimming with answers no matter how brief the exposure, literally constructing their percepts no matter how brief the input exposure might have been. And they did so in a strikingly conventional, even banal way. Unconventional inputs were typically conventionalized.

But interestingly, as exposure times were lengthened on successive trials, my subjects would characteristically get stuck with the percepts they'd constructed on earlier, briefer exposures. Their perceptions, in a word, were attempted interpretations of what was being exposed – hypotheses about the "world" in which they found themselves. Eventually, with a long enough time exposure, they'd see the picture or design or word correctly (but often with a gasp of surprise, having been earlier well convinced that they had "seen" it correctly on a briefer exposure).

In a word, they were not just passively "receiving" the presented input, but constructing it and doing so along quite conventional lines. They were attempting to "make sense" as best they could – and getting stuck in their conventionalized constructions. It would sometimes take twice as long for them to recognize a display correctly as it would take a subject who had not been through those very brief exposures. Plainly, they were victims of their own earlier efforts.

All of which led me to formulate what I called a hypothesis theory of perception: that perceiving was guided by, steered by hypotheses about what was to be conventionally expected. So, for example, eight-letter pseudowords that were distant approximations to English took a much longer exposure time to be recognized than ones that more closely approximated conventional English letter sequences. Words (and pseudowords) are processed with the expectation that they conform to spelling conventions or to social convention generally. And so, for example, dirty words (and lewd pictures) take much longer to recognize than conventionally "proper" ones if you start the sequence of exposures way down below threshold level. Subjects get stuck with their wrong, early hypotheses.

But note one other thing. Once a subject has been tachistoscopically exposed to a lewd picture or dirty word, he will more easily recognize such pictures or words when subsequently presented to him. I asked one of our undergraduate subjects why he thought this was so. "Good Lord," he said, "you don't expect to be shown dirty pictures in a Harvard lab, do you? But then things change." And that remark from that seventeen-year-old freshman led me to another line of work – and to a refinement of the hypothesis theory.

It had to do with the nature of expectancy. Let me put it this way. Your expectations are both situationally determined (you do not expect to be shown dirty pictures in a tachistoscope in a respectable Harvard laboratory) and more generally determined both by your own personal characteristics and by the social customs of your own culture or subculture, even granting that the two often interact in what the French like to call your *deformation professionelle.* I sometimes look at the world passing by as a seasoned old New Yorker, sometimes as a psychologist law professor, sometimes as an adventurer. And how I do so will depend on whom I am with, on what I am doing, and other circumstantial matters.

How can a psychologist ignore such obvious matters in studying human behavior? And do our conventional psychological methods of research – the laboratory, the conventional interview, standardized tests, and the rest – take them into account? A psychologist can learn a lesson or two from the anthropologist, the sociologist, even the historian. We will never understand human behavior simply by studying it in vitro or out of context, only in the here-and-now, without taking account of the historical compromise that always exists between the Established and the Possible.

Why, for example, is the United States the only country left in the Western world that still punishes capital crimes with the death penalty? Public opinion polls indicate that Americans are no more in favor of such a practice than people in any other country. How come, then, do we go on using this barbaric and demonstrably ineffective practice – ineffective, for it is known that states that still use the death penalty do not thereby reduce their capital crime rate. My colleague David Garland has just published a stunning book on this baleful topic (*Peculiar Institution*, Cambridge: Harvard University Press, 2010) and it is plain that the persistence of this barbaric practice depends upon a false appeal to people's "concern about public welfare" (p. 63). Capital punishment is presented as part of a war against crime. We kill people in wars, don't we? Here is a verbatim citation of a prosecutor's typical argument before the jury in a murder trial, cited by Garland (p. 63): "I say to you we're in a war again in this country, except it's not a foreign nation, it's against the criminal element in this country. [The defendant, William Brooks, is a] member of the criminal element, and he's our enemy." So, the administration of justice is converted into a "war on crime," and, as in war, your duty is to destroy the enemy. Not to do so is unpatriotic.

Garland, the author of that book, is a Scotsman, a lawyer, and a sociologist, all of which help him be a shrewd psychological observer of the American scene. But he also senses the importance of storytelling. As he rightly notes, it is the genre of narrative that was central to the prosecuting attorney's appeal to the jury. A murderer, like an enemy combatant, deserves nothing better than death. Not simply retribution, but deadly warfare: Put your enemy to death.

So to return now to what psychology should include, or more generally, on what psychology should be modeled. I would definitely include the part-literary, part-anthropological, part-historical study of everyday ways of classifying the events we must live with. Indeed, this is a lesson that is being learned in virtually all disciplines concerned with the human condition – even in that most rigid discipline of law and jurisprudence.

Let me turn now to a related matter already hinted at. It has to do with how a culture's ways become internalized, incorporated in our individual ways of conceiving of the world, how we become "members" of a culture and internalize its ways as features of our

Selves – "self-formation," or however you wish to characterize it. It is the domain of what we usually call developmental psychology, a field that has made enormous progress over the last quarter-century thanks principally to dialectic between two approaches. Let me call one of them the Piagetian approach, and the other the Vygotskian.

Piaget was concerned principally with structure, how our knowledge of the world is put together in an orderly fashion, first in a particularized and highly concrete way and then increasingly organized into transformably abstract structures open to a wide range of construals and reconstruals. How, in a word, do we organize our encounters with the world in a way that honors the particularity of experience yet conserves the structure we impose upon it. What are these conservational processes that take us from concrete particularity to a more abstract and enduring way of structuring experience – how do we get from mere appearance to a deeper, more continuous sense of "reality."

Vygotsky's program was quite different. His principal concern was with the processes involved in the socialization of experience, how experience becomes socialized in a manner that permits us to relate our mental activity to the socially relevant ways of the culture in which we must live.

We have come to recognize that both emphases are needed in a properly balanced psychology – especially in developmental psychology. And increasingly we are becoming aware of how important it is to take both perspectives into account: our attachment to the Established and our search for the Possible.

REFERENCES

Garland, D. (2010). *Peculiar institution: America's death penalty in an age of abolition*. Cambridge, MA: Harvard University Press.

8

Schooling and Literacy in Mind and Society

DAVID R. OLSON

It was Aristotle who taught us that it was the human capacity for speech that made man the rational animal and it was writing that made him civilized. Both of these claims are now seen as tropes, exaggerated clichés. Rationality seems not to be the exclusive possession of human beings, and social order, civilization, is clearly not the exclusive possession of written cultures. Yet it remains a fact that modern societies see literacy and education as central to their survival and parents see literacy and schooling as essential to the development of their children. These beliefs and concerns cannot be ignored and require that we ask why, precisely, literacy and schooling matter to persons and to societies.

A bit of history can introduce us to the problem. Until about 1300 in the West, reading was not seen as an independent way of acquiring knowledge; reading was tied to memorization and oral delivery. Scholars would commit a written text to memory and only then begin to use that remembered text as an object of reflection and analysis. Quintillian, a fourth-century Roman philosopher, for example, claimed that reading preceded interpretation. For us moderns, the two are intertwined (Carruthers 1990; Green 1994). Until the sixteenth century, reading was taught independently of writing, writing being the preserve of the guilds. When writing did enter the common school, it was as "handwriting, learning to form letters correctly; composition, the deliberate shaping of linguistic forms, continued to be thought of as an oral skill.

Writing as composition began much later. Composition in the Middle Ages was a part of rhetoric, the oral art of persuasion. Indeed, until recently writing was the preserve of teachers of composition, who were well aware of the fact that the road from oral or speech competence to written or literate competence was rocky indeed. Years of tutorial and practice are required to learn the conventions of the written form including such simple matters as punctuation and sentence structure, as well as the more complex matters of logical structure and genre. But teachers of composition also noted that it was not simply a matter of learning to "write down" what one thought or said; the knowledge of and competence with oral forms, contra most linguists, was not so elaborate and not so standard either. Composition has become a matter of learning to use language in a more reflective and self-conscious way, to speak as if one were writing. In this way, habits of writing have come to influence spoken patterns of thought and action.

Psychologists have been slow to grant that writing is an important and distinctive form of language. When writing was granted some significance the question became, How does this transition to literacy come about? As is now widely acknowledged, the transition to literacy starts long before children are taught the mapping between letters and phonemes. Reading to children is important but just what is being learned from being read to remains unclear. Part of the significance of being read to is that it introduces children to the fact that written discourse is indirect: That is, it is not directed at the reader – the reader is, as it were, a bystander (Nelson 1996; Olson & Torrance 2001). In reading the language is not "heard" but "overheard," insulating expression from the immediate context of reception. In this way written language shares some properties with quotation, that is, reported speech, a point I will return to. Some oral language games such as the old kindergarten game "Simon Says" may contribute in their small way to helping children learn, as Maragaret Donaldson (1978, p. 70) once said, "to pay scrupulous attention to the very words." But usually it comes down to schooling, to the explicit teaching and conscious learning of just how the marks on the page map onto the phonological, the lexical, and the syntactic properties of one's oral language. That reading is in part learning a mapping from speech to script has long been known. Indeed, historically, it was assumed that that was all that was required, that is, learning the code. What is new in our understanding is that the linguistic structures (phonemes, words, and sentences) are not consciously known, that is, "known as such," by prereading children and even nonreading adults. Learning to read and write is to discover something about one's spoken language. Literacy contributes to making speech and language into an object of explicit knowledge. Making knowledge explicit is the link of literacy, schooling, and society. How this could be so is the focus of this chapter.

LITERACY AND MIND

Explicitness is a mischievous notion that, to be useful, but to be examined carefully. To be explicit means more than that something is expressed or written down. Rather, it involves the reflexive or recursive notion that the language or thought becomes itself the object of thought. Linguists distinguish between *use*, using a language, and *mention*, making the language an object of citation or quotation or commentary. Psychologists more commonly discuss "mention" in terms of metaconcepts such as metalinguistics and metacognition. Such "meta" concepts make the linguistic structures that are used in the course of ordinary speech into structures that may be referred to and thought about. It is this reflexive process that makes implicit knowledge explicit.

Explicitness of linguistic knowledge is well enough known to teachers of grammar. Language in the classroom may be abstracted from use and conceptualized in terms of a set of grammatical rules that the grammar teacher may use to evaluate particular expressions. Rules and norms are the critical features of an explicit grammar. The rules of grammar serve as norms or standards against which any spoken or written performance may be judged. But what, then, is the nature of oral or spoken linguistic competence?

There is an important argument in linguistics as to whether linguistic competence consists of the knowledge and application of a set of rules for generating an utterance in a context, what Chomsky called an "I-grammar." It is the implicit knowledge of these rules, it is said, that allows speakers not only to generate utterances but also to self-correct and to notice anomalies in the speech of others. But even if there are such rules, and this itself is a controversial view, these rules are implicit, neither known as such to the speakers of the language nor providing explicit grounds for judgments of the well-formedness or grammaticality of an utterance. Such rules as there are scoered by linguists. Indeed, the Grammar was first developed as a theory of written Latin "subject to due rules" (Green 1994, p. 45) and only later applied to vernacular languages. Once formulated, of course, these rules may be used prescriptively, as when grammar teachers say, "You can't say, "to Joe and I"; you must say, "to Joe and me"; you can't say, "for who"; you must say, "for whom"; and go on to provide a covering rule as to why this must be the case. What I mean by explicitness, then, is the conscious knowledge accessible to the speaker or writer of the rules of language that provide a norm or standard against which any oral performance may be judged. Just how such rules are involved in actual speaking, as opposed to metalinguistic judgment, remains unclear.

Here we may rely on an important distinction first made by Wittgenstein (1958) between a set of performances that may be "characterized or described by a rule" and those that are "generated by a rule." For a performance to be generated by a rule, one must know the rule and how to apply it. Further, this allows the possibility that a judgment may be made as to whether the rule was correctly applied. Rules for arithmetic or for chess or for logical proofs are clear examples of following formal, explicit rules. In regard to speech, it is not always so clear as to whether or not a speaker knows a rule as opposed to more simply having a habit (Pinker & Prince 1999). Some utterances just sound funny even when one cannot explain the oddness by appeal to a rule. The oddness is a product of one's implicit knowledge of the language. With an explicit grammar, one can retrieve the rule and make a judgment. Rules and procedures, known as such and applied mechanically in both production and judgment, are what I mean by explicitness; a computer program would be a paradigmatic example of such rule following.

If grammar is an explicit theory of the language, it may be argued that writing is the primary tool in the invention and, subsequently, the teaching of that grammar. On this view, writing is a primary means for creating an awareness of some of the important implicit properties of language. It does so through the invention of a technology. The alphabet is a simple, relatively explicit, technology. It involves a set of characters and a set of rules that, if followed, generate a sound pattern. Not reliably, as critics have often noted: "Hot" and "ought" ought to be spelled similarly but they are not. However, there is enough structure and enough agreement on the rules that it is possible to read aloud an unknown language that uses that alphabetic technology, and even a beginning reader can read nonsense letter sequences: What does "H-I-G" say?

But explicit rules apply not only to the sounds represented by the alphabet but to the other linguistic structures such as words and sentences. A writer must judge, Is "civilization" an English word? Samuel Johnson, the author of the first dictionary of English, thought it was not, whereas he thought that "civility" was a proper word. A writer has to decide; if he or she decides wrongly, the teacher (or editor) will point it out. A writer must ask him- or herself whether the subject of the sentence is missing or ask whether a particular pronoun has an antecedent, and so on. But furthermore, a writer must ask him- or herself whether the argument being made is clear, and whether or not there is appropriate evidence for the argument, and so on. All of these decisions are examples of knowing and applying rules to a production of a written product. The rules are perhaps not as explicit as those for baking a cake, but they are just as robust. Learning to write is learning to master this technology, this set of procedures or rules that are to be applied in the formation and revision of a product. Some of these rules may be picked up through reading and through oral debate, but they rely in large part on the advice and feedback from teachers, the experts in the tradition, as well as a good deal of practice. Schooling is an essential constituent.

There is now an abundance of research that examines what is involved in moving from oral competence to literacy (Tolchinsky, in press). Learning to read and write is not merely the acquisition of a set of skills but also learning about, that is, learning metalinguistically about, the language. Literate adults assume that their knowledge about language, that it consists of distinctive sounds, or syllables, of words and sentences, is available, as well, to children before they learn to read and that learning to read and write is a relatively straightforward matter of learning the written signs for these linguistic entities. It seems that their assumption is seriously misleading.

Berthoud-Papandropulou (1978), a student of Piaget, asked children, "Which is a longer word, 'train' or 'caterpillar'. Pre-reading children responded "Train", often adding "because caterpillars are tiny." This suggests that children are treating the word as transparent to the object referred to. One criticism of that finding was that, perhaps, children were not familiar with the word "word." Bruce Homer and I (Homer & Olson 1999) posed the question another way. We showed prereading children a card on which was written "Three little pigs," which we read to the children and had them repeat to us. Then we covered up one of the words and asked, "Now, what does it say?" to which many prereaders replied, "Two little pigs." When two of the words were covered the children suggested it said "One little pig." They took the written signs to represent individual objects rather than the words for those objects. Again this suggests that children identified the written forms with the objects referred to rather than the constituents of the oral expression. A critical process in learning to read, then, is to move the constituents that are implicit in oral language into consciousness so that visual signs may become associated with them.

The problem is illustrated in another way, following the lead of Emilia Ferreiro and her colleagues (Ferreiro & Teberosky 1982). Homer and I asked prereading children to write a series of expressions for us. When asked to write "Cat," for example, they typically replied, "I don't know how to write." When encouraged to try, they commonly went on to produce a single, short squiggly line, which they then read back as "Cat" or "A cat." you are writing then. When asked to write "Two cats," they went on to produce two squiggles. And similarly for "Three cats," they produced three squiggles. It is clear that they produced a sign for each of the cats, not a sign for each of the words. Again, the words to be written remained transparent and ignored. Consequently, when asked whether they could write "No cats," many children said they could not. One child smiled knowingly and moved the pencil around in the air without touching the paper and then announced, "There were no cats so I didn't write anything." In another task children were asked to write "A dog or a cat" in response to which one subject produced a single squiggle and announced it said "A dog." Prereading children tend not to recognize that the request to write requires that they take the language "offline" and think about the language rather than the meanings it is ordinarily used to convey.

Prereading children take written marks to represent the objects represented rather than the words of the expression. They tend to assume that written marks carry meanings in much the same way that drawings do, although the distinctive squiggles they produce clearly show that they distinguish drawing from writing. There are two inferences to be drawn from these observations. First, the words of the expression did not immediately offer themselves to consciousness as the entities to be represented by writing. Writing, it may be argued, is instrumental in bringing just those aspects of language into consciousness; only then can distinctive marks be associated with them. And second, it indicates that children have to learn the special relation between writing and language. Compare these two expressions:

Can you draw a cat?
Can you write "a cat"?

Only in the latter are you required to lift the expression out of its normal usage by marking it with quotation marks. The quotation marks indicate that the expression is mentioned rather than used. This is the link between writing and quotation that I alluded to earlier. Although quotation is a secondary device available in spoken language, it is a device, I suggest, that is primary to writing. Writing requires that one think of language as "offline."

Another way of making the same point is to suggest that writing is essentially a metarepresentational activity that raises aspects of language into consciousness. Different writing systems, of course, move different aspects of language into consciousness. Alphabets put phonemes; Chinese characters put morphemic syllables; and so on (Morais, Alegria, & Content 1987; Read, et al. 1986; Vernon & Ferreiro 1999). In each case, the writing system is a technology, an explicit set of rules for analyzing an utterance into categories suitable for explicit representation.

LITERACY AND SCHOOLING

This notion that writing is essential to making linguistic knowledge explicit may be applied to knowledge development in a schooled society. If one grants that literacy is an exercise in turning one's implicit knowledge of language into a set of explicit and rule governed categories, it becomes possible to see why modern education is more or less synonymous with literacy. This is not a necessary truth about education (literacy is not the only possible route to education), but it is a contingent truth, that is, a truth that holds for a modern technological and bureaucratic society in which literacy is more or less coterminous with education. Not only are reading and writing a matter of making knowledge explicit, but so is all school-based knowledge. Not only does this occur through learning algorithmic skills such as algebra or such formal systems as Newton's laws of motion, but also through all the school subjects that require that beliefs be held for reasons and that claims be supported by evidence. Schooling in large part is learning to "give reasons for your answers," an instruction that appears at the top of many school assignments and formal tests. Giving reasons is a matter of making knowledge explicit. It is insufficient to know how a thing works; one must also know "how you know," "what are your reasons for thinking," and the like. How do you know that "one-half of a half is a quarter"? "I just know" will not do; one must provide a suitable rule or algorithm. The algorithm is an explicit rule or set of rules. In their study of the effects of literacy and education among the Vai, a traditional society in Liberia, Scribner and Cole (1981) found that a major difference between schooled and unschooled children was their ability to and willingness to "give reasons" justifying their answers. The giving of reasons, which everyone can do in some contexts, becomes a primary concern of schooling: Concepts like reasons, evidence, causes, inferences, in a word, talk about knowledge. Not only what one knows but how one knows it is a central activity of schooling and a defining characteristic of schooled knowledge. And distinguishing one's assumptions from one's beliefs and hypotheses is an important aspect of understanding one's own and others' thoughts (Olson et al. 2006; Antonietti et al. 2006).

It is not a coincidence that this kind of explicit knowledge is tied up with writing and with schooling. Recipes, like computer programs and like mathematical proofs, are written documents. While much of the critical information is held in memory, much of it must be read or consulted in carrying out either practical or intellectual activities. Texts, including textbooks, are primary sources of such routinized and rationalized information, and the ability to read is the essential to access that information. Understandably, books and documents are fundamental to the educational enterprise; the dream that these may become obsolete because of the Internet is specious; education is learning to create and use documents including book length ones. Even the routine criticism of schools for their "bookishness" is only half-valid. Knowledge in a literate society is critically tied up in documents, books, and even computer programs.

Schools are the institutions in which children become familiar with the nature of rules and procedures, how they are formed, how they are applied not only in behavior but also in talking, reasoning, and writing. This, presumably, is the reason that teachers write a list of activities for the day on the corner of the blackboard. These rules provide the criteria teachers use in making and grading assignments. These rules mandate commands such as "Answer in full sentences," "Give reasons for your answers," "Contrast and compare," and the like. Schooling may be seen as a move from the implicit knowledge children take to school to the explicit knowledge expressed through the use of notations and the rules and regulations for their use.

To summarize to this point. Literacy and schooling matter because writing is the route to explicitness, that explicitness embodied in the technologies of our society. Just as writing is mastered by dissolving speech into elements that may be assembled according to fixed rules, so too the knowledge that writing is used to preserve and against which learners are to judge their own constructions and representations is composed of explicit categories and rules, rules that spell out conditions and causes and rules that spell out procedures for correct performance. The educator's role is to help students assess their productions in terms of these rules and procedures.

LITERACY AND SOCIETY

Not only are literacy and schooling important to making knowledge explicit and subject to systematic thinking, literacy and schooling bear a direct relation to the structures and procedures of a bureaucratic society. To most people "bureaucratic" is a pejorative term, reminding them of Joseph Heller's *Catch 22*, in which nothing could be done because of the network of self-refuting bureaucratic rules. Governmental reform is often couched in terms of cutting "red tape" or cutting bureaucracy. Indeed, bureaucracy can be evil, as the not-so-long-ago-exposed Stasi, the secret police of the former East Germany, showed (and was recently portrayed in the German film *The Lives of Others* (2007). But those dark cases may blind us to the more general fact that our lives in a modern society are completely bound up in bureaucratic rules and procedures. Institutional functions are described by economists in terms of "entitlements" and "obligations." Contracts and laws spell these out: If you do such and so, you will get such and so. Such bureaucratic rules apply equally to schooling: If you take a 6-credit course and submit a thesis, a university may confer a university degree. But only if one is duly registered, attends classes, turns in a certain number of papers, and so on. If high school or university students are asked why they are taking two math courses, they are unlikely to reply, "Mathematical functions are fascinating" and more likely to reply, "I need the credits." Earning credits by meeting one's obligations entitles one to certain privileges but only if the rules are applied appropriately and uniformly. That is what defines a bureaucracy.

Societal literacy, to borrow a concept from Georg Elwert (2001), is the kind of literacy that underwrites a modern bureaucratic society. It involves the formulation and implementation of explicit procedures for the ordering of activities in terms of rules, norms, formal procedures, or algorithms that are set out in codes, documents, and manuals. Examples include Robert's Rules of Order, the first attempt to spell out how to conduct a public meeting. But they also include constitutions, charters, contract law, rules for production, rules for interpretation of documents, and the like. Such rules depend not only on explicit procedures but in addition on mechanisms to monitor and enforce such rules. Personal honor is not enough to maintain a rule. The entire implementation of a bureaucratic state, whether ancient empire or modern democracy, is so ordered as to establish these rules and to see that they are carried out. Power goes hand in hand with procedure, but if the procedure is explicit and rule governed it may gain "the consent of the governed." Schools are essential to learning the rules of such a bureaucratic system and learning to respect and honor them.

Once one is alerted to the elaborate structures of rules and procedures of a bureaucratic society they are recognizable anywhere. Justice is handled not simply by punishing the guilty. The courts have the job of following accepted procedures to determine who is guilty. Before the judge makes a pronouncement, the plaintiff is merely the "accused," but once the judge has spoken, the plaintiff may be "guilty as charged." These elaborate, somewhat intricate procedures are what we grandly refer to as "the rule of law," the agreement that appropriate, fair, mechanical, transparent judgments will be made following explicit rules and procedures. Montaigne, a seventeenth-century philosopher, went so far as to claim that law was more important than justice, a view seconded by David Hume, who asserted that "we must have a government of laws and not of men."

Bureaucracies pertain not only to the economy and to systems of justice but also to the construction and legitimation of knowledge itself. One contributes to knowledge not only by getting a good idea, but rather by, first, having earned membership in a profession such as science, medicine, or education; by creating documents that meet the criteria of originality as defined by existing published work; of complying with accepted methods of argument and evidence, and having the product duly vetted by the guardians of the discipline, namely, the editorial boards of the primary journals of the discipline and the judgment of one's peers. The disciplines themselves exist because of the protection and resources they gain or are entitled to from the larger society in return for which they are obligated to provide the society with reliable knowledge. If they routinely fail, their right to exist will be abolished. The current rhetoric of school reform, including the charge that "schools are failing," carries with it the threat that if schools fail they will be closed – clearly an empty threat as no modern state would dare abolish schooling, for, as we have seen, schooling is essential to a bureaucratic state. They may, however, create a certain degree of alarm by issuing such threats.

Once we recognize the bureaucratic nature of modern society, it is easier to grant that the school's primary responsibility as an institution is to the larger society rather than to the children who attend it and, consequently, that the role of the school is to introduce learners to the bureaucratic structures of modern society, especially those devoted to the development of expertise and the acquisition of knowledge. This responsibility frequently conflicts with that of sustaining and encouraging the mental lives of individual students (Katz & Olson 2001), one of the issues around which debates about school reform revolve (see Olson 2003).

I have used the notion of explicitness as a way of spelling out the relation between the two sides of literacy that have usually been seen as oppositional. On the one hand, literacy and schooling may be viewed as altering persons in such a way that social changes follow. On the other hand, literacy and schooling may be viewed as introductions to ongoing social practices that in turn shape the habits and beliefs of the young. I have tried to spell out the link between personal literacy and "societal literacy" in terms of explicitness, explaining knowledge and practices in terms of explicit rules and procedures, procedures that organize not only our mental lives but our social organization.

The societal literacy of a modern bureaucratic society is what makes our literacy essentially coterminous with education. Bureaucratic, technological societies such as ours are organized around explicitness – formulations of rules and procedures for getting things done – a tradition devoted to developing and upholding an orderly society characterized by the "rule of law." Things must be done in accordance with stated, ideally agreed upon, rules and principles. Developing and implementing these rules may be described as a technology. Indeed,

Sigfried Gideon, the historian of technology, claimed that "technology is explicitness." In this sense bureaucracies whether of government or of knowledge are technologies. They are designed to provide an explicit and reliable routine for producing a standard product whether in the form of the judgment of a court or in the form of an advance in science.

So here is the link of literacy, mind, and society. Literacy is instrumental in formalizing knowledge and practices in terms of known, explicit rules that can be more or less mechanically applied by anyone trained in the use of those rules and procedures, residual ambiguity being resolved by courts and panels. Bureaucracies are the social systems that result from the application of these principles to complex social goals and problems. They allow the possibility that complex tasks can be dissolved into established rules and procedures carried out by persons trained to play particular roles. They are democratic to the extent that they operate by consent rather than by force and to the extent that the procedures involved are seen as transparent and fair. They are, thus, alternatives to both wise men and potentates.

These explicit rules and procedures apply not only to the society but to the mental lives of individuals. What I have argued is that the institutions of a bureaucratic society are themselves literate institutions. Bureaucracies not only use literacy, they embody the very practices of literacy, practices I have described in terms of explicit rules and procedures. Thus, literacy plays a role not only in consciousness of language and consciousness of mind, but also in the explicitness of arguments, the uses of evidence, and the forms of discourse appropriate to such specialized institutions as economics, law, science, and literature. Formal education is the primary means of introducing learners to these specialized institutions.

A modern bureaucratic society is often scorned for its impersonal attitudes and rigid procedures. "Rules are rules" is the refrain of the unreflective. Nonetheless, a society without documented and enforceable rules, laws, contracts, and agreements is neither by definition nor practice a "literate society." A literate society is one that is both societally literate, having in place the infrastructure for the systematic, bureaucratic management of social affairs, and personally literate, composed of a citizenry with the knowledge and willingness to participate fully in these governing institutions. Schools, through their literate activities, provide a bridge between these two.

REFERENCES

Antonietti, A., Liverta Sempio, O., Marchetti, A. & Astington, J. (2006). Mental language and understanding of epistemic and emotional mental states. In A. Antonietti, O. Liverta Sempio & A. Marchetti (Eds.) *Theory of mind and language in developmental contexts* (pp. 1–24). New York: Springer.

Berthoud-Papandropulou, I. (1978). An experimental study of children's ideas about language (p. 55). In A. Sinclair, R. J. Jarvella, & W. J. M. Levelt (Eds.) *The child's conception of language*. Berlin, Heidelberg, New York: Springer-Verlag.

Carruthers, M. J. (1990). *The book of memory: A study of memory in medieval culture*. Cambridge: Cambridge University Press.

Donaldson, M. (1978). *Children's minds*. Glasgow: Fontana/Collins.

Elwert, G. (2001). Societal literacy: Writing culture and development. In D. R. Olson & N. Torrance (Eds.) *The making of literate societies* (pp. 54 67). Oxford: Blackwell.

Ferreiro, E., & Teberosky, A. (1982). *Literacy before schooling* (K. G. Castro, trans.). Exeter, NH : Heinemann Educational Books.

Green, D. H. (1994). *Medieval listening and reading: The primary reception of German literature 800–1300*. Cambridge: Cambridge University Press.

Homer, B., & Olson, D. R. (1999). Literacy and children's conception of words. *Written Language and Literacy*, 2, 113–117.

Katz, S., & Olson, D. R. (2001). The fourth folk pedagogy. In B. Torff & R. J. Sternberg (Eds.) *Understanding and teaching the intuitive mind: Student and teacher learning* (pp. 243–263). Mahwah, NJ: Lawrence Erlbaum Associates.

Morais, J., Alegria, J., & Content, A. (1987). The relationships between segmental analysis and alphabetic literacy: An interactive view. *Cahiers de Psychologie Cognitive*, 7, 415–438.

Nelson, K. (1996). *Language in cognitive development: Emergence of the mediated mind*. Cambridge, England: Cambridge University Press.

Olson, D. R. (2003). *Psychological theory and educational reform: How school remakes mind and society*. Cambridge: Cambridge University Press.

Olson, D. R., Antonietti, A., Liverta Sempio, O., & Marchetti, A. (2006). The mental verbs in different conceptual domains and in different cultures. In A. Antonietti, O. Liverta Sempio & A. Marchetti (Eds.) *Theory of mind and language in developmental contexts* (pp. 31–64). New York: Springer.

Olson, D. R., & Torrance, N. (2001). *The making of literate societies*. Oxford: Blackwell.

Pinker, S., & Prince, A. (1999). The nature of human concepts: Evidence from an unusual source. In R. Jackendoff, P. Bloom & K. Wynn (Eds.) *Language, logic, and concepts* (p. 221). Cambridge, MA: MIT Press.

Read, C. A., Zhang, Y., Nie, H., & Ding, B. (1986). The ability to manipulate speech sounds depends on knowing alphabetic reading. *Cognition*, 24, 31–44.

Scribner, S., & Cole, M. (1981). *The psychology of literacy*. Cambridge, MA: Harvard University Press.

Vernon, S. A., & Ferreiro, E. (1999). Writing development: A neglected variable in the consideration of phonological awareness. *Harvard Educational Review*, 69(4), 395–415.

Wittgenstein, L. (1958). *Philosophical investigations* (G. E. M. Anscombe, trans.). Oxford: Blackwell.

9

Teaching Writing to Undergraduate Psychology Students as Socialization to a Genre

PIETRO BOSCOLO

In the United States and several European countries, the teaching of writing has an important role in higher education – although this role differs depending on whether it is located *inside* or *outside* the disciplines of a course of study (Carter 2007). When *outside* disciplines, writing is usually taught in first year (First Year Composition [FYC]) as a general ability, basically unrelated to the disciplines that characterize a specific degree in higher education. Since the 1990s, there has been long debate about FYC and the underlying view of writing. The claim of teaching writing genres out of context, as a "general" academic ability, has been criticized in particular from a social-constructivist perspective (e.g., Freedman 1995; Russell 1995). The gist of the criticism is that the teaching of writing should be related to the scientific communities represented in the domains of higher education, closely connected to the activities – problems, theories, and methods – that characterize each community. However, in FYC courses, teachers of English are asked to prepare students for academic genres outside, and independently of, research work and reflection about findings and theories (Downs & Wardle 2007; Wardle 2009). Instead, teaching writing *inside* the discipline means relating writing and knowing; that is, different disciplines or groups of disciplines are characterized by different ways of knowing and writing. According to this perspective, writing is viewed as part of a discipline: in Carter's (2007) words, "A specialized conception of disciplinary knowledge is integrated with a specialized conception of writing" (p. 387).

243

The inside versus outside distinction – or dichotomy – does not seem to fit the syllabuses of universities, such as those in Italy, that do not include the teaching of academic writing, unless requested by a member of faculty particularly interested in the question (as in the case of the present author). However, neglect of writing instruction does not mean that writing is not important in Italian higher education – here I refer in particular to the master's degree in psychological disciplines, in which the role of writing is relevant. In psychology departments, undergraduate students attending master's courses have to write a dissertation related to a discipline of a specific degree. In the dissertation, conducted under the guidance of a supervisor, students have to analyze either the results of an empirical study or a review of a topic and are expected to demonstrate the level of psychological knowledge and methodological competence achieved during five years (three plus two) of academic study. A dissertation based on empirical research is valued as a potentially original work by both professors and students, whereas a review is considered to be a less demanding task. The master's thesis is different from the doctoral dissertation, which concludes the student's participation in a Ph.D. program after the master's degree – although writing a master's dissertation based on empirical research work is also demanding. On the one hand, the writing instruction that students receive in high school is not sufficient to allow them to deal effectively with this type of work, which represents a new genre and includes argumentative, descriptive, and expository writing. On the other, as mentioned, at university they receive neither "general" writing instruction such as FYC nor any specific training in dissertation writing except from their supervisors. The supervisor's guidance includes bibliographical and methodological assistance and indications about structural aspects of the dissertation, but he/she is usually less concerned with writing. Of course, there are professors who guide students in the writing of their dissertation closely, in particular when students appear to be promising future scholars. However, in general, faculty does not view writing as an important aspect of undergraduate education, but as a skill that students should have learned in high school. Students, in turn, view the dissertation as their last examination, very different from the previous ones, mostly because the dissertation focuses on a research topic and discipline of their choice. Thus, although there are students who want to conclude the dissertation as soon as possible to get their degree and find a job, most students have expectations about the dissertation and foresee its complexity but are not very aware of the difficulties.

This chapter is aimed at analyzing some crucial aspects of teaching how to write a master's dissertation in psychology. It is based on the assumption, justified by the author's experience of teaching academic writing to undergraduate psychology students for several years, that writing a master's dissertation requires students to learn a new genre. Learning a new genre implies, for adult writers, not only acquiring or "tuning" new knowledge and skills, but also modifying some beliefs about writing previously acquired during their school education, which often conflict with the new acquisitions.

LEARNING TO WRITE AT UNIVERSITY

The discontinuity between university and high school writing regards instructional and assessment practices, on the one hand, and the functions and context of writing, on the other. Regarding the teaching aspects, university students lack the regular practice of writing and teacher feedback that characterizes writing instruction in previous school grades. Moreover, written examinations based on open questions are not fruitful occasions for writing, since professors' assessments focus on the quantity of knowledge demonstrated by students rather than on the linguistic quality of their responses. Regarding the functions of writing, in general the role of writing in higher education cannot be compared with written compositions and reports in high school (Boscolo, Arfè, & Quarisa 2007; Lea 1998; Lea & Street 1998; McCune 2004; Säljö 1997). It is in the master's dissertation that the discontinuity is most apparent. The function of the dissertation is novel to students, who have to give an account not only of what they have learned, as when taking an examination, but also of what they have "become" through their university studies. In fact, a student has to learn to adapt his/her textual competence to new problems of scientific communication and argumentation.

In order to write the dissertation, undergraduate students should acquire knowledge, abilities, and awareness related to three types of competence. First, they have to give a structure to the dissertation, which, in the case of a dissertation based on an empirical study, is a sequence starting with the theoretical framework and ending with a discussion of findings. This sequence, described in *The Publication Manual of the American Psychological Association* (VI ed. 2010), is the aspect of the dissertation that undergraduates are more concerned with initially: Knowing the structure of the dissertation seems to be the first step toward achieving the goal! In fact, the structure itself is only partially meaningful if it is not "filled" with research work. The second type or level of competence regards text organization, that is, a set of cognitive and linguistic operations that are much more complex than those of high school written compositions. From the cognitive point of view, writing the theoretical framework requires reading, selecting, and organizing information from various sources, a more complex operation than discourse synthesis in high school (Spivey 1996). However, the main source of difficulty regards the pragmatic and rhetorical aspects of writing. In the dissertation a student has to describe/narrate his/her work and support a point of view: that is, to demonstrate the validity of a hypothesis and the appropriateness of a method as well as underlining the relevance of findings and justifying possible methodological limitations. This requires the use of communication strategies aimed at facilitating the reader's understanding, on the one hand, and highlighting the critical points of the study, on the other. In fact, at university many students have to learn the use of paragraphing and text organization, which they should have mastered during high school years. Limited textual competence is particularly apparent in the theoretical framework and the discussion, where the author summarizes his/her work as well as its merits and limitations.

The third aspect regards dissertation writing as an opportunity for the student to participate in the scientific community, in which he/she has so far been only a peripheral member. This is in fact the most extraneous aspect of students' experience, and the gap between this and high school writing becomes particularly evident. In high school, a student has to demonstrate the quality of his/her learning and writing in terms of knowledge, coherence, and personal commitment, while in the dissertation he/she has to display a personal research work, conducted with the conceptual and methodological tools, and written according to the norms, of the international scientific community of psychologists. Although the research findings may be modest, through the dissertation the student should become aware of the relevance of this work to his/her identity as a psychologist. Of course, the three types of learning experience – structure, text writing, and participation – are closely connected to one another. On the one hand, respecting structure and using appropriate writing tools are basic requisites for the expression of a scholar's identity in writing. On the other, expressing one's identity through writing is possible only if the norms of the international community, including expert use of textual and rhetorical tools, are respected. The use of these tools, however, requires overcoming some beliefs about writing and, in particular, about the nature of text.

STUDENTS' BELIEFS ABOUT ACADEMIC WRITING AND TEXT

Over the past three decades, many studies have been conducted on the beliefs of students at different school levels about learning and the acquisition of knowledge. Regarding students' beliefs about academic writing, two main approaches have emerged: surface and deep

(Lavelle 1993, 1997; Lavelle & Guarino 2003). The surface approach is characterized by the belief that learning is basically memorizing, and writing is the reproduction of knowledge. The deep approach to writing is characterized by the belief that knowledge is not transmitted, but constructed; thus, writing implies personal elaboration of knowledge. The surface and deep approaches clearly recall the *knowledge telling* and *knowledge transforming* constructs, respectively, which, according to Bereiter and Scardamalia (1987), characterize novice and expert writers. When *telling* his/her knowledge, the writer does not set him/herself any communicative goal, but limits him/herself to exposing what he/she knows about a topic through the search for information in memory. Instead, knowledge is *transformed* when it is adapted to a communicative goal: for instance, to support a personal point of view and convince the reader of its value. On the basis of this distinction, many undergraduate students could be considered knowledge tellers!

Lavelle's conceptualization of students' beliefs has been basically confirmed by other scholars, who have adopted different terminology, but the same superficial/deep approach distinction (Campbell, Smith, & Brooker 1998; Smith, Campbell, & Brooker 1999). White and Bruning (2005) investigated the relationship between university students' implicit beliefs about writing and the quality of their written essays, starting with Schraw and Bruning's (1996, 1999; Schraw 2000) model of reading beliefs. According to this model, students have two different approaches to reading: *transmissional* and *transactional*. In the transmissional approach, information flows from the text to the reader without any personal elaboration. Instead, in the transactional approach, a reader construes the meaning of a text according to his/her prior knowledge and reading goal. The text meaning is a dynamic relationship that involves the writer, the text, and the reader. White and Bruning (2005) applied the transmission-transaction distinction to writing, analyzing university students' beliefs about essay writing by means of an inventory. Two factors emerged from the factor analysis:

transmission and transaction. Writers with transmissional beliefs seem to view writing as a way of sending information, with little or no critical or personal integration. They show little affective and cognitive commitment when writing, and their written production shows poor idea development and text organization. Instead, students with transactional beliefs are cognitively and emotionally involved during the writing process and seem to conceive writing as a tool for the critical elaboration of knowledge. They also write better essays than students with a transmissional approach.

The knowledge telling versus transforming distinction, extensively cited by cognitively oriented writing researchers over the past three decades, has great merit, particularly with regard to its first pole. The knowledge-telling construct has proved to be an excellent metaphor for how novice writers express their ideas and concepts. They retrieve knowledge from memory, select information to be used according to the assignment, and keep the text basically coherent. However, they are not concerned with having the reader understand or interacting with them. Whereas "telling" effectively accounts for the limitations of novice writers, "transforming" emphasizes the cognitive aspect of expert writing – using knowledge flexibly – but neglects the linguistic/ rhetorical aspect. An expert writer is one who can compose a message in which information is not only coherent, but also organized to enable the reader to understand the writer's message. As well as implying a mature use of knowledge, this ability implies the use of linguistic and rhetorical strategies, through which the reader is "accompanied" through the text and his/her understanding is facilitated. In other words, while knowledge telling indicates a cognitive operation of recalling information in which language is of limited importance, in knowledge transforming, the information is not in fact transformed, but adapted to the communicative goal of the writer. That is, it is a matter of *dispositio*, which is not only a cognitive operation, but also, and more importantly, a rhetorical one. In general, the superficial/ deep distinction, while useful in outlining two "styles" of writing (and learning), leaves open the question of how to facilitate the transition from the negative to the positive pole: in other words, how to overcome "superficial" attitudes and foster students' will and ability to write a "deep" essay. This transition requires an adequate use of text organization, which, in turn, requires students to modify their beliefs. Two students' beliefs about the text as emerging from students' writing and classroom discussions will now be analyzed.

Many undergraduate students of psychology seem to have a "static" view of text, in which two beliefs are integrated: one about the relationship between knowledge and writing, the other about writing as an individual rather than a social activity. Also because of the strong influence of the cognitive approach in several psychological domains, and the limited importance given to writing in higher education, students seem to believe that thinking and writing are basically equivalent. Their experience of examinations, in which the exposition of knowledge is sufficient for a satisfying result regardless of the quality of text, confirms this belief. Students' use of knowledge telling reflects the belief that not only does the quality of a text depend on a writer's knowledge, but also a text is just a sequence of sentences, not, as etymology indicates, an interlacing. The introductory chapter of the dissertation, in which the theoretical framework of the study is presented, may help clarify what I mean by the static versus dynamic views of text. The theoretical framework is aimed at presenting a research domain with its different, and often conflicting, perspectives, and at highlighting the "niche," according to Swales's (1990) metaphor. This refers to the more limited literature about a topic in which the specific problem is positioned, as well as the reasons that require and justify occupying the "niche," such as the scarcity of studies and/or conflicting findings of previous studies. Thus, the framework is a path that the reader has to be guided through, toward the research questions and hypotheses. This seems to be, and in fact is, a linear route, where linearity is not an intrinsic feature of the text, but the outcome of the writer's ability to take into account and relate the various aspects of a topic and translate them into a well-framed and organized textual sequence, thanks, in particular, to the appropriate use of connectors. In terms of processes, this "dynamic" view of text implies the writer's willingness to revise and reorganize the text continually to keep it coherent, clear, and convincing. This is what I mean by the argumentative dimension of academic writing, a concept that I often stress in class ("Writing at university is *always* argumentative") and that for students represents a real experience of conceptual change.

Students are made aware of this feature of the theoretical framework through writing exercises: for instance, by constructing the framework of a study they have already conducted in a workshop related to one of the courses attended and discussing its features with the professor and other students in the class. In general, reading exemplar texts is a fruitful practice for learning to write: Exemplar texts are examples of knowledge telling, and good texts are published papers. This use of "efferent" reading of good texts is a new experience for students (Rosenblatt 1978), who, when reading a research report, usually focus on the contents (methodology, results, conclusions) and rarely, or never, on the writer's descriptive and argumentative ability. Obviously, this change in the view of reading and its relationship to writing also has to be strengthened through further appropriate reading and writing practice.

TEACHING INTERTEXTUALITY

The second belief – about the individual nature of writing – is also related to the static view of text. According to this belief, what an individual writes depends on his/her more or less "innate" ability, and on the quality and quantity of his/her cognitive and linguistic tools. The perspective of writing as a sociocultural activity is another source of cognitive change for students. Writing is a social activity not only because it is a tool of communication, but also because, when writing, we use words and sentences and refer to texts already used and written by others. This is the meaning of intertextuality: As Bazerman (2004) argues, "Intertextuality is the mechanism through which we write ourselves in the social text and the social text writes us" (p. 54). The concept of discourse community is related to intertextuality (Fairclough 1992): a complex system of individuals who share genres, language, a corpus of theories and concepts, values, and goals and interact through various media, in particular written language. This is the most irksome aspect for students to realize: that what we write is never – or is only partially – "ours," because we cannot ignore or avoid what has been written by others. Most students have been taught to recognize intertextual links when reading narrative and poetry in high school. However, they are accustomed to viewing those links as relationships among literary works, quite distant from their own writing. Now, in their own writing, students have to realize that for a writer, intertextuality is a need and a duty. When producing a scientific text as a dissertation, a student cannot ignore what has already been written on the same research problem or a very similar one and must take into account other scholars' hypotheses, findings, and conclusions; posing a research problem means recognizing what others have – or have not – found. Intertextuality also implies the duty of making apparent to readers the sources from which hypotheses have been elaborated. Students should be made aware that intertextuality is a basic aspect characteristic of writing as a social activity (Nelson 2008; Spivey 1997).

This is also the occasion to discuss with students the fuzzy boundaries between intertextuality and plagiarism. If all we write – and say – has already been written (or said) by somebody else, how is it possible to produce an "autonomous" text? How can we teach intertextuality to students and make them aware of the difference between this and plagiarism? I think that a correct use of texts written by others can be taught from two points of view: the reader's and the writer's. Regarding the reader's perspective, students should be taught to read a psychological paper, chapter, or book that identifies the author's debts to other scholars and the ways he or she recognizes them. Intertextuality has several dimensions (Bazerman 2004). One dimension regards the more or less explicit relationship between two texts: Are they integrated into each other, as in discourse synthesis, or they are distinct but compared? A second dimension regards the form of the intertextual link, which may be a direct quotation, or an indirect one (a paraphrase), or the use of concepts and terms currently employed in psychological discourse, and the more or less conventional phrases with which articles often begin (e.g., "Over the past three decades numerous studies have been conducted into..."). A third dimension regards the distance between texts: the intratextual reference ("As said at the beginning of the paper...") and the reference to "distant" texts, that is, texts written long ago, or different in genre or theoretical perspective. For instance, when presenting recent questions of psychology, many authors cite the work of ancient philosophers who first dealt with a question. Last, intertextual material can be used with different functions: to support an idea or hypothesis or to contrast it. Students can be trained to recognize the intertextual links in their own and others' texts, and to practice the various forms of intertextuality in a text written by them. In the classroom, discussing text relationships can also help teachers and students clarify the relationships between intertextuality and authorship, on the one hand, and intertextuality and plagiarism, on the other.

Regarding the writer's perspective, a student's intertextual awareness is built through writing practice in which he/she learns to summarize, synthesize, and paraphrase. One could object that a student should already have mastered these skills in high school. However, university differs from high school in that these operations, at university, are used to compare authors and theories justified by research work. A critical point in writing a dissertation is the management of references, of whose function students are not always aware. The use of references should be the object of specific teaching, aimed at inducing students not only to respect American Psychological Association (APA) norms, but also to understand the relationship between the writer and the community of discourse. Many students think that a dissertation is improved with more references, which, in fact, are often copied. Students should be made aware that references have several functions: to help a reader frame a problem correctly within international literature, to guarantee the correctness of what is written (many constructs, when used out of a theoretical framework, may be generic or misleading); and, last, to prevent plagiarism. Through references, the author identifies his/her indebtedness to other authors, but also, by using constructs, critically discussing ideas, and commenting on findings, he/she confronts them.

WRITING AND IDENTITY

According to Ivanič (1998), "Writing is an act of identity in which people align themselves with socio-culturally shaped possibilities for self-hood, playing their part in reproducing or challenging dominant practices and discourses, and the values, beliefs and interests which they embody" (p. 32).

Writing a dissertation not only requires the student to modify his/her beliefs about writing. Learning a new genre also implies having a different motivation to write. Over the past decades many studies have been conducted on the motivational aspects of writing, and particularly on the conditions (task, topic, context) that can make writing attractive or interesting to students at various school levels (see Bruning & Horn 2000; Boscolo 2009; Hidi & Boscolo 2006, 2007 for reviews). However, a student's motivation to write his/her dissertation is quite different from motivation to write a composition in previous school grades, and more complex than mere interest in the topic, self-efficacy, or self-enhancement. At university a student carries out a task he/she has chosen, under the guidance of a supervisor, who suggests – or imposes – a research method and checks the validity of results. Therefore, writing is no longer a discipline that can be perceived as more or less interesting or threatening. Through writing, for the first time a student relates actively – not only as an observer or user, by reading and studying – to the discourse community in which he/she is now only a peripheral participant (Lave & Wenger 1990). Writing a dissertation requires the student to use critically what he/she has learned and to present and value the results of his/her study and be aware of the importance of this work for the formation of his/her identity as a psychologist.

Due to constraints, a student may view the rules and norms of academic/scientific writing as a limitation on the free expression of his/her thought. Helping students find an identity through writing means making them become aware that through academic writing they appropriate the discourse practices that characterize a sociocultural context. The dissertation reproduces the discourse practices of the scientific psychological community, filtered through the scientific orientations of local research groups. In one department, psychology may have an experimental orientation, whereas in another the orientation may be clinical-qualitative. Subsequently, the "formal" constraints of scientific writing may be different in relation to different epistemological perspectives. Ivanič (1998) distinguishes several types of identity in relation to writing. The self as an author is the one more pertinent to the present discourse. According to this type of identity, the writer views him/herself as an author, and the way he/she appears to be the author of what is written represents his/her identity as a writer. The self as author also includes the writer's voice, that is, in the case of the dissertation, his/her opinions and positions regarding psychological research. In a dissertation, these positions may be the same as those of the cited authors or be different. After all, writers also differ in how they claim responsibility for what they write. Analyzing how students try to express their voice when writing can provide a good opportunity for clarifying the concept of the self as an author. For instance, formulating the hypotheses or research questions of a study is a moment of awareness and reprocessing for the student. Often these hypotheses and questions may be imposed on the student by the research group in which he/she is a temporary participant through his/her supervisor. The way hypotheses are written and justified can be evaluated in terms of theoretical coherence, as when we read or review a paper. They can also be considered, however, in terms of the student's commitment to outlining a research work in which he/she believes. The final part of the dissertation, where the author discusses his/her work, underlining its merits and limitations, also lends itself to this dual analysis, in terms of quality of findings and the writer's identification process.

An enlightening example of author's voice is offered by Ivanič (1998), who justifies her use of metaphor in writing:

> In some places, particularly towards the end of sections, I allow myself to use slightly more allusive and/or metaphorical language, leaving a bit more to the reader's imagination than is common in academic language: I think this makes for slightly more interesting reading, and also conveys the commitment I feel towards some of the issues I am writing about: I hope it balances the impression I may be giving of myself elsewhere of being pedantic and impersonal. (p. 31)

These words illustrate the meaning of posing oneself as an author: being aware and believing in what one writes and, on the basis of this trust and awareness, trying to "approach" the audience, not only to convince them. In this search for an identity, in which writing means posing oneself as an author, is the meaning of the motivation to write in university.

TO CONCLUDE: THE TEACHING OF WRITING FROM *OUTSIDE* TO *INSIDE* DISCIPLINES

At the beginning of the chapter two opposing positions on the teaching of writing in higher education were mentioned: inside the discipline versus outside. Now, which pole of the inside/outside distinction does the view of teaching writing outlined in the chapter fit better? I think that the reply should be, Both. Teaching how to write a dissertation requires teaching the general rules and constraints according to which a paper has to be written, in keeping with a "normative" view of academic writing, which, at least initially, may be extraneous to the writing experience of students. However, writing is *inside* the psychological disciplines, since through these rules and constraints students are made aware of the formal structure of a genre and realize that writing is an instrument for connecting their work to the scientific community of psychology.

REFERENCES

Bazerman, C. (2004). Intertextuality: How texts rely on other texts. In C. Bazerman & P. Prior (a cura di) *What writing does and how it does it* (pp. 83–96). Mahwah, NJ: Lawrence Erlbaum Associates.

Bereiter, C., & Scardamalia, M. (1987). *The psychology of written composition.* Hillsdale, NJ: Lawrence Erlbaum Associates.

Boscolo, P. (2009). Engaging and motivating children to write. In R. Beard, D. Myhill, J. Riley & M. Nystrand (Eds.) *The Sage handbook of writing development* (pp. 300–312). London: Sage.

Boscolo, P., Arfè, B., & Quarisa, M. (2007). Improving the quality of students' academic writing: An intervention study. *Studies in Higher Education, 32,* 419–438.

Bruning, R., & Horn, C. (2000). Developing motivation to write. *Educational Psychologist, 35,* 25–37.

Campbell, J., Smith, D., & Brooker, R. (1998). From conception to performance: How undergraduate students conceptualise and construct essays. *Higher Education, 36,* 449–469.

Carter, M. (2007). Ways of knowing, doing, and writing in the disciplines. *College Composition and Communication, 58,* 385–418.

Down, D., & Wardle, E. (2007). Teaching about writing, righting misconceptions: (Re)envisioning "First-Year Composition" as "Introduction to Writing Studies." *College Composition and Communication, 58,* 552–584.

Fairclough, N. (1992). Discourse and text: Linguistic and intertextual analysis within discourse analysis. *Discourse and Society, 3,* 193–217 (In A. Jaworski & N. Coupland (Eds.) (1999), *The discourse reader* (pp. 183–211). London, New York: Routledge).

Freedman, K. (1995). Educational change within structures of history, culture and discourse. In R. W. Neperud (Ed.) *Context, content and community in art education.* New York: Teachers College Press

Hidi, S., & Boscolo, P. (2006). Motivation and writing. In C. MacArthur, S. Graham & J. Fitzgerald (Eds.) *Handbook of writing research* (pp. 144–157). New York: Guilford.

Hidi, S., & Boscolo, P. (2007). (a cura di). *Writing and motivation*. Oxford: Elsevier.

Ivanič, R. (1998). *Writing and identity*. Amsterdam, Philadelphia: John Benjamins.

Lave, J., & Wenger, E. (1990). *Situated learning: Legitimate peripheral participation*. Cambridge: Cambridge University Press.

Lavelle, E. (1993). Development and validation of an inventory to assess processes in college composition. *British Journal of Educational Psychology*, 68, 395–407.

(1997). Writing style and the narrative essay. *British Journal of Educational Psychology*, 67, 489–499.

Lavelle, E., & Guarino, A. J. (2003). A multidimensional approach to understanding college writing processes. *Educational Psychology*, 23, 295–305.

Lea, M. (1998). Academic literacies and learning in higher education: Constructing knowledge through texts and experience. *Studies in the Education of Adults*, 30, 156–171.

Lea, M. & Street, B. (1998). Student writing in higher education: An academic literacies approach. *Studies in Higher Education*, 23, 157–172.

McCune, V. (2004). Development of first-year students' conceptions of essay writing. *Higher Education*, 47, 257–282.

Nelson, N. (2008). The reading-writing nexus in discourse research. In C. Bazerman (Ed.) *Handbook of research on writing* (pp. 435–450). New York, London: Lawrence Erlbaum Associates.

Publication manual of the American Psychological Association (6th ed.). Washington, DC: American Psychological Association.

Rosenblatt, L. M. (1978). *The reader, the text, the poem*. Carbondale: Southern Illinois University Press.

Russell, D. (1995). Activity theory and its implications for writing instruction. In J. Petraglia (Ed.) *Reconceiving writing, rethinking writing instruction* (pp. 51–77). Mahwah, NJ: Lawrence Erlbaum Associates.

Säljö, R. (1997). Talk as data and practice: A critical look at phenomenographic inquiry and the appeal to experience. *Higher Education Research & Development*, 16, 173–190.

Schraw, G. (2000). Reader beliefs and meaning construction in narrative text. *Journal of Educational Psychology*, 92, 96–106.

Schraw, G., & Bruning, R. (1996). Readers' implicit models of reading. *Reading Research Quarterly*, 31, 290–305.

Schraw, G. & Bruning, R. (1999). How implicit models of reading affect motivation to read and reading engagement. *Scientific Studies of Reading, 3,* 281–302.

Smith, D., Campbell, J., & Brooker, R. (1999). The impact of students' approaches to essay writing on the quality of their essays. *Assessment & Evaluation in Higher Education, 24,* 327–338.

Spivey, M. (1996). Integration of visual and linguistic information: Human data and model simulations. Ph.D. Dissertation, University of Rochester.

Spivey, N. N. (1997). *The constructivist metaphor: Reading, writing, and the making of meaning.* San Diego, CA: Academic Press.

Swales, J. M. (1990). *Genre analysis: English in academic and research settings.* Cambridge: Cambridge University Press.

Wardle, E. (2009). "Mutt genres" and the goal of FYC: Can we help students write the genres of the university? *College Composition and Communication, 60,* 765–789.

White, J. M., & Bruning, R. (2005). Implicit writing beliefs and their relation to writing quality. *Contemporary Educational Psychology, 30,* 166–189.

10

Experiencing Pictorial Artworks: The Role of Intersubjectivity

FEDERICA SAVAZZI, GABRIELLA GILLI, AND
SIMONA RUGGI

THE COMPLEXITY OF AESTHETIC EXPERIENCE

Images are able to catch our attention and involve us in the world they depict – a world of sensations, emotions, and thoughts. Of the variety of images to which we are exposed in our daily life, art images have the power to move the observer in an even stronger way than other images. According to Arnheim (1981), art is a quality present in all objects, whether artificial or natural, provided that they are endowed with "expressive dynamics." "Expressive dynamics," as opposed to the practical quality, is the distinctive feature of the artistic quality. However, differently from common artifacts, artistic images represent the purest and most intense example of that "art phenomenon" present *in nuce* in all objects. Therefore, a work of art shows particular formal features and triggers in the observer a variety of processes ending in an aesthetic evaluation.

The aesthetic behavior connected to a work of art consists of a feeling through the senses (*aisthanomai* = I feel, I perceive with my senses, I comprehend) as well as of comprehension of something that has been created in a complex, ordered, and rigorous way that means "artistically" made (*arë* = to articulate, to ordinate). Consequently, a common view within cognitive sciences and psychology is to consider aesthetic experience as characterized by a peculiar and complex weaving of perceptive, emotional, and cognitive processes (Jacobsen 2006; Leder, Belke, Oeberst, & Augustin 2004; Massironi 2000; Argenton 2008).

Furthermore, aesthetic experience is regarded as having several different processing levels: from the immediate response of the beholder to the perceived visual features of the artwork, to the explicit aesthetic judgment. More specifically, the makeup of an aesthetic experience may be subdivided into five levels: mere observation; the attitude to appreciate aesthetic entities; the experience, namely, one's response to the perceptual artifact; an objective appraisal of whether or not the artistic object is liked; and the aesthetic judgment, or an explicit evaluation of the artistic value of a work of art (Gallese 2012, oral speech). Whereas the first processing levels are based on unconscious and automatic mechanisms, the final levels are strongly influenced by conscious and deliberated processes of evaluation (Di Dio & Gallese 2009; Gallese & Di Dio 2012).

Scholars from different fields, such as philosophers, psychologists, and neuroscientists, have sought answers to questions such as "What happens when we experience a work of art?" and "How can aesthetic experience be described?"

Some authors call for an interdisciplinary approach for an "integrative science of aesthetics" (see, for example, Shimamura 2012, p. 3). Nevertheless, differences in approaches and theories are still relevant: Researchers often propose competing explanations for the aesthetic response phenomenon (for a philosophical systematization of different theories of art, see Casati 2008).

In the field of cognitive sciences, different perspectives have dealt with the components characterizing the complex phenomenon of aesthetic experience in visual art, specifically with respect to paintings (for a recent review of the different approaches, see Shimamura & Palmer 2012). By focusing on the experience of the beholder, some of them conceive aesthetic response as simply an individual and intrapsychic phenomenon. Such approaches to aesthetics can be distinguished on the basis of the processing level on which they claim the aesthetic experience is rooted. There are positions that give relevance to the unmediated response to the visual characteristics of an artistic stimulus at a physiological/neural level (Zeki 1999; Jacobsen 2006; Livingstone & Hubel 2002; Biederman & Vessel 2006; Ramachandran & Hirstein 1999). However, other approaches recognize as the primary place of aesthetic experience the higher cognitive processes of understanding that lead to the formulation of an explicit aesthetic judgment (Crozier & Chapman 1984; Child 1969; Eysenck 1988; Argenton 1996). Moreover, depending on the specific theoretical frame considered, bottom-up factors (concerning the visual and structural characteristics of the artwork, such as color and symmetry, and referring to the route of information processing from sensory signals to knowledge) and top-down cognitive processes (the cognitive feedback from one's cultural background and knowledge) are conceived of as exercising different influences on the aesthetic experience.

This chapter focuses on one of the differences between approaches to the aesthetic phenomenon, the difference concerning the identification of the fundamental level of the aesthetic process and the relational aspects that provide the basis of experiencing art. We compare a cognitive model with a neuroaesthetic one, namely, the communicative theory of art (Freeman 1995, 2004, 2010) and the embodied model of aesthetic experience (Freedberg & Gallese 2007).

Both of these theoretical positions strongly stress the inherently relational and intersubjective nature of aesthetic experience (which is not considered only an intraindividual experience of the beholder). However, these theories significantly confront each other on (1) the level of aesthetic experience crucial to its definition: cognitive versus. prerational; (2) the kind of aesthetic involvement: intellectual versus emotional; and (3) the philosophical conception of intersubjectivity that gives foundations to each theory: mind reading versus embodied simulation.

First, the communicative theory of art (Freeman 1995, 2004, 2010) argues that art experience is an intrinsically intersubjective enterprise in that it triggers hermeneutic reasoning about the artist, the referent (world), and the beholder him/herself. This theory considers as essential in making an aesthetic evaluation the ability of the beholder to theorize the relationships among the elements involved in the art system. Moreover, the cognitive comprehension of the artwork varies as a function of the developmental stage of the viewer (Parsons 1987). In contrast, the embodied theory (Freedberg & Gallese 2007) argues that aesthetic experience is rooted in the activation of universal neural structures responsible for the embodied simulation of actions, emotions, and bodily sensations. These neural mechanisms are the same as those responsible for the human predisposition to the interaction and recognition of the actions, emotions, and sensations of others. Furthermore, differently from approaches that consider art appreciation as related exclusively to the activation of the visual cortex (e.g., Zeki 1999), this position stresses the role of the multimodal simultaneous activation of various sensory and perceptive pathways, all responsible for the deep emotional response to art.

Therefore, the power of the work of art to engage its beholder is considered in different ways by the cognitive approach and by the embodied approach to art appreciation. In the first perspective, engagement with the artwork derives from an understanding of its meaning considering the intentionality it involves. In the second perspective, a work of art engages the beholder by emotionally arousing him/her.

Finally, these two theories of art are subtended by conceptions of intersubjectivity that differ in the levels and complexity of the mental contents that are at the basis of intersubjective exchanges and art appreciation. On the one side, the communicative theory of art identifies the fundamental mechanism for an understanding of others' internal states in the cognitive ability of "mind reading," which is a voluntary and introspective reflection on others' mental states (Baron-Cohen, Tager-Flusberg, & Cohen 2005). In contrast, the embodied approach identifies the mechanism behind the comprehension of others' experiences in an automated, unconscious, and prereflexive process of reproducing others' internal states (Gallese 2003; Gallese, Eagle, & Migone 2007).

The following sections of the chapter discuss these two theories. Their shared – though differentiated – proposals of aesthetic experience as a relational enterprise are explained. Additionally, the philosophical and psychological conceptions of intersubjectivity to which the two approaches appeal are compared.

COMMUNICATIVE THEORY OF ART

The theoretical framework of the communicative theory of art is cognitivism. In this view, art is a way to clarify our mental life to ourselves and is not just a set of pleasant objects (Parsons 1987). Art is a manifestation of high-quality human cognition: Its production and experience are the outcomes of skills, knowledge, procedures, and expectations. Art is considered to promote in the beholder complex interpretative processes. According to Parsons, "people respond to paintings differently because they understand them differently" (1987, p. 1).

Consequently, aesthetic responses to works of art are primarily based on the cognitive mastering, or cognitive apprehension, of the art itself. In fact, cognitive models consider aesthetic experience as a "challenging situation to classify, understand and cognitively master the artwork successfully" (Leder et al. 2004, p. 493).

This understanding of the meaning of a work of art is also strongly affected by cultural and relational influences.

Regarding cultural influences, art is considered a product of a slow evolution and cultural construction. A work of art is always realized within a specific cultural context, which is an extremely relevant feature of artistic interpretation. Therefore, a complete interpretation of a work of art needs to take into consideration the specific cultural context in which it has been realized. Furthermore, our present conception of art and its producers is itself the outcome of a slow cultural evolution and construction. For example, the notion of beauty is not simply related to different historic periods: Even during a single period and within the same country, different aesthetic ideals may coexist (Eco 2004).

Considering the relational influences, paintings not only allow a viewer to see a meaningful representation, but also allow people to communicate reciprocally. In fact, a working definition of representational depiction should include the notion of "someone's attempt to communicate, preserve, or express" something (DeLoache, Pierroutsakos, & Troseth 1997, p. 3). This means that the cognitive mastering of a painting is almost invariably subordinated to communication because "communication is not confined to exchanging utterances or gestures; instead there is a variety of cultural devices whereby we try to bridge the gap between minds and between physical and mental realities" (Freeman 2004, p. 374).

INTERSUBJECTIVE CONNOTATION OF THE COMMUNICATIVE THEORY OF ART

The development of a mental metarepresentational capability is considered essential in understanding others' intentions. Yet, how can people transmit and communicate their own internal representations to understand and be understood by others? According to this approach, the communication of internal states is often mediated by cultural tools such as language or notation systems. In this sense, "there is something about the architecture of the human mind that enables children and adults also to produce external notations, that is to use cultural tools for leaving an intentional trace of communicative and cognitive acts" (Karmiloff-Smith 1992, p. 139). One of these notation systems is art, which is one of the most powerful media that enable people to communicate features internal to the mind, such as intentions and emotions. Indeed, art is conceived as a set of symbolic cultural devices or intermental realities. Thus, artistic artifacts can be seen as representational mediators for communication.

The communicative function of artworks is what precisely gives two main potentialities to paintings: to indicate the external referents and, at the same time, to evoke the mind frame of the artist (Callaghan 2003). Thus, to comprehend an artistic artifact means to reason on the network of intentionality involved in the production of and response to art. In this sense, because Searle (1983) considers intentionality as the human mind's capability to be about or to stand for states or affairs in the external world, art is a notation system to which the intentional states of the artist and the observers are directed.

The acquisition of an interpretative theory of art should be based on the development of a Theory of Mind (ToM) through which the beholder becomes able to formulate hypotheses about his own and others' mental states, such as desires, beliefs, and feelings (Freeman 2004). As is well known, Theory of Mind is a social understanding ability whose possession allows people to comprehend their own and others' mental states to make sense of and predict their and other people's behavior (Wimmer & Perner 1983). ToM enables children and adults to comprehend others' attitudes, intentions, thoughts, and feelings to make others' behavior predictable and meaningful (Fonagy & Target 2001) and to answer and behave in appropriate ways in response to the different relational situations that may occur.

Therefore, Theory of Mind offers an interpretative paradigm to a critical reading of the artistic phenomenon. This paradigm is aimed at understanding how art is interpreted because it argues that the ability to master an "external" system of representations implies a mental representation of the intentionality of all actors involved in the artistic phenomenon, that is, the artists and the viewers.

In the words of Freeman (2011), "Pictorial competence is communicative in nature: we now add that it springs from emergent cross-talk between mechanisms serving two core domains: (a) domain-specific representations of theory of mind, and (b) one strand of domain-specific naïve physics, namely intuitive optics. A prime function of intuitive optics is to understand the minds of the other users of that same optics" (p. 424).

DEVELOPMENT OF A THEORY OF ART

A relationship between the development of the child's Theory of Mind and his/her theory of art has been hypothesized (Browne & Wooley 2001; Freeman 2000, 2010; Richert & Lillard 2002). As for Theory of Mind, children develop a theory of pictures through a process of acquisition characterized by progressive normative stages. These developmental stages are based on children's comprehension of the relationships existing among all four terms constituting the "art system," namely, Artist, Viewer, Picture, and Referent-world (Freeman 1995). In fact, the four entities can contract six relationships among themselves. Through these relationships, an interpretation of the mental intentions of others is possible.

This process produces an "encounter of minds," that of the Viewer and that of the Artist: "An Artist is the agent behind the production of the Picture...; the Viewers make assumptions about how the appearances of things relate to the appearances of Pictures of those things, and to the ways in which picture-producers generate the artefact" (Freeman 2004, p. 361). Thus, to analyze the development of a child's theory of art is to "engage with one strand of the child's journey toward a grasp of subjectivity" (Freeman 2010, p. 208).

Children develop an increasingly broad theory of art framework. This interpretative activity is a lifelong endeavor (Freeman 1995, 2004; Parsons, 1987). First, they focus mostly on subject matter. Many studies (for example, Räsänen 2003) supported Parsons's (1987) view that, at the beginning of aesthetic development, the artist is seen as an imitator of perceptible reality, judging the artwork is not distinguished from judging its maker, and judgment on the picture is "collapsing" on judgment on reality.

Later, children include concepts concerning the artist's expressive abilities. Because intentionality is one of the fundamental aspects of aesthetic reasoning (Bloom 2004), the key element for understanding the artwork is precisely the intent of the artist (Freeman & Parsons 2001). Finally, children may become aware of their own interpretative activities as viewers. In fact, essential to the definition of art phenomenon is the presence of a public (Bloom 2004).

With regard to the development of a theory of art, Freeman (2012) is now studying the relationship between drawing and the outside world, and a child's pictorial imagination. There is evidence that younger children show both a rigidity and a flexibility in the manner in which they represent to themselves how a drawing is a pointer to properties of things in the outside world, a rigidity in that a pointer is fixed by the act of naming: younger children do not change their opinion on what a minimalist drawing represents, such as a circle or a line, when they are told that the drawing was made with the intent of the creator to represent a certain thing; a flexibility in that children can imagine the same drawing as representing more than one pointer; for example, a circle can refer to a "real" lollipop or to a "real" balloon. "Maybe that mentality is an important advance in pictorial reasoning" (Freeman in press).

Gelman and Ebeling (1998) gave further support to the importance of the comprehension of intentionality in judging a painting. In an experiment, they asked two- and three-year-old children to name simple tempera paintings. Half the children were told that paintings were intentionally made ("When John was painting in art class, he used some paint to make something for his teacher. This is what it looked like"), and the other half were told that the paintings were accidentally made ("When John's dad was painting the house, John accidentally spilled some paint on the floor. This is what it looked like"). They found that the first half of the children named the shape represented in the painting, whereas the other half of the children described the material used to draw. Thus, the way a painting is made is significant to its comprehension: Children consider the work of art to be the intentionally made painting and not the accidentally made one (Bloom 2004).

There is also evidence that children are slowly able to consider how another observer could interpret their drawings; thus, they consider a representation as an object of communication. In fact, seven-year-old children, but not younger children, consider the possibility of improving their own pictorial representation after having completed it (Golomb 1992).

This change is so evident that it can be found not only in the pictorial production but also in the pictorial active vision (Freeman 1995). In fact, the child slowly becomes aware of the modes of expression, the potential role of the artist, and the interpretive possibilities of the user. The development toward realism represents a profound intersubjective change. In fact, from this moment on, the child considers the needs and beliefs of others, and there is a conceptual progress underlying the recognition of the expression of multiple minds in pictorial representations.

For example, reasoning related to the determinants of beauty changes with increasing age. Children only slowly consider a painting beautiful independently of the object represented because of the skillfulness of the artist. Afterward, the comprehension of the viewer himself/herself becomes an essential component in judging beauty. A painting is even more beautiful because it pleases the eye of the beholder. In this sense, children start to consider the possibility of individual differences in the aesthetic perception of different beholders.

Children around five years of age subjected to false belief tasks and questioned on their opinions about the artist believe that the mood of the painter is reflected directly in the "mood" of his/her productions. In other words, a happy artist will create necessarily a happy painting (Callaghan & Rochat 2003). However, ten-year-old children in judging the emotions that a work of art transmits consider the technical skills of the artist and his/her intention to produce a certain mood in the observer (Freeman & Sanger 1993). If a painter represents a sad face, this does not necessarily mean that he/she feels sad in turn.

In conclusion, children turn to the mind of the artist to understand fully the work of art "in an attempt to make sense of a world run by others" (Freeman in press).

EMBODIED THEORY OF ART APPRECIATION

David Freedberg and Vittorio Gallese (2007) have advanced a new theoretical hypothesis to explain the aesthetic empathetic engagement with images based on evidence from neuroscience. These authors stated that art is relevant for human beings because of its power to attract and emotionally engage the beholder. In fact, even though they recognize that aesthetic experience enables modulation by different contextual factors (such as historical and social components) that may lead to an articulated aesthetic judgment, the authors argue against the primacy of cognition in one's responses to art. According to them (Freedberg & Gallese 2007), when speaking about aesthetic experience, it is essential to focus primarily on the feelings of empathetic engagement with what is depicted in the works of art. As the authors pointed out, this attention to the emotional engagement with art is not new; it was already introduced in the nineteenth century when German scholars used the notion of empathy (*Einfühlung*) in the field of aesthetics. Only later was this concept transferred from the field of aesthetics to that of the psychology of interpersonal relations by Lipps (1903).

Freedberg and Gallese (2007) proposed that aesthetic experience is not always informed by cognition and cultural stocks, but it is always rooted in the activation of embodied universal mechanisms that operate at a precognitive level and that are responsible for the empathic perception of visual artworks. In fact, they argued that the feelings of empathy arising when observing visual art may consist not only of "the empathetic understanding of the emotions of represented others" but, most probably, of "a sense of inward imitation of the observed actions of others in pictures and sculptures" (p. 197). Therefore, they suggested that empathy is an essential constituent of the aesthetic experience and, most striking, that empathy is based on mirroring neural mechanisms.

Specifically, their hypothesis is that the aesthetic connotation of works of art substantially derives from the activation of an innate mirroring system in the motor areas of the brain. This system is responsible for simulating at a prerational level the actions, feelings, and emotions evoked in the beholder by paintings and sculptures. More precisely, this neuronal system allows the content of the painting and the visible gestures of the artist to activate internal representations of the bodily states associated with that stimulation, as we were acting or feeling the same actions or emotions evoked by the painting. Because of this internal functional mechanism of simulation, we make sense of others' actions, emotions, and sensations at a prerational level.

It is well known that mirror neurons were discovered in the premotor cortex of the macaque brain (area F5) (Gallese et al. 1996; Rizzolatti et al. 1996). They are active both when the monkey performs a finalized motor act, such as grasping objects with the hand or mouth, and when it observes another individual performing similar motor acts. Subsequently, these mechanisms have been identified in humans (see Gallese, Keysers, & Rizzolatti 2004; Rizzolatti & Craighero 2004; for a review, see Gallese & Sinigaglia 2011).

As highlighted by Gallese (2010b), the mirroring mechanisms are not confined to the domain of actions, and findings show that these mechanisms are responsible for various functions. In fact, they are able to mediate the understanding of the purpose of an action even when this purpose is not completely visible and, therefore, its ultimate goal can only be imagined (Umiltà et al. 2001). In addition, these mechanisms are responsible for understanding the intentions behind the actions of others and the reason for an action (Iacoboni et al. 2005), and they are related to the domain of emotions and feelings (Gallese 2005, 2006).

INTERSUBJECTIVE CONNOTATION OF THE EMBODIED THEORY OF ART

Gallese (2010b) claims that the work of art is not an object in itself; it takes its essence as a function of the intersubjective social relationship in which it is immersed. In this view, intersubjectivity has a purely phenomenological connotation, not so much in reference to the intentional relationship between communicative partners by means of a notational system as in reference to the common transcendental subjectivity of the entire viewing public (Husserl 1960).

Because of the intersubjective relationship between the artwork and the beholder, the former is able to move by evoking an embodied simulation of actions and feelings in the beholder.

In fact, according to Gallese (2006), the activation of a shared neural state realized in two different bodies because of the mirroring system is a direct account of "experiencing" another person's state. The activation of a shared mental state provokes the surfacing of similar sensations evoked in the observer "as if" he were doing the same thing; the "objectual other" becomes "another self" (intentional attunement, Gallese 2006). This mechanism allows an implicit and direct form of understanding of the actions of others (Gallese et al. 1996), which is not considered to be based on the exclusive mediation of higher cognitive strategies that provide for the application of sophisticated deductive processes (embodied simulation, Gallese 2005).

The theoretical explication of social engagement with others derived from the findings of the subpersonal activation of resonance systems, mirror neurons, and shared representations is known as the "embodied simulation" hypothesis (Gallese 2005). Implicit simulation theorists argue that the mirroring subpersonal processes themselves are just a nonconscious and prereflexive simulation of the other's intentions. Our experience of others is underpinned by the activity of "mirror matching neural circuits," which are interpreted as "simulation routines, as if processes enabling models of others to be created" at the functional level (Gallese 2001, p. 45).

This approach conflicts with the mind reading approach. In fact, embodied approaches that consider Theory of Mind perspectives, such as "theory theory" and "simulation theory," account for "neither our primary and pervasive way of engaging with others nor the true basis of our folk psychological understanding, even when narrowly construed" (Gallagher & Hutto 2008, p. 17).

Theories on embodiment refuse to interpret intersubjectivity as a higher cognitive mind reading capability because they consider intersubjectivity a predisposition given to human beings from birth and engraved in the body itself.

Differently from "standard simulation" theory (Gordon 1986, 2005; Harris 1989; Goldman 1989, 2005) that considers social understanding as the result of a deliberate and conscious cognitive effort aimed at simulating the mental states hidden in others' behavior by relying on introspection, "embodied simulation" (Gallese 2003, 2005, 2006) considers simulation as a process that remains entirely at a subpersonal level, "a mandatory, non-conscious, and pre-reflexive mechanism that is not the result of a deliberate and conscious cognitive effort aimed at interpreting the intentions hidden in the overt behaviour of others, as implied by the theory-theory account" (Gallese et al. 2007).

In sum, we do not just see the intentional behavior of others – an action, an emotion, or a sensation. By means of embodied simulation, we are able to develop a specific phenomenal state of "intentional attunement," an internal representation of the body states associated with the observed actions, as if we were acting out the same explicit behavior.

EMBODIED SIMULATION DURING AESTHETIC EXPERIENCE

According to this view, aesthetic experience associated with visual works of art is a complex process that starts with scanning the visual artwork. It is then subjected to further processing levels and allows the beholder to "perceive-feel-sense" (Di Dio & Gallese 2009, p. 682) a work of art because the visual processing is conceived to be an active multimodal way of perceiving. In fact, perceiving a painting is seen as an intentional relational act between the beholder and the artistic object that encompasses not only vision but also other senses, such as touch and the emotional sphere. This complex process is caused by the simultaneous activation of different neuronal systems, such as visual and sensorimotor areas. It is precisely the activation of multiple and parallel circuits that instantiate mirror properties responsible for the simulation of actions, emotions, and corporeal feeling sensations in response to artworks (Gallese 2010a) that is considered crucial to the surfacing of an aesthetic experience.

There are two aspects of a painting that contribute to activating a mirroring neuronal simulation: "the content of art works, in terms of the actions, intentions, objects, emotions, and sensations portrayed in a given painting or sculpture" and the "quality of the artwork in terms of the visible traces of the artist's creative gestures, like brush work, chisel marks, and signs of the movement of the hand" (Freedberg & Gallese 2007, p. 199).

Thus, it has been hypothesized that even when an artwork has no recognizable representational content, it may still activate an empathic involvement of the beholder with the traces of the gestures that the artist has made to create that artwork. In this case, the internal simulation evoked by the work of art is that of the motor action that produced those artistic signs on the table (Freedberg & Gallese 2007; Gallese 2010a).

In this view,

> What we see is not simply patterns of colour and shape. We see traces of human activity. Western-historical scholarship has long recognized something of this, notably the power of the drawn line as a mark or trace of the artist's activity, a power that has encouraged talk of the line as emblematic of the artist's genius. But in most

plastic art-making practices we see traces of the artist's activity, most obviously in brushworks or marks on surfaces, that records the process of shaping of solid material…, or in the pattern of a woven basket, blanket or rug, all of which, being three-dimensional structures rather than mere patterns on a surface, provide detailed record of the maker's activity. (Smith 2012, p. 119)

In further aesthetic processing levels, these precognitive mechanisms may be modulated by factors such as context, individuals' interest in the artwork, prior knowledge, and familiarity. In fact, the authors recognize that the explicit evaluation (aesthetic judgment) of a work of art, which is the most cognitive aspect of aesthetic engagement, may be affected by social and cultural aesthetic canons. Nevertheless, the authors argue that "no esthetic judgment is possible without a consideration of the role of mirroring mechanisms in the forms of simulated embodiment and empathetic engagement that follow upon visual observation" (Gallese & Freedberg 2007, p. 411).

There are some critical issues with respect to this conception of art experience. Some doubts about the relevance of mirror systems for aesthetic experience of static artwork may arise. Nevertheless, studies on mirror neurons in humans have shown that even the observation of static images leads to simulation in the observer's brain. In fact, mirror neurons have been demonstrated to be activated not only by viewing actual dynamic human actions (Buccino et al. 2001) but also by dynamic information from static pictures of individuals in motion (implicit motion). Urgesi et al. (2006) found a selective activation of the motor system during the observation of images of human actions. Their study showed changes in muscle responsiveness only during the observation of implied motion hands versus still hands but not of nonbiological entities with (e.g., waterfalls) or without (e.g., icefalls) implied motion. Proverbio, Riva, and Zani (2009) found that mirror neurons respond to static images representing more or less dynamic actions. More recently, Calvo-Merino, Urgesi, Orgs, Aglioti, and Haggard (2010) found that specific motor areas are activated by the perception of images representing human bodies in dance postures but not by images showing objects.

Several studies within psychology and neuroaesthetics found evidence compatible with this theoretical hypothesis (Di Dio, Macaluso, & Rizzolatti 2007; Massaro et al. 2012; see Di Dio & Gallese 2009; Gallese & Di Dio 2012). In one of these studies (Di Dio et al. 2007), the neuronal activity of laypersons was registered using functional magnetic resonance imaging (fMRI) as they observed reproductions of classical and Renaissance sculptures representing human figures. Sculptures were presented in the original version and in an altered version in which the Golden Beauty proportions were modified. Results showed that viewing original sculptures elicited the activation of motor areas (ventral premotor cortex and posterior parietal cortex). The activation of these areas was interpreted as the motor resonance most likely elicited by the implied motion represented in the sculptures.

CONCLUDING REMARKS

A dichotomy between mirroring processes (or low-level mind reading) and mentalizing (or high-level mind reading) has been stated (Goldman 2006), claiming that these processes are strongly and qualitatively different. Mentalizing would be more cognitive, reflective, and controlled and less reflexive and automatic than mirroring; such an interpretation supports the incompatibility of the ToM approach with the embodiment approach (Goldman 2009; Clay & Iacoboni 2011).

Explanations based on neural mirroring should be "triangulated" (Smith 2012, p. 80) with phenomenological and cognitive approaches to the aesthetic experience.

The communicative theory of art is primarily centered on considering one's cognitive mastering of the message conveyed by what is represented in an artwork. Dealing with the development and the nature of aesthetic reasoning and evaluation may neglect the emotional engagement of the beholder. The cognitive approach deemphasizes the capacity of visual artworks to arouse perceptual or emotive responses in the beholder because art production and appreciation are considered as directly associated with cultural patterns and cognitive faculties.

In contrast, the embodied approach to art, even if it considers the emotional engagement central in the aesthetic experience, has been criticized as being of marginal relevance for aesthetics (Casati & Pignocchi 2007). In fact, the neural bases of empathic responses to art are not constitutive of aesthetic response tout court, or, more precisely, of aesthetic judgment and appraisal. Although the findings on mirroring systems are key elements in the comprehension of "psychological significance of sharing the same body with other people," still "the perception of similarity is not enough to provide the motivation for engagement and communication or to explain the responsive emotions that fuel engagement" (Reddy 2008, p. 21).

Similarly, the neural evidence (supporting the embodied simulation), in suggesting that we "feel" and understand the action depicted in the artwork through a "direct mapping" onto the premotor cortex, does not speak for itself: It cannot fully explain the aesthetic experience.

The authors of the approach also recognize this deficiency:

> We did not suggest that the activation of mirror or canonical neurons was sufficient for esthetic appraisal or for judgments about artworks. Our claim was that canonical and mirror neurons often have a crucial role in esthetic responses – because of their role in various forms of simulated embodiment that are relevant in considering esthetic responses, and that offer the basis for understanding the neural substrate of empathetic reactions to works of art. … We claimed that embodied and empathetic responses, too long neglected, have a much wider role in esthetic responses than hitherto acknowledged. (Gallese & Freedberg 2007)

A word to the wise: Today, there is no unique, conclusive theory able to explain the wide variety or responses shown by subjects when experiencing works of art. "Grand theories are surely hopelessly premature in their grandiosity" (McManus 2011, p. 186).

Nevertheless, comparing and discussing different theories and their research results is worthwhile, and it can orient and guide in the field of cognitive sciences the research programs on aesthetics.

One such possible research program could be on the role that intersubjective and relational processes play in the nature and development of aesthetic engagement. Given the renowned crucial role of intersubjectivity, we have attempted to present how these processes have been interpreted, discussed, and studied within two different theoretical perspectives. Further research will shed light on the nature and evolution of the intriguing intersubjective experience of art.

REFERENCES

Argenton, A. (1996). *Arte e cognizione. Introduzione alla psicologia dell'arte.* Milano: Raffaello Cortina.

   (2008). *Arte e espressione. Studi e ricerche di psicologia dell'arte.* Padova: Il Poligrafo.

Arnheim, R. (1981). *Arte e percezione visiva.* Milano: Feltrinelli.

Baron-Cohen, S. E., Tager-Flusberg, H. E., & Cohen, D. J. (2005). *Understanding other minds: Perspectives from developmental cognitive neuroscience* (2nd ed.). New York: Oxford University Press.

Biederman, I., & Vessel, E. (2006). Perceptual pleasure and the brain: A novel theory explains why the brain craves information and seeks it through the senses. *American Scientist, 94,* 249–255.

Bloom, P. (2004). *Descartes' baby: How the science of child development explains what makes us human.* New York: Basic Books.

Browne, C. A., & Wooley, J. D. (2001). Theory of mind in children's naming of drawings. *Journal of Cognition and Development, 2,* 389–412.

Buccino, G., Binkofski, F., Fink, G. R., Fadiga, L., Fogassi, L., Gallese, V., Seitz, R. J., et al. (2001). Action observation activates premotor and parietal areas in a somatotopic manner: an fMRI study. *European Journal of Neuroscience, 13*(2), 400–404.

Callaghan, T. C. (2003). Nascita e primo sviluppo della rappresentazione grafica. *Età Evolutiva, 76,* 51–63.

Callaghan T. C., & Rochat P. (2003). Traces of the artist: Sensitivity to the role of the artist in children's pictorial reasoning. *British Journal of Developmental Psychology, 5,* 415–445.

Calvo-Merino, B., Urgesi, C., Orgs, G., Aglioti, S. M., & Haggard, P. (2010). Extrastriate body area underlies aesthetic evaluation of body stimuli. *Experimental Brain Research*, 204(3), 447–456.

Casati, R. (2008). Che cosa spiega una teoria dell'arte (What does a theory of art explain)? In M. Bresciani Califano (Ed.) *Paradossi e disarmonie nelle scienze e nelle arti* (pp. 137–158). Firenze: Olschki.

Casati, R., & Pignocchi, A. (2007). Mirror and canonical neurons are not constitutive of aesthetic response. *Trends in Cognitive Sciences*, 11, 10, 410.

Child, I. L. (1969). Esthetics. In G. Lindzey & E. Aronson (Eds.) *The handbook of social psychology* (vol. III, pp. 853–916). Reading, MA: Addison Wesley.

Clay, Z., & Iacoboni, M. (2011). Mirroring fictional others. In E. Schellekens & P. Goldie (Eds.) *The aesthetic mind: Philosophy and psychology* (pp. 313–332). Oxford: Oxford University Press.

Crozier, W. R., & Chapman, A. J. (1984). *Cognitive processes in the perception of art*. Oxford: Elsevier.

DeLoache, J. S., Pierroutsakos, S. L., Troseth, G. (1997). The three R's of pictorial competence. In R. Vasta (Ed.) *Annals of child development* (pp. 1–48). Bristol, PA: Jessica Kingsley.

Di Dio, C., & Gallese, V. (2009). Neuroaesthetics: A review. *Current Opinion in Neurobiology*, 19(6), 682–687.

Di Dio, C., Macaluso, E., & Rizzolatti, G. (2007). The golden beauty: Brain response to classical and renaissance sculptures. *PloS One*, 2(11), e1201.

Eco, U. (2004). *Storia della bellezza*. Torino: Bompiani.

Eysenck, H. J. (1988). Personality and scientific aesthetics. In F. Farley & R. Neperud (Eds.) *Foundations of aesthetics art and art education*. New York: Praeger.

Fonagy, P., & Target, M. (2001). *Attaccamento e funzione riflessiva: Selected papers of Peter Fonagy and Mary Target*. Milano: Raffaello Cortina.

Freedberg, D., & Gallese, V. (2007). Motion, emotion and empathy in esthetic experience. *Trends in Cognitive Sciences*, 11, 197–203.

Freeman, N. H. (1995). Teoria della mente, teoria delle rappresentazioni pittoriche: un progresso concettuale nell'infanzia. *Età Evolutiva*, 50, 111–117.

Freeman, N. H. (2000). Communication and representation: Why mentalistic reasoning is a lifelong endeavour. In P. Mitchell & K. Riggs (Eds.) *Children's reasoning and the mind* (pp. 349–366). Hove: Psychology Press.

Freeman, N. H. (2004). Aesthetic judgment and reasoning. In E. Eisner & D. Day (Eds.) *Handbook of research and policy in art education* (pp. 359–378). Mahwah, NJ: Lawrence Erlbaum Associates.

Freeman, N. H. (2010). Children as intuitive art critics. In C. Milbraith & C. Lightfoot (Eds.) *Art and human development* (pp. 185–212). Hove: Psychology Press.

Freeman, N. H. (2011). Varieties of pictorial judgment: A functional account. In E. Schellekens & P. Goldie (Eds.) *The aesthetic mind: Philosophy and psychology* (pp. 414–426). Oxford: Oxford University Press.

Freeman, N. H. (2012). A sense of pictorial possibility: Minimalist drawings by you and other people A sense of pictorial possibility. In A. Farneti & I. Riccioni (Eds., *Proceedings of Arte, psiche e società:. Processi cognitivi e implicazioni sociali nella creazione e fruizione dell'arte*, 15–16 novembre 2011. Brixen: Libera Università di Bolzano. Roma: Carocci.

Freeman, N. H., & Parsons, M. J. (2001). Children's intuitive understandings of pictures. In B. Torff & R. J. Sternberg (Eds.) *Understanding and teaching the intuitive mind: Student and teacher learning* (pp. 73–82). Mahwah, NJ: Lawrence Erlbaum Associates.

Freeman, N. H., & Sanger, D. (1993). Language and belief in critical thinking: Emerging explanations of pictures. *Exceptionality Education Canada*, 3, 43–58.

Gallagher, S., & Hutto, D. (2008). Understanding others through primary interaction and narrative practice. In J. Zlatev, T. Racine, C. Sinha & E. Itkonen (Eds.) *The shared mind: Perspectives on intersubjectivity* (pp. 17–38). Amsterdam: John Benjamins.

Gallese, V. (2001). The "shared manifold" hypothesis: From mirror neurons to empathy. *Journal of Consciousness Studies*, 8, 5–7, 33–50.

(2003). The roots of empathy: The shared manifold hypothesis and the neural basis of intersubjectivity. *Psychopathology*, 36(4), 171–180.

(2005). Embodied simulation: From neurons to phenomenal experience. *Phenomenology and the Cognitive Sciences*, 4, 23–48.

(2006). Intentional attunement: A neurophysiological perspective on social cognition and its disruption in autism. *Brain Research: Cognitive Brain Research*, 1079, 15–24.

Gallese, V. (2010a). Mirror neurons and art. In F. Bacci & D. Melcher (Eds.) *Art and the senses* (pp. 441–449). Oxford: Oxford University Press.

Gallese, V. (2010b). Corpo e azione nell'esperienza estetica: Una prospettiva neuroscientifica. In U. Morelli (Ed.) *Mente e bellezza: Mente relazionale, arte, creatività e innovazione* (pp. 245–262). Torino: Umberto Allemandi & c. editore.

Gallese, V. (2012, May 16). *Il corpo nell'esperienza estetica: Una prospettiva neuroscientifica.* Lecture at Università Cattolica del Sacro Cuore di Milano.

Gallese, V., & Di Dio, C. (2012). Neuroesthetics: The body in aesthetic experience. In V. Ramachandran (Ed.) *Encyclopedia of human behavior* 2nd ed. San Diego, CA: Academic Press.

Gallese, V., Eagle, M. N., & Migone, P. (2007). Intentional attunement: Mirror neurons and the neural underpinnings of interpersonal relations. *Journal of the American Psychoanalytic Association, 55*(1), 131–176.

Gallese, V., Fadiga, L., Fogassi, L., & Rizzolatti, G. (1996). Action recognition in the premotor cortex. *Brain*, 119, 593–609.

Gallese, V., & Freedberg, D. (2007). Mirror and canonical neurons are crucial elements in esthetic response. *Trends in Cognitive Sciences*, 11(10), 411–411.

Gallese, V., Keysers, C., & Rizzolatti, G. (2004). A unifying view of the basis of social cognition. *Trends in Cognitive Sciences*, 8, 396–403.

Gallese, V., & Sinigaglia, C. (2011). What is so special about embodied simulation? *Trends in Cognitive Sciences*, 15, 512–519.

Gelman, S. A., & Ebeling, K. S. (1998). Shape and representational status in children's early naming. *Cognition*, 66, B35–B47.

Goldman, A. I. (1989). Interpretation psychologized. *Mind and Language*, 4, 161–185.

Goldman, A. I. (2005). Imitation, mind reading, and simulation. In S. Hurley & N. Chater (Eds.) *Perspectives on imitation: From neuroscience to social science*. Vol. 2: *Imitation, human development, and culture* (pp. 79–93). Cambridge, MA: MIT Press.

Goldman, A. I. (2006). *Simulating minds: The philosophy, psychology, and neuroscience of mindreading*. New York: Oxford University Press.

Goldman, A. I. (2009). Mirroring, Mindreading, and Simulation. In J. A. Pineda (Ed.) *Mirror neuron systems* (pp. 311–330). New York: Humana Press.

Golomb, C. (1992). *The child's creation of a pictorial world*. Berkeley: University of California Press.

Gordon, R. (1986). Folk psychology as simulation. *Mind and Language*, 1, 158–171.

Gordon, R. (2005). Intentional agents like myself. In S. Hurley & N. Chater (Eds.) *Perspectives on imitation: From neuroscience to social science*. Vol. 2: *Imitation, human development, and culture* (pp. 95–10). Cambridge, MA: MIT Press.

Harris, P. L. (1989). *Children and emotion: The development of psychological understanding*. Oxford: Blackwell.

Husserl, E. (1960). *Meditazioni Cartesiane e discorsi parigini*. Milano: Bompiani.

Iacoboni, M., Molnar- Szakacs, I., Gallese, V., Buccino, G., Mazziotta, J., & Rizzolatti, G. (2005). Grasping the intentions of others with one's own mirror neuron system. *PLoS Biology*, 3(3), 529–535.

Jacobsen, T. (2006). Bridging the arts and sciences: A framework for the psychology of aesthetics. *Leonardo*, 39(2), 155–162.

Karmiloff-Smith, A. (1992). *Beyond modularity: A developmental perspective on cognitive science.* Cambridge, MA: MIT Press.

Leder, H., Belke, B., Oeberst, A., & Augustin, D. (2004). A model of aesthetic appreciation and aesthetic judgments. *British Journal of Psychology*, 95, 489–508.

Lipps, T. (1903). Einfühlung, innere Nachahmung, und Organ-empfindungen. *Archiv für die gesammte Psychologie*, 1, 185–204.

Livingstone, M., & Hubel, D. H. (2002). *Vision and art: The biology of seeing.* New York: Harry N. Abrams.

Massaro, D., Savazzi, F., Di Dio, C., Freedberg, D., Gallese, V., Gilli, G., & Marchetti, A. (2012). When art moves the eyes: A behavioral and eye-tracking study. *PLoS ONE* 7, 5: e37285. doi:10.1371/journal.pone.0037285

Massironi, M. (2000). *L'Osteria dei Dadi Truccati: Arte, psicologia e dintorni.* Bologna: Il Mulino.

McManus, I. C. (2011). Beauty is instinctive feeling: Experimenting on aesthetic and art. In E. Schellekens & P. Goldie (Eds.) *The aesthetic mind: Philosophy and psychology* (pp. 169–189). Oxford: Oxford University Press.

Parsons, M. J. (1987). *How we understand art: A cognitive developmental account of aesthetic experience.* Cambridge: Cambridge University Press.

Proverbio, A. M., Riva, F., & Zani, A. (2009). Observation of static pictures of dynamic actions enhances the activity of movement-related brain areas. *PloS One*, 4(5), e5389.

Ramachandran, V., & Hirstein, W. (1999). The science of art: A neurological theory of aesthetic experience. *Journal of Consciousness*, 6(6), 15–35.

Räsänen, M. (2003). Interpreting art through visual narratives. *Landscapes: The Art, Aesthetics, and Education*, 2, 183–195.

Reddy, V. (2008). *How infants know minds.* Cambridge, MA: Harvard University Press.

Richert, R., & Lillard, A. S. (2002). Children's understanding of the knowledge prerequisites of drawing and pretending. *Developmental Psychology*, 38, 1004–1015.

Rizzolatti, G., & Craighero, L. (2004). The mirror-neuron system. *Annual Review of Neuroscience*, 27, 169–192.

Rizzolatti, G., Fadiga, L., Gallese, V., & Fogassi, L. (1996). Premotor cortex and the recognition of motor actions. *Cognitive Brain Research, 3,* 131–141.

Searle, J. R. (1983). *Intentionality: An essay in the philosophy of mind.* Cambridge: Cambridge University Press.

Shimamura, A. P. (2012). Toward a science of aesthetics: Issues and ideas. In A. P. Shimamura & S. E. Palmer (Eds.) *Aesthetic science: Connecting minds, brains, and experience* (pp. 3–30). New York: Oxford University Press.

Shimamura, A. P., & Palmer, S. E. (Eds.) (2012). *Aesthetic science: Connecting minds, brains, and experience.* New York: Oxford University Press.

Smith, M. (2012). Triangulating aesthetic experience. In A. P. Shimamura & S. E. Palmer (Eds.) *Aesthetic science: Connecting minds, brains, and experience* (pp. 80–106). New York: Oxford University Press.

Umiltà, M. A., Kohler, E., Gallese, V., Fogassi, L., Fadiga, L., Keysers, C. & Rizzolatti, G. (2001) "I know what you are doing": A neurophysiological study. *Neuron, 31,* 155–65.

Urgesi, C., Moro, V., Candidi, M., & Aglioti, S. M. (2006). Mapping implied body actions in the human motor system. *Journal of Neuroscience: The Official Journal of the Society for Neuroscience, 26*(30), 7942–7949.

Wimmer, H., & Perner, J. (1983). Beliefs about beliefs: Representation and constraining function of wrong beliefs in young children's understanding of deception. *Cognition, 13,* 103–128.

Zeki, S. (1999). *Inner vision.* Oxford: Oxford University Press.

11

Does Culture Shape the Professional Self? An Exploration of Teachers' Narratives

EMANUELA CONFALONIERI AND SARAH MIRAGOLI

INTRODUCTION

Before actually beginning the job, I thought teaching would have been easier. I thought that it was more or less about entering a classroom, attempting to explain things to children and going home. And that was about it. I was wrong. It is totally different, because when a teacher enters a classroom he/she has to attune him/herself to each student. Before I started I thought that I would have had to consider the group while I now know that it is important to consider all their different individual issues.

Human thinking is moved by a profound need to give meaning to reality. An account of the series of events that make up a person's life can give meaning to an otherwise complex set of personal experiences and a network of different life meanings (Bruner 1986, 1990; Rosenwald & Ochberg 1992; McAdams 1993), as seen in the preceding teacher's narrative. The research presented in this article was devised to investigate via narratives teachers' professional self (or the cluster of attitudes, knowledge, and expertise) (Kelchtermans 1993) with a focus on the development of that professional self.

The narrative or life story connects actions and thoughts that encourage new perspectives and points of view (McEwan & Kieren 1995; Witherell & Noddings 1991) (for example, the preceding teacher's learning that it is the teacher who adjusts himself to herself to the student). The process of remembering life experiences requires an appropriate personal language, which amalgamates thoughts, words, images, and beliefs (Smorti 2007). Smorti's (2007) making-meaning process for interpreting narratives represents a dialogue between mental representations and symbolic and linguistic representations. Autobiographies and life stories confer on events, choices, and personal motivation a shared meaning that is framed into all life experiences (for example, the earlier teacher's perspective before and after beginning to teach). Narratives can be used to interpret and classify one's experience by organizing events according to a logical principle. Furthermore, narratives organize and shape the experiential flow in a harmonic linguistic process (Smorti 2007).

Some researchers (Holstein & Gubrium 2000; Moss, Springer, & Dehr 2008; Philpott 2011; Somers & Gibson 1994) conceive narratives as "ontological narratives," highlighting the fact that narrators give meaning to their experiences with their narrative by attributing a logical structure (e.g., goals, aims, means, successes, and failures) and achieving an understanding of one's self (Lieblich, Tuval-Mashiach, & Zilber, 1998) (e.g., the teacher's understanding of each student's individual perspective as changing her views of what it meant to be a teacher). Therefore, through narratives, individuals raise self-awareness by reflecting on their life path.

Recently, human development fields have used narratives or life stories to help professionals to reflect on and evaluate their personal and professional experiences (e.g., Beauchamp & Thomas, 2009; Bullough, Mortesen Bullough, & Blackwell Mayes 2006; Forrest, Keener, & Harkins 2010; Kelchtermans & Vandenberghe 1994, 1996; Loughran et al. 2004; Soreide 2006).

The development and awareness of a professional identity can be adequately expressed through narrative processes (Clarke 2008; Moss, Springer, & Dehr 2008; Wetherell, Taylor, & Yates 2001) while professional expertise and professional attitudes of teachers develop around stories (Craig 2007; Holstein & Gubrium 2000; Soreide 2006). In those narratives, teachers conceive of themselves as active agents and developers of their own professional experiences (Liu & Xu 2011). They express expectations, aspirations, perceptions, professional codes, opinions, beliefs, and values through narratives (Clandinin & Connelly 1998; Forrest, Keener, & Harkins 2010). A narrative or life story approach may be effective for teachers as these narratives tell the story of their career. In so doing, they are able to frame their everyday experience of being a teacher. This everyday experience is made of personal experiences, beliefs about education, and beliefs about the social and intellectual capacities of children and how all of these interact and change (Moss, Springer, & Dehr 2008).

Being a teacher also means being part of a social environment and of a network of social interactions (students, colleagues, families). Narratives put into words cognitive understanding of a specific and shared social, cultural, and personal context (Amsterdam & Bruner 2000; Bruner 1990, 1996; Hermans & Kempen 1993; Liu & Xu 2011; Polkinghorne 1988; Sarbin 1986). Although the development of professional identities is an individual process, self-representations are rooted in social experiences, in others' expectations (positive or negative) (Bruner 1986, 1990, 1996; Philpott 2011). This multidimensional perspective transforms narratives into a powerful analysis and exploration tool through which teachers' narration becomes an amalgamation of beliefs about education, cultural points of reference, personality traits, as well as internal and external motivations (Clandinin & Connelly 2000; Clandinin et al. 2007; Forrest, Keener, & Harkins 2010; Hollingsworth 1994; Johnson & Golembek 2002).

A NARRATIVE INVESTIGATION OF TEACHERS' PROFESSIONAL SELF

This study was devised to investigate teachers' professional self, defined as a cluster of identity (attitudes, knowledge, and expertise) that is the outcome of cognitive, affective, and actionlike phenomena

(Kelchtermans 1993) via narratives or life stories with a focus on the development and changes of their professional self.

The teachers' professional self, as conceived by Geert Kelchtermans (1993), individuates core characteristics of teachers' professional identity. Kelchtermans identifies two core elements to study professional identity:

1) *Professional self* is articulated both retrospectively and prospectively and is divided into several subcategories: *Descriptive – Self-image, Evaluating – Self-esteem, Will – Motivation, Normative – Performance perception*
2) *Subjective education theory* is expressed by *knowledge* and *beliefs*

According to Kelchtermans, teachers' professional self has to be understood within a multidimensional interpretative framework. The teachers' professional self is located in a cultural and social context, which has been construed through professional experiences. Teachers are continuously involved in an active learning process and in an ongoing redefinition of their self and of their expertise, and these processes are shaped by giving meaning to everyday experience.

Teachers are often challenged in their problem solving abilities and in their affective involvement, and therefore being a teacher implies great personal engagement. Teachers often recall memories of past activities in order to plan and program future activities.

Given the key characteristics of the teaching profession, autobiographical methods that take into account context and culture and capture subjective views and are framed into temporal sequences may be an effective and meaningful tool to investigate teachers' professional identity.

For this research, a semistructured interview that was designed to elicit participants' narratives that were consistent with our research goal to investigate the development of teachers' professional self within a social context was used. We expected that interview content would be different for elementary, secondary, and high school teachers.

Method

Procedure

Teachers completed a one-hour semistructured interview to explore their professional experiences and their implicit personal theories of education. Tape-recorded and transcribed interviews were coded by two independent judges; interrater reliability was calculated (K = .81). Content analysis was performed on the interviews and three macrocategories (self-image, motivations, self-esteem) that represented professional self were identified and two microcategories (behavioral dimensions, metareflective dimensions) representing participants' implicit education theories (see Table 11.1).

Participants

Ninety-six teachers (eleven male and eighty-five female) from Northern Italian schools, ranging from 25 to 60 years old (M = 42.7; *SD* = 7.8) participated. Of the participants 46.9 percent have been working as teachers for less than fifteen years; 26 percent of the participants were primary school teachers, 26.1 percent secondary school teachers, and 47.9 percent high school teachers. High school teachers were subdivided into two groups; 23 percent worked in classical studies high schools and 24.9 percent worked in professional high schools.

Results

Descriptive statistics revealed that teachers' professional profile (see Table 11.2) was defined by the following dimensions:

1. *Self-image*: Teachers narrate their stories through the *vulnerability* dimension, which is elicited when the social context struggles to give them a specific role. Teachers describe their professional behavior (*behavioural dimension*) as being careful

about their communicative style and about their listening skills. When prompted regarding knowledge, they think about their profession (*metareflective dimension*), teachers mostly rely on themselves (*self-reference*), and they use they "teaching style" conceived as knowledge acquired across many years of professional experience.

2. *Motivation*: Teachers define motivation as a personal journey for professional satisfaction (*personal motivation*). Professional growth was the most powerful motivation for continuing a difficult professional routine.

3. *Self-esteem:* Others enter teachers' autobiographies when teachers talk about self-esteem, which is based on negative and positive socially promoted perceptions (*social dimension*).

In summary, the teachers' professional profile that emerged from autobiographies presents strong traits of ambivalence. Teachers perceive themselves as vulnerable and eager for positive feedback if they feel they have performed well. Teachers root their professional profile in a relationship dimension; however, they are mostly self-reliant and they use their past experiences to define their existing professional identity.

Autobiographies were analyzed using the preceding categories. The variable "school level" was controlled in the analysis and a univariate analysis of variance was conducted.

Self-Image. The category "self-image" refers to any potential changes of teachers' self-perceptions that may have occurred in their professional career. The changes may have occurred in relation to the psychological experience of their everyday professional activity and their perception of role identity. Table 11.3 shows mean values by school levels – of the four dimensions that account for how the professional self has evolved.

There was no significant effect of school level on the transformation of self-image.

TABLE 11.1 *Categories representing professional self and implicit education theories*

Professional self: *Self-image*	Implicit education theories: *Behavioral dimension*	Implicit education theories: *Metareflective dimension*	Professional self: *Motivation*	Professional self: *Self-esteem*
Affectivity stands for the perception of a personal and direct involvement with students, greater emotional predisposition, and a careful attention to students' specific developmental needs; narratives present the "affective" predisposition through a greater role flexibility, which is expressed through certain sensitivity for emotional aspects	*Discipline* embodies subject knowledge, an awareness of conceptual and multidisciplinary aspects, learning outcomes, and related assessments	*Theoretical background* refers to textbooks, journals, training courses that contribute to teachers' teaching styles	*Extrinsic motivation* describes situations when the decision of becoming a teacher was based on practical advantages or on contingencies	*Self-efficacy* represents the awareness of being able to organize professional activities to manage different school scenarios. Self-efficacy evokes judgments about personal abilities – reinforced by positive experiences – previous successes, skills, and effective strategies to achieve curriculum goals
Professional profile stands for a better confidence about the teaching role, which embodies both professional expertise and self-awareness as an authority figure	*Communicative dimension* indicates the ability of delivering material effectively by adapting the material to students' abilities and needs and conveying the importance of critical thinking	*Self-reference* expresses the tendency to use internal states (sensitivity, intuition, past experiences) to shape one's teaching style	*Personal motivation* characterizes a professional choice based upon pleasantness/unpleasantness of everyday activities and the possibility for professional growth	*Self-esteem* refers to teachers' self-assessment; it implies a judgment on views of teaching profession, attitudes toward the job, attitudes toward colleagues and students

Role identification concerns a gradual adherence to the professional role in terms of awareness of the meaning and utility of the work; also, it refers to the discovery over time of pleasant aspects of teaching	*Relational dimension* indicates teachers' ability to establish a monitored relationship with their students, one that takes into account peculiarities of school context	*Significant interactions* embeds personal exchanges at school (colleagues, parents, students)	*Relational motivation* refers to relational qualities; in this case, the professional dimension is conceived as a mutual exchange with colleagues, students, and parents Professional gratification is achieved through relationships	*Social dimension* refers to teachers' perception of colleagues' and students' judgements about their professional self Teachers' self-perception depends on positive and negative contextual reactions
Vulnerability refers to changes of social representations of teachers that influenced teachers' self-imag. Narratives express "vulnerability" through accounts of a sense of inadequacy regarding current social expectations, changes of students' needs, and less societal sympathy for teachers	*Personal qualities* refers to dispositions and attitudes that may favor teaching provision	*Institutional characteristics* refers to narrative accounts of institutions, curriculum criteria, deadlines, administration, staff meetings that are part of teachers' everyday activities	*Group motivation* refers to a social commitment which is felt as a mean to promote universal values, changes in the education system and at a societal level	

TABLE 11.2 *Narrative categories and professional profile*

Self image	
Affectivity	1.03
Professional profile	1.06
Role identification	0.85
Vulnerability	**1.43**
Behavioral dimension	
Discipline	0.90
Communicative dimension	**1.25**
Relational dimension	1.08
Personal qualities	0.73
Metareflective dimension	
Theoretical background	1.08
Self-reference	**1.51**
Significant interactions	1.31
Institutional characteristics	1.03
Motivation	
Extrinsic motivation	1.45
Personal motivation	**1.84**
Relational motivation	1.71
Group motivation	0.32
Self-esteem	
Self-efficacy	0.78
Self-esteem	1.21
Social dimension	**1.46**

TABLE 11.3 *Mean values disaggregated by school levels*

	Transformation of self-image		
	Primary school N = 25 Mean	Secondary school N = 25 Mean	High school N = 46 Mean
Affectivity	1.36	1.12	0.80
Professional profile	1.48	1.48	1.74
Role identification	1.00	0.96	0.72
Vulnerability	1.36	1.32	1.52

The first category ("affectivity") represents the perception of a personal and direct involvement with students, a greater emotional predisposition, and a careful attention to students' specific developmental needs. Narratives present the "affective" predisposition through a greater role flexibility, which is expressed through sensitivity to emotional aspects that are connected to the scholastic life. In this study, narratives of primary school teachers were more affective than others. Following are several narrative excerpts of how "affectivity" is being expressed:

- *Before actually beginning the job, I thought teaching would have been easier. I thought that it was more or less about entering a classroom, attempting to explain things to children and going home. And that was about it. I was wrong. It is totally different, because when a teacher enters a classroom he/she has to attune him/herself to each student. Before I started I thought that I would have had to consider the group while I now know that it is important to consider all their different individual issues.*
- *I consider myself to be good at listening. I listen. I listen a lot in my relationships. A person who is able to go beyond an explicit behaviour, which could be the child's reaction to something else. A good teacher should be careful about hidden behaviour triggers and about children's psychological well-being and a bit less attentive about punctuality and pragmatism.*

The category "professional profile" represents greater confidence about the teaching role, which embodies both professional expertise and self-awareness as an authority figure. Narratives display this category through accounts referring to better theoretical knowledge, a better personal view of curriculum development, a more effective communicative style, and a more accurate set of strategies to deal with the class group. All participants were particularly conscientious about this aspect. Following are narrative excerpts concerning the "professional profile."

- *There was a time when I was demotivated because as a young professional I used to mistakenly become overly attached to students. I used to think that students should have always met my expectations. Thus, I was often disappointed either when a rule was not respected or when assignments were not done properly.*
- *I had to search for skills that I didn't have. I first had to develop my personal abilities before students were eventually able to develop their own.*

The category "role identification" concerns a gradual adherence to the professional role in terms of awareness of the meaning and utility of the work. It also refers to the discovery, over time, of pleasant aspects of teaching. In this study, primary school teachers expressed this category more often in their narratives. Following are several narrative excerpts of "role identification."

- *I have changed since my first day. I entered a classroom without any experience and I was not aware of being in front of children. I was thinking to deal with adults and, therefore, I used to communicate with them as if they were adults. I have learned that I need to talk to them in a very simple manner and not to take anything for granted. I try to have in mind that they do not know anything and so everything needs to be explained to them.*
- *Actually there have been many changes and probably nothing is granted and certain in this profession and this is something I have become aware of over the years.*

The category "vulnerability" refers to changes of social representations of teachers that influenced teachers' self-image. Narratives express "vulnerability" through accounts of a sense of inadequacy regarding current social expectations, changes of students' needs, and less societal sympathy for teachers. High school teachers expressed a greater concern for vulnerability. Following are narrative excerpts that express "vulnerability."

TABLE 11.4 *Mean values disaggregated by school levels*

	Behavioral dimension		
	Primary school N = 25 Mean	Secondary school N = 25 Mean	High school N = 46 Mean
Discipline	0.52*	1.56*	0.74*
Communicative dimension	1.08	1.04	1.46
Relational dimension	1.00	0.84	1.26
Personal qualities	0.40	0.96	0.78

***$p < .001$; ** $p < .01$; *$p < .05$

- *If one considers gratification coming from students and colleagues, then those are positive; however if one considers the macro level and all the negative news from the Ministry (and I am not only talking about salary issues) then…. [doesn't finish thought] I think I would be able to have a permanent position in the school system. I am not able to see myself doing any other job; however I am not able to find anything, from what we hear, that would let me believe that I will have a permanent job one day.*
- *I predict an uncertain future, because I am not able to understand what direction the school is taking, in terms of employment opportunities, number of students, possibility of having some autonomy, which does not exist, or perhaps it's my fault and I am not informed enough.*

Behavioral Dimension. This category refers to the necessary resources teachers need to accomplish their duties, and the key abilities for teachers to work at their best. Table 11.4 shows mean values against the four dimensions describing this category and disaggregated by school levels.

"Discipline" embodies subject knowledge, an awareness of conceptual and multidisciplinary aspects, learning outcomes, and related assessments. In this study, three school levels show statistically significant differences ($p < .05$). Secondary school teachers account more often for a disciplinary dimension followed by high school teachers and by primary school teachers. Following are narrative excerpts in which "discipline" is being expressed.

- *I believe that a teacher has to first develop specific subject knowledge and its related competencies.*
- *Teachers need to know much more than what they actually explain in the classroom, because teachers have to learn how to select relevant information and material for their students. Therefore, it is necessary to have a content-based expertise rather than knowledge based on information and news without any self-reflection.*

The "communicative dimension" indicates the ability to deliver material effectively by adapting it to students' abilities and needs and conveying the importance of critical thinking. Primary and secondary teachers had similar views on the communication dimension. High school teachers were more likely to mention this dimension in their narrative than primary and secondary school teachers. A similar picture emerged regarding the "relational dimension." The relational dimension indicates teachers' ability to establish a monitored relationship with their students that takes into account the age of the students. Following are narrative excerpts in which a "relational dimension" is expressed.

- *As for a relational point of view, a good teacher should be capable of establishing some sort of cooperation, but not a highly competitive environment.*
- *A teacher should be able to mediate in the classroom; he/she should be able to encourage collaborative work. A good teacher is a person who hermeneutically draws out the best of each student. All students have value.*

The final dimension is "personal qualities," that is, dispositions and attitudes that may favor the teaching provision. In the sample, secondary school teachers more often provided narrative accounts of this aspect.

TABLE 11.5 *Mean values disaggregated by school level*

	Metareflective dimension		
	Primary school N = 25 Media	Secondary school N = 25 Media	High school N = 46 Media
Theoretical background	0.96	0.80***	1.30***
Self-reference	2.20*	1.00*	1.41*
Significant interactions at school	1.52	1.04	1.35
Institutional characteristics	0.96	0.56**	1.33**

***$p < .001$; **$p < .01$; *$p < .05$

Metareflective Dimension. This category explains the interpretative framework teachers use to plan and implement their curriculum activities. Table 11.5 shows mean values disaggregated by four category dimensions and school levels.

The first category ("theoretical background") refers to textbooks, journals, training courses that contribute to teachers' teaching styles. This study revealed a significant difference ($p < .001$) between high school and other teachers with high school narratives representing more descriptions that fit this category (especially if they are compared with secondary school narratives). Some excerpts are presented in the following:

- *I think that the college really contributed to my development. My teaching style, on one hand, is based on my experience as a student; on the other hand, it is based on my practical experience.*
- *I think that theories are important; however, theory needs to be combined with practical activities. We are not theoretically well prepared, and, I think, this is something we lack. I don't think that practical activities are enough if they are not accompanied with good theoretical bases.*

"Self-reference" expresses the tendency to use internal states (sensitivity, intuition, past experiences) to shape one's teaching style. This aspect is significantly ($p < .05$) more often present in primary school teachers. It is worth noting that secondary school teachers are those who use less self-reference in their curriculum activities. Excerpts that follow provide some example of self-reference:

- *I believe that teachers communicate who they are, some of their values, through their sympathy, listening skills, their ability to consider the contribution of each student.*
- *I do not have particular points of reference. I developed my personal teaching styles. For example, I often use the experience I had when I was on a temporary job… because I was in a big group of teachers and I took from them things I liked.*

The category "significant interactions at school" embeds personal exchanges at school (colleagues, parents, students). In the study, this aspect characterized primary school teachers more than others. Some narrative excerpts provide examples of this category:

- *When I begin to teach in a new curriculum, I count on colleagues who have some seniority and, therefore, several years of experience.*
- *An important aspect of my work regards my colleagues. I learnt how to work in a team and everything is about supporting each other. I would say that the team is a great source of information and support.*

Finally, the category "institutional characteristics" refers to narrative accounts of institutions, curriculum criteria, deadlines, administration, staff meetings that are part of teachers' everyday activities. This aspect is significantly present in high school teachers ($p < .01$), especially compared to secondary school teachers.

Motivation. This category refers to narrative accounts of teachers' motivation. Table 11.6 shows mean values disaggregated by four dimensions of this category distributed by school levels.

The category "extrinsic motivation" describes situations when the decision of becoming a teacher was based on practical advantages or

TABLE 11.6 *Mean values as a function of education level*

	Motivation		
	Primary school N = 25 Mean	Secondary school N = 25 Mean	High school N = 46 Mean
Extrinsic motivation	0.96***	1.32	1.78***
Personal motivation	1.48*	1.12*	2.43*
Relational motivation	1.56	1.24	2.04
Group motivation	0.48	0.28	0.26

***p < .001; **p < .01; *p < .05

on contingencies (for instance, the desire for having a part of the year work-free, financial security). More specifically, high school teachers (especially if they are compared with primary school teachers) more often identify this motivation in their narratives (p < .001). Narrative excerpts highlight how teachers use this type of motivation:

- *I was not aware of whether I would have been good at teaching. Perhaps I initially chose this profession because I was lazy.*
- *At the beginning there was a financial reason, which is silly, but I was not living in a university town and I wanted to stay there.*
- *Teaching allows you to provide educational training and offers a three-month holiday: therefore, there is a long period to recharge one's batteries.*

"Personal motivation" dimensions characterize a professional choice based upon pleasantness/unpleasantness of everyday activities and the possibility for professional growth. Narrative analyses show a significant use of this motivation among high school teachers (p < .05) and primary school teachers. Narrative excerpts that follow represent how teachers use this type of motivation:

- *I became a teacher because I really like this job. I like doing it, I like the preparation involved, I like to think about something different, and this makes me feel more alive.*

- *My professional choice was aimed at finding something I liked: here I am; I found a job involving children (I like children) and teaching (I like teaching).*

"Relational motivation " refers to relational qualities. In this case, the professional dimension is conceived as a mutual exchange with colleagues, students, and parents. Professional gratification is achieved through relationships. This motivation was significantly more present in high school teachers. Finally, the last category ("group motivation") refers to a social commitment that is felt as a means to promote universal values, changes in the education system and at a societal level. The following narrative excerpts represent how teachers use this type of motivation:

- *Being a teacher means to feel a certain omnipotence to change the world, to have the possibility to follow everyone and everything, to provide better life conditions to all children.... Certainly, I have learned from experience to evaluate the limits of my actions and that others have their own identity and they are not my creation.*
- *I like children very much; I think that children are our future; it is not rhetorical, and I think that children could save us... in a sense that if we succeed in passing positive values on to them ... then the world can change.*

Self-esteem. This category is related to their overall self-esteem and their professional self-esteem. Table 11.7 shows mean values for the three category dimensions by school level.

The first category (self-efficacy) represents the awareness of being able to organize professional activities to manage different school scenarios. "Self-efficacy" evokes judgments about personal abilities, reinforced by positive experiences such as previous successes, skills acquired, and effective strategies that were used to achieve curriculum goals. This category was described by references to titles, professional development, and student achievements. In this study, primary school

TABLE 11.7 *Mean values disaggregated by education level*

	Self-esteem		
	Primary school $N = 25$ Mean	Secondary school $N = 25$ Mean	High school $N = 46$ Mean
Self-efficacy	0.80	0.64	0.85
Self-esteem	1.40	1.40	1.00
Social dimension	0.96***	1.20	1.87***

***$p < .001$; **$p < .01$; *$p < .05$

teachers used this category the most. Narrative excerpts that follow are representative of self-efficacy:

- *Probably I realized that I made the right choice because I was able to establish a relationship with children, with the class.*
- *I believe I am a good teacher because I am able to have a relationship with students: I am able to manage my knowledge and to deliver a lecture.*

The second category ("self-esteem") refers to teachers' self-assessment. It implies a judgment on views of the teaching profession, attitudes toward the job, attitudes toward colleagues and students. Narratives highlight statements of cultural values (work commitment, sympathy, etc.) and statements of overall self-satisfaction as teachers. Primary school and secondary school teachers presented this category more than high school teachers in their narratives. Narrative excerpts that follow are representative of self-esteem:

- *I try to do my best when I work; I am not afraid of children; therefore I think I do my best to work well.*
- *I think I am patient. And I like children anyway; I know how to approach them.... Those qualities make me continue to do this job.*
- *I am an extroverted person, I like socializing, and I like spending time with children: I think those are a teacher's best qualities.*

Finally, the category "social dimension" refers to teachers' perception of colleagues' and students' judgments about their professional self. Teachers' self-perception depends on positive and negative contextual reactions. High school teachers are more careful ($p < .001$) than other teachers (especially primary school teachers). The excerpts that follow are representative of the social dimension.

- *As I still see many of my previous students... many are happy to see me; therefore I think, "What I did was not in a vacuum."*
- *I really care about my popularity among students regarding school activities.*
- *My self-image depends on my students' perception of me.*

DISCUSSION AND CONCLUSION

The concept of professional identity may be defined as a representational cluster of theories, attitudes, and beliefs about the self and professional activities (McCormick & Pressley 1997). In education, the professional identity is characterized by relational traits that are connected to the self and subjective characteristics that each individual believes he or she has (Beijaard, Meijer, & Verloop 2004; Clandinin et al. 2007; Knowles 1992; Nias 1989). Those aspects influence the way teachers perform their activities, their teaching style, and their attitudes with regard to institutional and social changes (Beijaard et al. 2004; Liu & Xu 2011).

Narrative accounts showed differences in teachers' professional stories (Clandinin et al. 2007). Differences regarded expectations; opinions about how a good teacher should be influence contextual and personal experiences of everyday activities. More specifically, the study presented here highlighted different teachers' profiles according to school levels.

Although the institutional context may be the same, all the actors involved understand and use narrative resources differently and develop their professional identity according to different situations (Davies & Harrè 2001; Holstein & Gubrium 2000). In accordance with the literature (Beijaard, Verloop, & Vermunt 2000; Forrest, Keener, & Harkins 2010), results showed that self-perception might influence self-efficacy, professional development, and abilities to face societal and school changes.

Primary school teachers (N = 25) seem to use a pedagogical approach (Beijaard 1995) in which relational aspects are more important than curriculum activities (Beijaard & De Vries 1997). They have a deep emotional involvement with their students, and they believe that emotional availability is the crucial element in the teacher-student relationship. Furthermore, primary school teachers are focused on students' psychological well-being and their good development (Soreide 2006). They find inside themselves their motivations and drive to overcome everyday difficulties. Primary school teachers have become gradually more aware of their social role, and they consider their profession as a mission. For this reason, they use their internal states as a point of reference (sensitiveness, intuition, past experiences), and their assertiveness encourages them to achieve professional goals. They are also very open to all other actors involved in the education system (colleagues, students, parents) and they consider their profession as a chance for personal growth.

Secondary school teachers (N = 25) are concerned with disciplinary actions and multidisciplinary activities involved in the learning process. Professional activities are focused upon personal qualities, attitudes that may support curriculum activities and encourage self-esteem. Curriculum and disciplinary aspects are the most important framework to orientate their profession and their sense of security (Goodson & Cole 1994).

High school teachers (N = 46) develop their professional identity around their curriculum and subject competencies, around their communication skills and their theoretical knowledge. Institutional aspects are crucial for their work, and teacher-student relationships are approached with a psychoeducational view. In this frame, teachers are self-aware of being authority figures and a point of reference for their students. High school teachers find their motivation in external events related to practical activities or to contingencies. They also find their motivation in internal states (cultural and personal). Furthermore, they perceive themselves as not so prepared to face new societal and student expectations; they also feel that their role is not recognized by the society.

In conclusion, teachers' professional identity is developed around different factors and multifaceted knowledge (Antonek, McCormick, & Donato 1997; Beauchamp & Thomas 2009; Clandinin et al. 2007; Cooper & Olson 1996; Knowles 1992). Interpretative processes of their experience favor a dynamic understanding of their identity (Beijaard et al. 2004; Day 1999; Forrest, Keener, & Harkins 2010; Kerby 1991). The ability to lead the classroom is another crucial aspect in defining teachers' representation of their pedagogical approach and of their relational style with students (Coldron & Smith 1999). Professional identity cannot, therefore, be defined as a static and stable construct over time. Professional identity varies across time, culture, and social context, and it can be defined as a process through which teachers learn strategies and methodologies to teach effectively (Clarke 2008). Teachers use a style that is attuned to their way of being and are actively involved in shaping their role in the school system and their professional self.

REFERENCES

Amsterdam, A., & Bruner, J. (2000). *Minding the law*. Cambridge, MA: Harvard University Press.

Antonek, J., McCormick, D., & Donato, R. (1997). The student teacher portfolio as autobiography: Developing a professional identity. *Modern Language Journal*, 81(1), 15–27.

Beauchamp, C., & Thomas, L. (2009). Understanding teacher identity: An overview of issues in the literature and implication for teacher education. *Cambridge Journal of Education*, 39(2), 175–189.

Beijaard, D. (1995). Teachers' prior experiences and actual perceptions of professional identity. *Teachers and Teaching: Theory and Practice*, 1, 281–294.

Beijaard, D., & De Vries, Y. (1997). Building expertise: A process perspective on the development or change of teachers' beliefs. *European Journal of Teachers Education*, 20, 243–255.

Beijaard, D., Meijer, P. C. & Verloop, N. (2004). Reconsidering research on teachers' professional identity. *Teaching and Teacher Education*, 20, 107–128.

Beijaard, D., Verloop, N., & Vermunt, J. (2000). Teachers' perceptions of professional identity: An exploratory study from a personal knowledge perspective. *Teaching and Teacher Education*, 16, 749–764.

Bruner, J. (1986). *Actual minds, possible words*. Cambridge, MA: Harvard University Press.

(1990). *Acts of meaning*. Cambridge, MA: Harvard University Press.

(1996). *The culture of education*. Cambridge, MA: Harvard University Press.

Bullough, R., Mortesen Bullough, D., & Blackwell Mayes, P. (2006). Getting in touch: Dreaming, the emotions and the work of teaching. *Teachers and Teaching: Theory and Practice*, 12(2), 193–208.

Clandinin, D., & Connelly, F. (1998). Stories to live by: Narrative understandings of school reform, *Curriculum Inquiry*, 28, 149–164.

(2000). *Narrative inquiry: Experience and story in qualitative research*. San Francisco: Jossey Bass.

Clandinin, D., Huber, J., Murphy, M., Murray Oarr, A., Pearce, M., & Steeves, P. (2007). *Composing diverse identities: Narrative inquires into interwoven lives of children and teachers*. New York: Routledge.

Clarke, M. (2008). *Language teacher identities: Co-constructing discourse and community*. Clevedon, UK: Multilingual Matter.

Coldron, J., & Smith, R. (1999). Active location in teachers' construction of their professional identities. *Journal of Curriculum Studies*, 31(6), 711–726.

Cooper, K., & Olson, M. (1996). The multiple "I's" of teacher identity. In M. Kompf, W. Bond, D. Dworet & R. Boak (Eds.) *Changing research and practice: Teachers' professionalism, identities and knowledge* (pp. 78–89). Washington, DC: Falmer Press.

Craig, C. (2007). Story constellations: A narrative approach to contextualizing teachers' knowledge of school reform. *Teaching and Teacher Education*, 23(2), 173–188.

Davies, B, & Harrè, R. (2001). Positioning: The discursive production of selves. In M. Wetherell, S. Taylor & S. Yates (Eds) *Discourse theory and practice*. London: Sage.

Day, C. (1999). *Developing teachers, the challenge of lifelong learning*. London: Falmer Press.

Forrest, M., Keener, T., & Harkins, M. (2010). Understanding narrative relation in teacher education. *Asia-Pacific Journal of Teacher Education*, 38(2), 87–101.

Goodson, I., & Cole, A. (1994). Exploring the teacher's professional knowledge: Constructing identity and community. *Teacher Education Quarterly*, 21(1), 85–105.

Hermans, H., & Kempen, H. (1993). *The dialogical Self: Meaning as movement*. San Diego, CA: Academic Press.

Hollingsworth, S. (1994). *Teacher research and urban literacy education*. New York: Teacher College Press.

Holstein, J., & Gubrium, J. (2000). *The self we live by: Narrative identity in a postmodern world*. New York: Oxford University Press.

Johnson, K., & Golembek, P. (2002). Teachers' *narrative inquiry as professional development*. New York: Cambridge University Press.

Kelchtermans, G. (1993). Biographical methods in the study of teachers' professional development. In I. Carlgren, G. Handal & S. Vaage (Eds.) *Teachers' minds and actions: Research on teachers' thinking and practice* (pp. 93–108). London: Falmer Press.

Kelchtermans, G. (1996). Teacher vulnerability: Understanding its moral and political roots. *Cambridge Journal of Education*, 26(3), 307–330.

Kelchtermans, G., & Vandenberghe, R. (1994). Teachers' professional development: A biographical perspective. *Journal of Curriculum Studies*, 26(1), 45–62.

Kerby, A. (1991). *Narrative and the self*. Bloomington: Indiana University Press.

Knowles, G. (1992). Models for understanding pre-service and beginning teachers' biographies: Illustrations from case studies. In I. Goodson (Ed.) *Studying teachers' lives* (pp. 99–152). London: Routledge.

Lieblich, A., Tuval-Mashiach, R., & Zilber, T. (1998). *Narrative research: Reading, analysis and interpretation*. London: Sage.

Liu, Y., & Xu, Y. (2011). Inclusion or exclusion? A narrative inquiry of a language teacher's identity experience in the "new work order" of competing pedagogies. *Teaching and Teacher Education*, 27(3), 589–597.

Loughran, J., Hamilton, M., LaBoskey, V., & Russell, T. (2004). *International handbook of self-study of teaching and teacher education practices*. Dordrecht, Nederlands: Kluwer Academic.

McAdams, D. (1993). *The stories we live by: Personal myths and the making of the self*. New York: Morrow.

McCormick, C., & Pressley, M. (1997). *Educational psychology: Learning, instruction, assessment.* New York: Longman.

McEwan, H., & Kieren, E. (1995). Introduction. In H. McEwan & K. Egan (Eds.) *Narrative in teaching, learning, and research.* New York: Teachers College Press.

Moss, G., Springer, T., & Dehr, K. (2008). Guided reflection protocol as narrative inquiry and teacher professional development. *Reflective Practice,* 9(4), 497–508.

Nias, J. (1989). Teaching and the self. In M. Holly & C. McLoughlin (Eds.) *Perspective on teacher professional development* (pp. 151–171). London: Falmer Press.

Philpott, C. (2011). Narrative as a cultural tool for experiential learning in initial teacher education. *Storytelling, Self, Society,* 7(1), 15–35.

Polkinghorne, D. (1988). *Narrative knowing and the human science.* New York: University of New York Press.

Rosenwald, G., & Ochberg, R. (1992). *Storied lives.* New Haven, CT: Yale University Press.

Sarbin, T. (1986). *Narrative psychology.* New York: Praeger.

Smorti, A. (2007). *Narrazioni: Cultura, memorie, formazione del Sè.* Firenze: Giunti.

Somers, M., & Gibson, G. (1994). Reclaiming the epistemological: Narrative and the social construction of identity. In C. Calhoun (Ed.) *Social theory and the politics of identity.* Oxford: Blackwell.

Soreide, G. (2006). Narrative construction of teacher identity: Positioning and negotiation. *Teachers and Teaching: Theory and Practice,* 12(5), 527–547.

Wetherell, M., Taylor, S., & Yates, S. (2001). *Discourse theory and practice.* London: Routledge.

Witherell, C., & Noddings, N. (1991). Prologue: An invitation to our readers. In C. Witherell & N. Noddings (Eds.) *Stories lives tell: Narrative and dialogue in education* (pp. 1–12). New York: Teachers College Press.

12

Commentary: Exploring Symbolic Spaces: Writing, Narrative, and Art

JENS BROCKMEIER AND BRUCE D. HOMER

Whereas animals are determined by their nature, human beings transcend their organismic limits and create boundless universes of symbolic meanings. This idea runs through the Western history of thought from Aristotle to modern philosophical, psychological, and anthropological theories of humans' cultural nature." Humans are symbolic animals, as Ernst Cassirer (1944) put it in his *Essay on Man*. Cassirer argued that "in the human world we find a new characteristic which appears to be the distinctive mark of human life. ... Man has, as it were, discovered a new method of adapting himself to his environment" (1944, p. 24). In addition to the biological systems of exchange by which animal species are adapted to their environment, Cassirer saw a further, specific human link that he called the "symbolic system." Taking an evolutionary stance, he explained how this system has transformed the whole of human life: "As compared with the other animals Man lives not merely in a broader reality, he lives, so to speak, in a new dimension of reality. ... No longer in a merely physical universe, [he] lives in a symbolic universe" (1944, pp. 24–25). The ecological niche of humans' cultural existence is not a space of perception and response but a space of symbolic construction.

As has often been pointed out, language is the hub of humans' symbolic constructions. Yet besides language, Cassirer was interested in art, myth, religion, ritual, and other cultural practices of imagination that he conceived of as interacting in manifold ways. "They are," he wrote, "the varied threads which weave the symbolic net, the tangled web of human experience. All human progress in thought and experience refines upon and strengthens this net" (Cassirer 1944, p. 25). As a consequence, humans do not live in a world of immediate material reality but in a self-created universe of meanings, a symbolic space. As we have enveloped ourselves, in Cassirer's view, in linguistic forms, scientific concepts, mathematical abstractions, artistic images, mythical narratives, and religious rites, we cannot see or hear anything except what is part of this symbolic space.

Cassirer's conceptualization of this space elaborates ideas familiar with both the European Enlightenment (Verene 2011) and pragmatist symbol theorists from North America like Charles S. Peirce and Nelson Goodman. Goodman, in particular, emphasized both the constructive nature of human world making and the plural structures that shape our symbolic worlds, as he outlined in his books *Ways of Worldmaking* (1978) and *Languages of Art* (1968). Art and art phenomena have always played a crucial role in this kind of thinking about human symbol and sign systems, which can be traced back in an even longer tradition, a tradition that has often crossed and blurred the line between theoretical and artistic languages (Brockmeier 1999). Cassirer himself was especially influenced by the art historian and cultural theorist Aby Warburg. Founder of the Library for Cultural Studies in Hamburg in the 1920s – a library that carried out this interdisciplinary "symbolic approach" – Warburg was one of the pioneers of a cultural approach to cognitive, affective, and aesthetic phenomena that in today's language could be called multimedia, multimodal, and multisemiotic. To Warburg, images, objects, and rituals were important practices of intellectual and cultural representation equal to language; he saw them as forms of writing realizing similar comparable functions.

This line of thought also reverberates in Vygotsky's early study, *Psychology of Art* (1971) and – building on Vygotsky and the cultural-historical school of psychology – in the project of a *Cultural Psychology* as outlined by Jerome Bruner (1990), Michael Cole (1996), and others. As Bruner states in his contribution to this volume, psychology studying humans' potential of symbolic meaning making must go beyond rigidly conceived disciplinary borderlines, drawing, among others, on "the part-literary, part anthropological, part-historical study of everyday ways of classifying the events we must live with" (p. 9). As already indicated, language and, by extension, narrative play a pivotal role in this project, and it is not least for this reason that narrative psychology has often been viewed as crucial in exploring not only stories and other forms of linguistic discourse, but also the more comprehensive way narrative practices bind the individual into a cultural world while binding the meaning of this world into the individual's mind (Brockmeier 2012).

It is again Bruner, one of the protagonists of a culturally oriented narrative psychology, who reminds us not only of the necessity and scope, but also of the limitations of this perspective. There is, he maintains in his chapter in this volume, a dynamic pervading the symbolic universe of our existence that goes far beyond the linguistic dimension. The human condition, on this view, is defined by a more general dialectics. On the one hand, we are shaped by our biological nature as a species living under particular physical conditions in a particular physical environment; on the other, we are shaped by the "symbolically rich cultures that we humans construct and in terms of which we live our lives communally." While we as a species are limited biologically in our human condition, we are at the same time "liberated from that condition by our striking capacity to go beyond it," imagining and symbolically creating "'possible worlds' that transcend that condition." Following Bruner, we thus have to conceive of the symbolic spaces we inhabit as dynamic constructions, constantly moved by the tension between our attachment to the Established and our search for the Possible.

Against the backdrop of these thoughts, we suggest understanding the ideas and results presented in the chapters of this book that form its second part, Narratives, as inquiries into different symbolic or semiotic systems that are part of the cultural environment of human mind and life. The symbolic spaces primarily investigated range from linguistic ones such as writing, literacy, and narrative to pictorial representations and the experience of art. As far as language is concerned, the particular aspects under examination have become the focus of academic attention only recently; we are talking about a time frame of a few decades, while other dimensions of language have been investigated for centuries. What is more, the aspects at stake have only recently been identified as "epistemic subjects" at all, as phenomena that are taken to exist on their own and to be worth systematic examination.

One is *literacy*. Literacy's historical rise and its psychological impact on and through the social institution of schooling are explored by David R. Olson. The question Olson raises is why, precisely, literacy and schooling matter to persons and to societies. His answer is that writing, as a social practice, linguistic form, and symbolic space, is a primary site for creating an awareness of important symbolic qualities and structural properties of language, both written and spoken. As individuals and as civilization, we have only become conscious of these qualities and properties because we have learned to write and to read: that is, because we have learned to live in the symbolic space of literacy.

A second, closely related aspect of language and of literacy is examined by Pietro Boscolo. Boscolo examines how *writing* is linked to knowing and how a new type of writing – academic writing – presumes and creates not just new knowledge but a new kind of knowing. Studying how university students of psychology learn to write a dissertation, he found that mastering this format of academic literacy requires students to learn a hitherto unknown genre, a new mode of writing and thinking. Yet learning a new genre implies not only acquiring new knowledge and skills, but also modifying beliefs about language and writing previously acquired during high school, which often conflict with the new symbolic space the university students are about to capture. All this goes beyond a narrow, technical understanding of writing that Boscolo calls "transmissional" because it assumes that writing transmits information through a text from the writer to the reader. Instead it demands and fosters the emergence of a novel ("transactional") way of thinking about language and its complexities. This occurs in tandem with a novel kind of motivation and a novel approach to social relatedness, especially in and through texts ("intertexuality"). It even involves the idea of a new identity of the student as a writer, as someone who is expected to pose him/herself as an author.

Another subject that figures prominently within the horizon of human symbol systems but was long neglected in psychology, education, and other social sciences is *narrative.* Analyzing the stories teachers tell about their "professional selves," Emanuela Confalonieri and Sarah Miragoli claim that these self-defining narratives are essential in shaping professional identities, and not only professional ones. They put together "clusters" of experiences, knowledge, and values; they navigate professional codes, aspirations, and beliefs; and they provide a personal genre, although drawing on cultural models. Unlike the academic genre Boscolo deals with, this personal or individual genre offers a space for reflecting on fundamental issues of one's life, raising a sense of self, self-awareness, and in fact chosen and created identity.

Finally, Federica Savazzi, Gabriella Gilli, Simona Ruggi broaden this spectrum of symbolic possible worlds by drawing our attention to the symbolic space of the "art phenomenon." Within this space, they maintain, particular art forms such as pictorial or sculptural are meaning-constituted enterprises that create and convey their meanings according to specific notation systems. As members of cultural communities, we learn to read these notation or meaning systems as forms of writing established and codified in diverse traditions. In this way, art has become "one of the most powerful media that enables people to communicate features internal to the mind, such as intentions and emotions. Indeed, it is conceived as a set of symbolic cultural devices" (or "cultural tools"), namely, as "inter-mental realities, that promote an 'encounter of minds.'"

Joining perspectives from the history of art, aesthetics, and psychological areas such research on emotion, Theory of Mind, and neurocognition, we learn of various approaches to aesthetic experience. More precisely, the focus is on the importance of experiencing pictorial artworks. Ultimately, the authors settle on the view common within cognitive sciences and psychology of art that aesthetic experience results from a peculiar weaving of cognitive, emotional, and intersubjective processes that determine how an artifact is perceived and interpreted. What is crucial in defining aesthetic experience, they propose, is that it is a symbolically mediated *emotional* response to art, a way to connect in which empathy is essential. In this way they contribute to, and at the same time keep open, the conversation about what counts as art. This conversation is never conclusive because – as we may add, turning again to Bruner's point – it, too, is subject to the ongoing dialectic between the Established and the Possible.

If we look at the spectrum of different symbol systems explored in these studies through the lens of Bruner we notice many features of these symbolic spaces that are indeed shaped by the tension between the culturally Established and the Possible. We can read them as case studies into different symbolic spaces in which established practices, genres, and experiences of symbolic activity are used and extended; in which the historical introduction of schooling and literacy, the learning of a new genre of writing, the telling of identity narratives, and the emotional experience of pictorial artworks allow people – individuals and entire societies – to extend the horizon of their particular symbolic universes, opening them to new, if perhaps minute, possibilities. This is one common characteristic. A second one comes into sight if we consider that all symbolic systems at stake are self-reflective. They are capable of referring to themselves, generating in this way an awareness or even consciousness of their own as forms of symbolic and semiotic mediation. More than this, it seems that this metasymbolic awareness plays a major role in the actual process of mediation, to such a degree as to be part of the very nature of symbolic or semiotic mediation.

This phenomenon has been studied in different contexts and under different names. Psychologists and linguists commonly discuss it in terms of metaconcepts such as metalinguistics and metacognition, as does David R. Olson in his chapter. Such "meta" concepts turn the symbolic structures into structures that may be referred to, used more consciously, and thought about. It is this reflexive process, Olson points out, that makes implicit knowledge, including knowledge about the symbolic process, explicit. The "going meta" of symbol systems is a theme in all chapters in this part of the book. Olson has even made the transformation of the implicit into the explicit the central point of his treatment of literacy – which he describes not only as a linguistic or psychological technology but also as embedded in social and societal institutions, first of all, of course, in schools.

It is important to keep in mind that explicit metalinguistic awareness is not the same as the awareness that the use of language inherently implies and needs. Surely we must know the grammatical rules of a language to speak it properly. But this knowledge does not necessarily presume or entail an awareness that also reflects the consciousness of language itself as a particular symbolic medium and practice. Olson's argument is that learning to read and write is not merely the acquisition of a set of skills but also a (metalinguistic) learning about language as an example of a general quality of symbolic systems. On this view, metalinguistic explicitness – the conscious knowledge accessible to the speaker or writer of the rules of language that provides a norm or standard against which any oral performance may be judged – is perhaps the most import result of literacy. "If grammar," Olson writes in his chapter, "is an explicit theory of the language, it may be argued that writing is the primary tool in the invention and, subsequently, the teaching of that grammar. On this view, writing is a primary means for creating an awareness of the important implicit properties of language." And this is not all. Literacy is not only key in developing consciousness of language and (self-reflective) consciousness of mind, it also plays a role in the explicitness of arguments, the uses of evidence, and the forms of discourse appropriate to such specialized institutions as law, science, economy, and literature.

Now to make the same point in the more comprehensive context of symbolic systems is to suggest that symbolic practices are essentially metarepresentational activities that bring aspects of the symbolic system into consciousness. We think that all chapters give support to this more generalized version of metacognition and metalinguistic awareness insofar as this mode of self-reflexivity applies not only to linguistic phenomena like writing and narrative but also to the symbolic phenomena of artistic and, especially, pictorial representation.

To explain this assumption in the context of what might be called a metasymbolic view we want to turn to a developmental perspective. In taking a look at the early development of oral and written language, we explain in some detail how children come to acquire metalinguistic awareness – as one form of metasymbolic awareness.

One of the most influential pioneers of the developmental study of the symbolic function was Jean Piaget. Piaget (1954) argued that small children first understand the world solely through their sensor-motor schemata, which define, and are defined by, what they can perceive and what they can do. True representational thought does not emerge until eighteen to twenty-four months, when children begin to use what Piaget considered the first real symbols to represent the world. This transition is marked by the advent of object permanence, that is, the understanding that an object continues to exist even after it can no longer be perceived. In Piaget's view, the point of the symbolic function is that the child learns that the absent object can be represented by a symbol.

A number of later studies, however, challenged the notion that young infants lack object permanence (e.g., Baillargeon 1993). And although there is some debate about the exact nature of infants' symbolic capabilities, today there is compelling evidence that rudimentary representational and symbolic abilities are already present much earlier, in fact from early on in life. By virtue of being immersed in the symbolic world of their culture, even very young children's representational capabilities are shaped by the dialectic between the culturally Established and the Possible, as well as by the metasymbolic nature of their culture's symbolic systems (Reddy 2008).

Children's symbolic abilities are intertwined with language well before they begin to speak themselves. Adults use language in the daily activities of toddlers to guide actions and highlight important aspects of their experiences. As children begin to acquire their first words, language is understood in relation to specific social experiences (Bruner 1983; Tomasello 2008). Young children fit word meanings to their existing preverbal concepts, which are derived from their manifold participatory interactions with adults (Nelson 2005). Gradually, these interactions (in which adults always use language) shape children's preverbal concepts to create more culturally uniform linguistic concepts. For Nelson (1996; 2005), this is one of the ways in which adults pass on the culturally Established through the symbolic space of language to children. At the same time, adults help them to enter the realm of the Possible. As children's linguistic and symbolic abilities increase, they learn to use words to refer mentally to and manipulate symbolic representations of objects or concepts. Vygotsky (1986), Piaget's great colleague and antipode, called this the social development of "inner speech," a process that even more opens up the symbolic space of the Possible.

There is considerable evidence that language mediates young children's symbolic activities in a variety of domains. For example, Tomasello, Striano, and Rochat (1999) found that children aged eighteen to thirty-six months engage in significantly more acts of symbolic play if an adult uses language while modeling symbolic play (e.g., saying, "Vroom! I'm driving my car!" while pushing a square block) than if only the action is modeled. Callaghan (2000) found that 2.5- to 3-year-olds' symbolic understanding of pictures was mediated by the degree to which language could be used by the children to represent the object in the picture. In both cases, researchers noted a marked increase in symbolic capabilities around age three.

During the third year of life children's symbolic capabilities flourish, and so does – we argue – their metasymbolic awareness, their knowledge (or at least sense) of the potentials of the symbolic system they use. DeLoache (2002) has explored the development of symbolic capacities in young children this age with her model task. In this task, children are shown a model of a room and shown that it corresponds to an adjacent actual room. A small toy (e.g., "Little Mickey") is hidden in the model, and children are told that a corresponding big toy (e.g., "Big Mickey") is hiding in the equivalent spot in the room. The children are then asked "to find big Mickey" on the basis of symbolic information they have acquired from the model. In numerous studies, DeLoache and her colleagues (e.g., DeLoache 1995, 2002) have found that it is not until around age three that children are able to understand the symbolic nature of the model. Further investigating the development of symbolic and metasymbolic understanding implied in this task, Homer and his colleagues have examined the role of language in children's performance on the model task (Homer & Nelson 2009; Homer, Petroff, & Hayward, 2012). They found that for young children, symbolic competencies in the DeLoache model task are mediated by language: Children's performance on the model task is improved when the use of language is supported (e.g., by prompting children to name hiding spots in the model before searching the room), and made worse when children's ability to use language is impaired (e.g., by using objects for which children cannot form unique verbal labels).

The use of narrative is another way in which language mediates children's development, widening their access to symbolic worlds. The stories we tell to and with children as well as the stories children tell on their own – be they realistic, fictional, anticipating future events, or involving past experiences – not only shape the way in which children experience and navigate the cultural worlds in which they live, but introduce them to imaginary worlds, to scenarios of fantasy and fiction, "to worlds, they never knew," as Nelson (2007, p. 177) characterize it. In Nelson's account of the specific symbolic quality of narrative one important aspect of stories is that they introduce characters in imaginary situations "children seem to have little problem relating to, even in the most fantastic animal stories" (2007, p. 177). What is more, narrative plays a crucial role in leading children into a new experiential space, a social space Nelson calls a "community of minds" (2007, p. 212). Since narrative practices always involve imagining the minds of others – whether the minds of storytellers, the minds of the addressees of one's own storytelling, or the minds of the protagonists and characters within the story worlds – they open the way to a community not just of minds but of *different* minds. That is, they allow the child symbolically to encounter and engage with others and other minds, in fact with entire "cultural knowledge systems" (Nelson 2007, p. 212) or, in Cassirer's words, with different "symbolic worlds" that go far beyond the personal range and lead into Bruner's "possible worlds." In her explanation of narrative as the developmental hub of children's symbolic activities, Nelson therefore suggests a broad notion of narrative practices in the preschool years that comprise cultural narratives such as children's stories, myths, folktales, fables, and gossip, as well as symbolic play and games: "All contribute to narrative consciousness and thus to being a member of the community of minds where these practices originate" (2007, p. 212).

Further effects of the dialectic between the culturally Established and the Possible, as well as the metasymbolic nature of language, are evident in studies that have more specifically examined the effects of narrative on children's development. For example, variations in the ways in which mothers reminisce with their young children have been linked to subsequent differences in the ways in which children recall their own prior experiences. Fivush (2008) found that mothers who extensively elaborate their memories with their children also provide more details on emotional and psychological aspects of past events than less communicative and elaborative mothers; as a consequence, children of "elaborative mothers" develop greater autobiographical narrative skills. There are also cultural variations in reminiscing styles, with European and American mothers tending to elaborate more overall and focus more on the emotional aspects of past events, whereas Asian mothers tend to focus more on societal rules, morals, and family settings (Wang 2001; Leichtman, Wang, and Pillemer 2003). These differences are reflected in the autobiographical narratives of children, which are similar across cultures in young children but show significant differences related to maternal reminiscing style by the end of the preschool years (Han, Leichtman, & Wang 1998; Wang 2003).

Symbolic and metasymbolic mediation is not limited to spoken language – written language has similar effects. Writing systems are by their very nature metarepresentational: To learn to read and write is to come to understand how one's culture represents spoken language in script (Olson 1994). To do so requires a deliberate analysis of oral language. This idea was expressed by Vygotsky (1986), who claimed that in learning to read and write, children must "take cognizance" of the structure of spoken language. However, as Olson (1994) has pointed out, not all aspects of spoken language are captured in written language, and therefore, in learning to read and write, children are becoming explicitly aware of those implicit structures of language that are represented in writing. In other words, children become aware of the aspects of speech that are codified by their culture's script.

A number of studies also have linked children's acquisition of literacy to the development of various aspects of metalinguistic awareness (see Homer 2009). For example, children's ability to identify words in spoken language is predicted by their awareness of words as a unit of text (Homer & Olson 1999). There is also evidence that exposure to letters and knowledge of letter names and sounds facilitate children's development of phonological awareness (Blaiklock 2004; Foy & Mann 2006) – which is one additional component contributing to children's development of metalinguistic awareness, that is, the metasymbolic knowledge of the symbolic nature or language.

Although we have only mentioned a few aspects of the development of children's symbolic and representational capabilities, primarily highlighting linguistic practices and forms of metalinguistic awareness, they may suffice to illustrate what we have called the metasymbolic view. From this metasymbolic point of view, we have read the chapters of this part of the book as case studies of different symbolic spaces, spaces in which a variety of practices and cultural formats of symbolic activity are used and in which they can be further explored. These case studies offer insights into a spectrum of symbolic worlds that we also have understood as "possible worlds," as worlds of human imagination that allow us to extend the cultural Possible. The spectrum of our symbolic worlds has ranged from schooling and literacy, and institutions that have specific genres and practices of writing and identity narratives, to the emotional experience of pictorial artworks. Our metasymbolic reading has been based on the assumption that all these different symbolic systems are self-reflective; this implies that they need and generate self-reflective abilities and practices. Such "meta" abilities and practices make the implicit explicit, and this includes the implicit knowledge of the symbolic function, as we have pointed out in our review of some essential moments in children's linguistic and metalinguistic development.

Besides the focus on the inherent dynamic of "going meta" of the human symbol function, we believe that the variety and diversity of symbol systems addressed in the chapters of this part of the book, as well as in our comments, move to the fore one more essential aspect of Cassirer's notion of humans as symbolic animals. In one of his earlier works, *Philosophy of Symbolic Forms* (1923–1929), Cassirer pointed out another quality of what he saw as humans' species-specific symbolic competence: We use not just symbols but a broad spectrum of *different* symbols, or, more precisely, symbolic systems. While the use of language arguably has been the evolutionary and culturally most momentous symbolic system, this achievement must not be seen in isolation but closely connected to other nonlinguistic symbolic forms and practices. In fact, one may say that it is the interplay and sometimes even fusion of different symbol systems that has given humans the cognitive and cultural edge over all other species. What is more, we mostly live in various symbolic modes simultaneously. Different symbol systems (and that includes sign systems) are not mutually exclusive. This is what makes the symbolic worlds of our culture – and with them, our minds – so incomparably complex. Using language or any other text or symbol system does not rule out the use of images and bodily movements, and the inclusion of other situational settings and performances; rather, these different practices typically merge and enhance each other (Brockmeier 2001). They also push each other, forming new fusions, combinations, and entanglements – for example, between the spoken and the written word, the word and the image, the image and the sound, the told and the enacted narrative, and the analog and the digital – again, continuously driven by the tension between our attachment to the Established and our search for the Possible.

REFERENCES

Baillargeon, R. (1993). The object concept revisited: New directions in the investigation of infants physical knowledge. In C. E. Granrud (Ed.) *Visual perception and cognition in infancy* (pp.265–315). Hillsdale, NJ: Lawrence Erlbaum Associates.

Blaiklock, K. E. (2004). The importance of letter knowledge in the relationship between phonological awareness and reading. *Journal of Research in Reading*, 27(1), 36–57.

Brockmeier, J. (1999). Ordnung und Imagination: Formen und Funktionen des mythischen Denkens in der Kunst (Order and imagination: Forms and functions of mythical thought in the arts). In H. W. Henze (Ed.) *Mythos und Musik: Neue Aspekte der musikalischen Ästhetik V* (*Myth and music: New aspects of musical aesthetics*, vol. V) (pp. 178–234). Frankfurt: Fischer.

Brockmeier, J. (2001). Texts and other symbolic spaces. *Mind, Culture, and Activity*, 8(3), 215–232.

Brockmeier, J. (2012). Narrative scenarios: Toward a culturally thick notion of narrative. In J. Valsiner (Ed.) *Oxford handbook of culture and psychology* (pp. 439–467). Oxford, New York: Oxford University Press.

Bruner, J. S. (1983). *Child's talk: Learning to use language.* New York, London: Norton.

(1990). *Acts of meaning.* Cambridge, MA: Harvard University Press.

Callaghan, T. C. (2000). Factors affecting children's graphic symbol use in the third year: Language similarity, and iconicity. *Cognitive Development,* 15, 185–214.

Cassirer, E. (1953–1957). *Philosophy of symbolic forms.* New Haven, CT: Yale University Press. (originally published 1923–1929).

(1972). *An essay on man:* An introduction to a philosophy of human culture. New Haven, CT: Yale University Press (originally published 1944).

Cole, M. (1996). *Cultural psychology: A once and future discipline.* Cambridge, MA: Harvard University Press.

DeLoache, J. S. (1995). Early symbol understanding and use. In D. Medlin (Ed.) *The psychology of learning and motivation* (Vol. 33, pp. 65–114). New York: Academic Press.

DeLoache, J. S. (2002) Symbolic development. In U. Goswami (Ed.) *Blackwell handbook of childhood cognitive development* (pp. 206–226). Oxford: Blackwell.

Fivush, R. (2008). Remembering and reminiscing: How individual lives are constructed in family narratives. *Memory Studies* 1(1), 49–58.

Foy, J. G., & Mann, V. (2006). Changes in letter sound knowledge are associated with development of phonological awareness in pre-school children. *Journal of Research in Reading,* 29(2), 143–161.

Goodman, N. (1976). *Languages of art: An approach to a theory of symbols.* Indianapolis: Hackett (originally published 1968).

(1978). *Ways of worldmaking.* Indianapolis: Hackett.

Han, J. J., Leichtman, M. D., & Wang, Q. (1998). Autobiographical memory in Korean, Chinese and American children. *Developmental Psychology,* 34(4), 701–713.

Homer, B. D. (2009). Literacy and metalinguistic development. In D. R. Olson & N. Torrance (Eds.) *The Cambridge handbook of literacy* (pp. 487–500). Cambridge: Cambridge University Press.

Homer, B. D., & Nelson, K. N. (2009). Symbols, signs and models: Language and the development of dual representation. *Journal of Cognition and Development,* 10, 115–134.

Homer, B. D., & Olson, D. R. (1999). Literacy and children's conception of language. *Language and literacy,* 2, 113–140.

Homer, B. D., Petroff, N., & Hayward, E. O. (2012). Linguistic mediation of children's performance in a new symbolic understanding task. *Journal of Cognition and Development* 14(3): 455–466.

Leichtman, M., Wang, Q., & Pillemer, D. P. (2003). Cultural variation in interdependence and autobiographical memory. In R. Fivush & C. Haden (Eds) *Autobiographical memory and the construction of a narrative self: Developmental and cultural perspectives*. Mahwah, NJ: Lawrence Erlbaum Associates.

Nelson, K. (1996). *Language in cognitive development: The emergence of the mediated mind*. New York: Cambridge University Press.

Nelson, K. (2005). Cognitive functions of language in early childhood. In B. D. Homer & C. S. Tamis-LeMonda (Eds.) *The development of social cognitive and communication* (pp. 7–28). Mahwah, NJ: Lawrence Erlbaum Associates.

Nelson, K. (2007). *Young minds in social worlds: Experience, meaning, and memory*. Cambridge, MA: Harvard University Press.

Olson, D. R. (1994). *The world on Paper*. Cambridge: Cambridge University Press.

Piaget, J. (1954). *The construction of reality in the child*. New York: Basic Books.

Reddy, V. (2008). *How infants know minds*. Cambridge, MA: Harvard University Press.

Tomasello, M. (2008). *Origins of human communication*. Cambridge, MA: MIT Press.

Tomasello, M., Striano, T., & Rochat, P. (1999). Do young children use objects as symbols? *British Journal of Developmental Psychology*, 17(4), 563–584.

Verene, D. P. (2011). *The origins of the philosophy of symbolic forms: Kant, Hegel, and Cassirer*. Evanston, IL: Northwestern University Press.

Vygotsky, L. (1971). *Psychology of art*. Cambridge, MA: MIT Press (originally published 1925).

(1986). *Thought and language*. Cambridge, MA: MIT Press (originally published 1934).

Wang, Q. (2001). "Did you have fun?" American and Chinese mother-child conversations about shared emotional experiences. *Cognitive Development* 16, 693–715.

(2003). Emotion situation knowledge in American and Chinese preschool children and adults. *Cognition & Emotion* 17(5), 725–746.

Concluding Remarks

ALESSANDRO ANTONIETTI, EMANUELA CONFALONIERI,
AND ANTONELLA MARCHETTI

The aim of this book has been to focus on a series of conceptual dimensions related to development and education, starting from the notion of "reflective thinking." Reflective thinking is an important knowing modality and procedure, a useful ability that allows us to face in an efficient and functional way many challenges embodied into reality. Reflective thinking is implied in different domains of development, such as metacognition, Theory of Mind, and narrative. It develops in various educational contexts – family, school, and university – that influence and define it in different ways. Furthermore, reflective thinking is enhanced by a lot of instruments and techniques (new technologies, oral and written productions, and artistic artifacts).

The various contributions of the book have been selected to erect a framework for the understanding of the role of metarepresentations and narratives in shaping our minds and changing them through the entire course of life. Reading these contributions and the commentaries to the two sections, we as editors have gained a deeper comprehension of some conceptual issues, and we would like to make them more explicit through this brief conclusion. Representations and Metarepresentations – giving the title to the first section of the book – should be better understood considering that what representation and metarepresentation are depends on the perspective we assume. Keywords in this scenario are the processes contributing to the construction and social representation of the world, the cultural meanings connected with technology and their influences on learning, and the role of context for the typical as well as the atypical development of Theory of Mind. Suggestions in this direction are offered in various chapters of the volume. For example, to solve a problem we obviously need a dynamic and changing-through-time representation of the problem itself, but this does not occur outside and independently of the "work" of social representations. So, when we solve a problem we deal also with a socially, historically, and contextually specific social representation of what is problem solving at school and at home, of what kind of abilities are required to solve that particular problem in that particular context, and so on. This implies that social representations (which develop – as every representation probably does – in the interplay between the intrapersonal and the interpersonal/social dimensions of experience) also act as metarepresentations, influencing the problem-solving activity from a higher level.

In the same sense, there are almost two meanings of "story retelling." During childhood, metacognitive language plays an important role in story retelling, and thanks to this activity children can meet mental states in action in a form that is similar to other cultural ways of representing mental life (novels, romances, movies, drawings, and the various forms of the arts). So metacognitive language is important for the development of narrative competence in childhood; at the same time, however, narrative competence acquires a more general, metarepresentational function when it is no longer employed to represent specific events in particular circumstances, but as the language to talk about human experience as a whole, that is, when narrative competence becomes the tool of narrative thinking. And as such, making sense to our lives is a matter of a continuous story retelling, which has its roots in the early stages of development.

Narrative processes are the specific topic of the second section of the book. Through its polysemic possibilities narrative can be also considered as a research device, able to enlighten the self dimensions and the educational processes involved in a wide set of activities ranging from literacy to the understanding of artistic artifacts. And what about the specific "places" of learning and instruction? In school settings as spaces of literacy, in universities as contexts where the future professional identities are built, what happens is not simply a growth and refining of reflective thinking of an isolated mind, but also the shaping of the selves of teachers and learners. Without the consideration of this intersubjective dimension an understanding of the processes of knowledge construction is not conceivable. The theme here is the importance of reflective thinking and narratives for cultural transmission. What we as human kind have learned through the centuries is offered at school and at the university in the form we can grasp in the present time; this "translation" and interpretation of culture shape our minds and, in doing so, shape our societies.

At the end of our excursus across the volume, should we think that this complex dynamics of circular causality responsible for the development of reflective thinking consists only (or mainly) of explicit, conscious, cognitively driven processes? A more articulated answer arises from some evidence gathered in the field of Theory of Mind as well as from some studies on aesthetic experience. The latter appears in fact to be grounded on prerational, embodied elements, which jointly contribute with cognitive elaboration to the final aesthetic appreciation; the former (Theory of Mind) is acquired and develops thanks to affective relationships with significant others. So, in both cases alterity is necessary to understand the world: Embodied simulation presupposes an alterocentric participation in others' experience, and Theory of Mind starts from and reaches the same target, that is, the mind of another, who must affectively sustain the child's development to be understood by the child.

Finally, narrative acts as a transitional representational device: In fact, it not only serves the goal of "presenting" the self in a conventional, symbolic form to ourselves and to others, but also promotes the mastery of psychic and social domains at the boundaries between reality and imagination. For this reason, the power of representations in narrative constitutes the links among the past, the present, and the future; among historical and possible selves and worlds: in short, a powerful resource for development and change.

We believe that the aim and challenge of the book have been successfully accomplished, offering new elements for reflection to readers. As researchers, we believe that it is fundamental to be aware of both perspectives that Bruner suggests in his chapter, that is, the "endless dialectic between the already Established and what we imagine to be Possible," in order to be mindful of the known, and at the same time curious and courageous explorers of new frontiers.

This book is dedicated to Olga Liverta Sempio: from her studies and her friendship we received a great lesson that continues to be a stimulus for our reflective thinking. We think that the concluding remarks we reported in this chapter match many of the core ideas which inspired Olga Liverta Sempio's work and thus we hope that she will share the message contained in the present volume.

INDEX

     Index